# POSING IN PARADISE

# POSING IN PARADISE

T.B. MARKINSON
MIRANDA MACLEOD

Posing in Paradise

Copyright © 2024 T. B. Markinson & Miranda MacLeod

Cover Design by Victoria Cooper

Edited by Kelly Hashway

This book is copyrighted and licensed for your personal enjoyment only. All rights reserved. No part of this publication may be reproduced, stored in a retrieval system, or transmitted in any forms or by any means without the prior permission of the copyright owner. The moral rights of the authors have been asserted.

This book is a work of fiction. Names, characters, businesses, places, events, and incidents are the product of the authors' imagination or are used fictitiously. Any resemblance to actual persons, living or dead, events, or locales is entirely coincidental.

# CHAPTER ONE

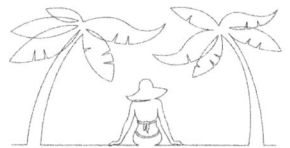

"Where the hell is the brown tweed suit for Alex Franklin's first scene tomorrow morning?" Gilly demanded the second I stepped foot in the wardrobe trailer. "If there's one more production delay, Dennis is going to fire the whole lot of us."

I blinked, adjusting to the dim light in the cramped trailer as the stale air closed in. Fired? With the state of my bank account, that would be catastrophic.

All around me, costumes hung in disarray. Shirts, pants, and dresses dangled crookedly on racks while accessories overflowed from plastic bins onto the floor. The small space was a whirlwind of clutter, a far cry from the orderly haven I strove to maintain.

Though I, as wardrobe supervisor, was the head of the department, Gilly, the costume designer for this production, technically outranked me. She loved to insist that no matter how tight a ship I ran, it could always be better. But, clearly, she'd gone on a tear trying to find the wayward garment with no concern for the chaos she left in her wake. I had little doubt I would be the one staying late to clean it all up.

I took a deep breath, pushing down my rising annoyance as my mind raced to remember where I had last seen the damn thing. "Are you sure it's not on the second rack behind Alex's name tag?"

"Don't you think I already checked there, Captain Obvious?" Gilly rifled through another pile, letting out an exasperated sigh as she came up empty-handed. "This movie is three weeks behind schedule. Way over budget. And everyone at the studio is demanding a blockbuster. Meanwhile, we're making a black and white rip off of a 1940s classic because our director thinks he's some sort of artistic genius. We're doomed."

"I swear it should be there," I insisted, trying not to let her negativity get to me. I needed this job too much to contemplate what I would do if the director actually did what Gilly thought he would and gave us all the sack. "I finished the alterations and steam pressed it myself this morning."

"It isn't here now."

On impulse, I grabbed the bag of dirty laundry one of the wardrobe assistants had gathered from the actors' trailers during the lunch break. I rummaged through it quickly, feeling a flicker of hope as I spied the familiar tweed fabric. "Found it!" I exclaimed, holding up the suit in triumph.

Gilly's expression went from relief to dismay in an instant. "There's a stain all the way down the front."

"You're joking." I inspected the suit with a growing sense of dread. Sure enough, a long streak of what looked like bright yellow mustard was smeared down the front of the once immaculate vintage tweed fabric. "What the hell? What kind of idiot eats mustard while in costume?"

Gilly snatched the suit from my hands, inspecting it with a critical eye. "This is exactly what we don't need right now," she snapped, her frustration palpable. "Dennis will have our heads for this."

"Let's not panic. I know exactly how to get this out." This was not an empty boast. My parents had owned a dry-cleaning business in my hometown of Waconia, Minnesota since before I was born. Stain removal was in my blood—a substance which, incidentally, could be removed from most garments with a mixture of cold water and table salt. Mustard, on the other hand, required more sophisticated supplies than I kept on hand. "I think our best bet is to bring it back to the studio dry cleaner and have them do a rush job before tomorrow's call time."

"No can do. Dennis wants to shoot this scene tonight instead of the morning. We'll have to pull a different costume and pray he doesn't notice." Gilly rummaged through the racks, grabbing a suit that was nearly identical to the ruined one, but at least a full size larger, if not two. "It's going to need a fitting and some lightning speed alterations, but I think this will work."

"Should I go get Alex?" Given how hot it was in our poorly ventilated trailer, I would welcome a chance to get fresh air into my lungs.

"She's on-set right now, filming a different scene." As she spoke, Gilly gave me the once-over, a sudden gleam in her eye making me want to run for cover. "You two are almost exactly the same size. You even have the same hair color."

I put a self-conscious hand to my plain brown bob. "A passing resemblance in hair color isn't exactly going to help us get the hem right."

"Trust me. I've been doing this long enough to know when bodies are the same size and shape. Here—" She thrust the skirt and jacket into my hands. "Put this on so I can start pinning."

"Here?" There wasn't enough space in this confined area for an ant to so much as don a tiny top hat, let alone for me to strip down and change clothing.

Gilly's frown suggested she'd come to the same conclusion. "No. Let's go to Alex's trailer."

"I don't know…"

It wasn't like Alex was the star of the film or anything. That honor belonged to the legendary Caroline Jacobs, who'd been my secret Hollywood crush ever since she'd come out as bisexual a few years ago. Not that I'd ever said more than two words to her despite working on this film together for weeks. To be honest, I'd mostly tripped over my own tongue and made a fool of myself in her presence. But Alex was an up-and-coming supporting actor known to have an attitude, and I had no desire to overstep any boundaries with her. I had enough experience with Hollywood to know how fickle the so-called talent could be.

"Come on, Margo. We're running out of time, and we can't risk Dennis finding out about this mishap."

Knowing she was right, I gave in without further protest. We wasted no time in making our way to Alex's trailer, my heart pounding with nerves as we approached the door. I attempted to express my objection as we entered without knocking, but Gilly remained indifferent to my concerns, engrossed in her phone screen.

"Damn it. I'm being summoned to Video Village." Her expression fell, and I couldn't blame her. Video Village was industry speak for the nerve center of the production, where the director, producers, and other key crew members huddled around monitors, dissecting every shot. Being called there without warning usually meant trouble. Had the director somehow had a premonition about the stained suit?

"Should we put this off until you're done?" I suggested

hopefully, eager to get away from a space that was equally as disorganized as our own trailer currently was, with makeup strewn across the small vanity and discarded costumes in piles on the floor.

No wonder the tweed suit had been ruined. Did Alex have no sense of respect for the wardrobe department at all? This type of blatant disregard was one more reason that, as much as I loved my job, I generally detested actors.

That my ex-girlfriend of five years had been an actor and had dumped me for her director the moment she'd found the smallest sliver of fame might have been the main reason, but the slovenly treatment of costumes was a close second.

Gilly shook her head, her eyes darting to the door. "No time for that." She hastily handed me the clothes. "Put those on and wait for me here. I'll be back as soon as I can." With that, she rushed out of the trailer, leaving me standing alone in the middle of Alex's space, clutching the costume pieces to my chest.

Fuming, I changed.

With my back to the door, I eyed my transformation in the mirror. Now that it was on my body, the suit wasn't nearly as big as it had looked on the hanger. After the placement of just a few strategic pins, every curve was accentuated in a way I wasn't used to but couldn't deny had an effect that was rather flattering. No wonder the movie stars in the 40s were so damn sexy.

Wandering away from the mirror, I noticed a glint of something shiny on the floor. A misplaced earring, no doubt, which I would've spent an eternity searching the wardrobe trailer for if I hadn't spotted it. Just as I bent to retrieve the object, the trailer door opened. Before I could turn around, a pair of arms had threaded around my waist. The owner's head buried into my neck, and a gruff voice that was equally likely to belong to a male or a female, whispered, "You look so beautiful I could eat you."

Startled by the unexpected intimacy, I jerked away. "Uh, you might have the wrong person."

"Oh my God. I'm so sorry. I thought you were someone else!" The person whipped around and dashed out the door before I could see who it was.

All I caught as the door slammed shut was a flash of firetruck red and a logo of some sort.

Funny how the costumes for this black and white film were so colorful. It was possible I was in shock.

I was only barely getting my wits back when Gilly burst through the door. "We have to get to the set for Caroline's last looks. Dennis has her doing the car scene."

"Caroline's on set today? I thought a stunt double was doing this scene."

My cheeks were still burning from the unexpected strange encounter moments earlier, but now the anticipation of coming face-to-face with the legendary star on such short notice added fuel to the flame. Sure, Caroline Jacobs was an actor, and I loathed actors. But she was also a goddess.

Exceptions had to be made for goddesses.

Glancing down, I realized I was still wearing the tweed suit. "Should I change?"

"No time, but you look fantastic. I think we did well."

In fact, I had been informed I looked good enough to eat. Not that I could tell Gilly that. And not like I was looking for anything remotely physical with anyone.

Not since Jenna.

It had been almost a year since she'd left, and I never wanted to be in a relationship again. Especially not with Hollywood types. The fact of the matter was the kind of fairy tale endings portrayed on the silver screen were nothing but filthy lies.

"No, no, no!" Dennis shouted within moments of our arrival on set. He grabbed the iPad, from which Gilly and I would monitor all the details of the scene, and began tapping furiously on the screen.

"What's wrong?" I asked.

"She needs a scarf." The director gestured to where Caroline Jacobs stood off to one side, her face a mask of frustration as she fumbled with the door of a vintage convertible.

I was momentarily taken aback by her stunning beauty, even at the height of her exasperation. The way the sunlight caught the golden highlights in her hair as she turned her head, the slight furrow of her brow as she struggled with the door handle—it was so captivating I almost forgot where I was.

For a moment, all I could do was gape at her like a lovesick fool. As if by instinct, I took a few steps backward so she wouldn't see me making an idiot of myself in this way. We hadn't even been introduced yet.

"A scarf?" Gilly's disbelieving tone snapped me out of my trance.

"I want it to float behind her as she drives off," Dennis explained. "It's a crucial part of the scene." This last part was called over his shoulder as he marched toward Caroline and the car.

If it was so crucial, why was it only being thought of now? But it wasn't my place to question, only to procure. I turned to Gilly, silently asking for guidance on how to proceed.

"Do we have a scarf picked out?" I inquired, hopeful for a quick fix.

Gilly shook her head, her brow furrowed. It was obvious

she didn't agree with the director's vision for the scene but knew better than to say so outright.

"Are we sure about this, Dennis?" I heard Caroline ask. Having let go of the car handle, she fidgeted with her necklace, twisting it so tightly I feared the chain would snap. "This car seems to have a mind of its own. If we add a scarf, it might be too distracting. Is this vehicle even safe to drive?"

Dennis glared at her, his own frustration evident even from several yards away. "Trust me, darling. The scarf will tie everything together, just like we discussed in the script reading. As for safety, my boys on the crew have assured me it's top-notch." Dennis offered a reassuring grin that was so false it made my stomach twist.

Caroline opened her mouth, her expression dubious. "I heard—"

"Enough complaining." Dennis cut her off before she could protest further, storming back toward Gilly and me. "Let's not waste any more time. Someone get me a scarf. Like yesterday! No one seems to understand that time is money!"

"Go to the trailer and grab every scarf you can find." Gilly gave me a shove, as if somehow all of this was my fault.

One thing about the vintage outfit I was wearing, it wasn't conducive to sprinting. Not that I let it stop me. All it took was recalling Gilly saying we'd all get fired to get my feet in motion. I sprinted to the trailer and returned in record time, huffing and puffing with my arms full of scarves.

"I got all that I could see. Although, I don't recommend this one." I dropped the objectionable scarf to the ground.

"That's perfect!" With a squeal of something like delight, which also sounded like a pig had been poked in the ass with a sharp stick, Dennis bent down to retrieve it.

"It's much too long," I said, only to be met with the director's steely eyes.

"Put it on her, now."

I swallowed hard as a sense of foreboding washed over me. But one look at Dennis's face told me not to argue, or I would face his wrath. What could I do? I made my way to Caroline, my hands trembling.

She stood beside the convertible, her head angled downward, ignoring my approach completely. Fine by me. The less I interacted with the talent, the better. That included both regular actors and goddesses alike.

As I lifted the scarf to drape it around her neck, holding it at my eye level in a way that obscured my face, Caroline turned her head slightly and let out a naughty giggle.

"You look amazing in that suit," she said, nearly stopping my heart. "I can't wait to get you out of it and have my way with you tonight."

She honest to God growled as she said this, which was sexy as fuck but also highly inappropriate considering she didn't even know my name. What the hell was going on with everyone on this set?

My arms dropped to my sides. But before I could make up my mind how to respond, realization spread almost instantly across Caroline's face.

"You're not you." Caroline's voice shook, and her blue eyes were impossibly wide. "I mean, you're not... never mind. I'm so sorry. I thought you were someone else. You must think me such a beast."

All I could do was laugh in what I hoped wasn't too maniacal a way. The scarf was still clutched in my hands, and I quickly placed it on her neck as I'd been instructed to do. "Funny thing. You're the second person to proposition me today since I put on this suit."

"Who the hell else propositioned you?" Caroline's demeanor changed instantly from embarrassment to fury. It was so disorienting, I struggled to find the right words to respond.

"I'm not..."

"Who was it?" This time Caroline's growl didn't have any trace of a sexy undertone. She sounded more like a rabid dog about to rip my face off. "Whoever it was, they were propositioning my fiancée."

I had no idea what she was talking about, but that didn't stop me from being terrified. Not knowing what else to do, I scanned all the bodies in the general vicinity, not seeing the firetruck red I'd glimpsed earlier. "I didn't get a good look. It all happened so quickly, leaving me stunned."

Not seeming to care about my explanation, Caroline stormed off before I could finish what I'd been about to say. The scarf trailed out behind her, and I had to admit, I could kind of understand Dennis's vision now that I saw it in action.

"Where the fuck are you going?" Dennis demanded as he chased after his star.

I was far enough away that I couldn't hear what was being said, but when I saw Caroline stop directly in front of Alex Franklin, I suddenly suspected I inadvertently might have gotten entangled in some sort of on-set love triangle.

Just my luck.

Caroline's face got redder and redder as she confronted Alex, her hands gesticulating wildly. It appeared to get ugly, with Alex shoving Caroline. *Should someone call the cops?*

Finally, Dennis pulled Caroline away by the scarf I'd given her, practically strangling the star of the film in the process. I could picture the tabloid headlines now. The woman was Hollywood royalty, her family legacy going back to 19th century London stage. Even I knew who she was, and who her mother was, and I generally didn't give a rat's ass about actors.

Hollywood people—a bunch of narcissistic and feckless jerks.

"I don't fucking care who's fucking who." With that, Dennis shoved Caroline behind the steering wheel of the car. "We can't burn daylight because of your pathetic love life." He looked over his shoulder. "Sunglasses. We need sunglasses."

Perhaps sensing I had reached my limit for the day, Gilly dashed forward with a pair that had seemingly materialized out of thin air.

Still visibly shaken, Caroline fired up the car, her expression the very definition of a scorned woman. Was she in character, or was this for real?

I knew one thing for sure, I was glad I was only wearing Alex's costume and wasn't literally in her shoes. From the look of things, Caroline Jacobs hated that woman with every fiber of her being. I couldn't blame her, knowing what it felt like the moment you learned of a loved one's betrayal. Perhaps I could smooth things over by making a voodoo doll of Alex. Not that I had made one of Jenna. Okay, I totally did, but I hadn't stabbed it with a pin in at least a couple of weeks.

Action was called, and Caroline punched the gas on the car, which fishtailed as it shot forward on the sandy road.

Dennis hopped up and down like a boy, urging her to go faster. "She needs to hit fifty to get her hair and scarf blowing in the wind."

I wasn't sure what speed she was at, but I watched through cracked fingers as the scarf I'd cautioned against swirled around Caroline's head, blinding her completely. A second later, the sickening sound of crunching metal filled the air as the vintage convertible Dennis had been so excited about plowed full speed into a tree.

## CHAPTER TWO

*I* pushed open the glass door and stepped from the palm-lined West Hollywood street into the dimly lit interior of Lumiere. It was my friend Asher's choice, the type of bar where the drinks cost more than a week's worth of groceries.

There was a time in my life when this would have been an exaggeration, my attempt at some self-deprecating humor. But after getting fired from my job because of the Caroline Jacobs scarf incident and unable to find anything new for the past six weeks, I was mostly living on ramen noodles and drinking that horror of horrors to any true Los Angelean: tap water. I couldn't even afford a lemon wedge to dress it up.

The electric energy of the trendy night spot pulsed around me as I made my way through the crowd in search of my friend. A group of women pushed past me, not even bothering to register disdain over my simple jeans and T-shirt. By contrast, they appeared ready to grace a runway with their effortlessly chic ensembles. It was clear from their total lack of acknowledgment that I was too far beneath them to actually exist in their world.

I comforted myself with the knowledge that their faces probably contained enough Botox and fillers to supply most of the plastic surgery clinics in the Midwest.

I finally spotted Asher at the far end of the bar, his nose practically pressed to the screen of his phone. He, too, wore a T-shirt and jeans but the type that only looked plain while actually costing a mint. With his tousled hair and whiter than white teeth, he would've fit in well with the women from earlier.

Except he wasn't a bitch. Catty, yes. But that was what I loved about him. My biggest regret of leaving the world of theater for film was how seldom I got a chance to catch up with my friend these days. It had been months since either of us had found time for more than the briefest of online chats, let alone a good old fashioned in-person meetup.

I slid onto the empty barstool beside him.

"Is this mine?" I eyed a tall, slender glass adorned with a delicate sugar rim, catching the glint of neon lights overhead.

"Who else would it be for?" Asher grinned as he set his phone to the side, giving me his full attention.

"Someone who could afford it?" My shoulders folded inward at the admission, shame creeping up from my stomach into my chest.

Asher offered a genuinely compassionate smile. "Still no luck on the job front?"

"I think I may be cursed. First, I lose my job because of some nepo baby with a stick so far up her ass she's going to need a proctologist to extract it. Now there's a goddamn director's strike. I mean, writers I get. Or even actors, if you're talking the background folks. But directors? What do those pampered princesses have to strike over? I honest to God don't know what I'm going to do."

"I wish I had work for you," he said, anticipating one of

my primary questions for the evenings before I had the chance to ask. "But—"

"I thought the strike only applied to film and television. Don't tell me theaters are dark, too." Now I felt guilty sucking down the fancy cocktail Asher had paid for.

"It's not that. We're booming, in fact. But my theater is only putting on nude productions this season."

"As in naked?" My eyebrows almost certainly reached deep into my hairline at that revelation. "You're the manager of a Shakespeare theater. What play could you possibly be doing in the nude?"

"The Scottish play," he replied, using the superstitious title for Macbeth that theater people often do for fear of cursing the production.

"Aren't there some rather intimate scenes with, like, a son and his mother?" I couldn't help but laugh awkwardly, which surprisingly eased the tension in my shoulders a bit.

"You're thinking of Hamlet. Although, I wonder if we could work that in. It's an exciting idea." Asher bounced on his stool, reminding me he had grown up in this twisted town instead of around salt-of-the-earth Midwesterners like me.

I shuddered. "I would say disturbing, but to each their own. Actually, having seen more than my fair share of actors in their birthday suits, I would've thought *Much Ado About Nothing* would have been a better choice."

Asher chuckled. "Good one, Margo."

"You sure you don't want to rethink that naked concept? I make a mean pair of pumpkin breaches, and not to brag, but nobody does a better bum roll than me." We both laughed, but soon my smile faltered as I remembered the current mess my life was in. Asher fixed me with a critical eye. "I know you're a great costumer, but damn. Why do you insist on dressing like a hobo in real life?"

"Money. Or lack thereof." I let out a long sigh. "It's not just my wardrobe that's suffering. I hate to admit this, but if things don't turn around soon, I'm going to have to pack it in and move back to Minnesota."

"Is that what you want, maybe?" Asher's voice was gentle with concern. "I know you've never cared for it here."

"A few years ago, I would have jumped at the chance to go home. California was Jenna's dream, not mine. I was just the sucker who couldn't say no. Now?" I shrugged, not sure quite how to put into words what I felt. "My parents are so proud of their daughter in Hollywood. I don't want to go home as a total failure."

"You are not a failure." He spoke in the way a bestie would to make me believe it. Almost. The thing I'd always loved about Asher was how he acted like an older brother willing and able to step in to protect me, mostly from myself.

"My accountant, if I could afford one, would tell you differently."

"Money isn't the only way to define success."

"Says the guy who can afford designer T-shirts," I said with a slight roll of my eyes. I wasn't exactly sure where Asher's money came from—certainly not from working in theater. I gathered he had plenty of it, or his family did, though I wasn't certain how I'd come to that conclusion since he rarely talked about his personal life. Maybe it was just his old money aura. I seemed to recall him mentioning a grandfather who had worked on Wall Street once upon a time.

"You've never told me what this latest film was you were working on or who got you fired. You want 'em whacked? 'Cause I know people." He cracked his knuckles to accompany his best gangster voice. Maybe I had the Wall Street thing all wrong, and his grandfather had been an underworld crime boss.

I leaned back in my chair, grateful for my friend's attempt to lighten the mood. "You know what? I appreciate the offer to have her whacked on my behalf, but let's just drop it. It's water under the bridge. I've been letting that woman live rent free in my head for too long. I don't even want to say her name." Or picture her in my head, because that did things to my body I wasn't proud of. Things that would be more in keeping with naked Shakespeare than a mob movie. What could I say? Crushes were hard to get over even when the bitch got you fired.

"Hey, given the price of rent in LA, you can't afford to be giving out free rooms like that. Not even up here." He tapped his temple, causing me to snort with laughter.

"Dude, Hollywood is the worst." I never pictured this as my life, and even now, I wasn't one to brag about what movies I worked on or who I got to see naked. Honestly, it all made me kinda sick to think about. All the fakeness and insincerity. Yet it paid the bills, so what did that make me? An enabler, at the very least.

Asher nodded his agreement. "I loathe Hollywood. It's why I love being in theater. I get to be the unseen puppet master in charge of it all."

"Yeah, that sounds like you. Any day now, you'll be adding evil super villain to your resume."

"Right after I add wedding planner," he said with a groan. "One of my cousins is planning this massive destination wedding in Hawaii, and my aunt somehow decided I'm the perfect man to help make her daughter's dreams come true."

"You and not the groom?"

"Between you and me, the dude's kind of a tool. But my cousin seems to like him, and my aunt's not the kind of woman you say no to."

"Oh, so she's the mafia boss?"

"Something like that."

"At least you get to flex those puppet-master skills in Hawaii." I drained the last of my cocktail with regret. It was so good, and I might never be able to afford another. I set it down with the reverence it deserved. "When's the big day?"

"Soon. Too soon." He took a sip of his drink as well, placing the empty glass beside mine. "Get this. I have to be there for ten days."

"Jesus. I suspected you were rich, but I never guessed you could afford to jet off to Hawaii for that long. You're getting us another round, buddy," I joked, but also I was kind of serious about wanting another drink.

"Ha, it's my cousin's family that has the serious moola, not me." His face fell.

"What's wrong?" Now I felt guilty about that whole second drink thing. Was he hiding his own set of money woes? I really was a shitty friend for not knowing more about his personal business. "Shit. I'm kidding about the drinks. They're like thirty bucks a pop."

"No, it's not that. It's just I may have met my match with this wedding. Usually, I love the stress of getting everything perfect, but there's a particular problem I'm at a loss to solve right now." His shoulders pulled inward.

I scooted forward on my seat, determined to be a better friend and provide a listening ear. "What's the problem?"

"Not a what but a who. The bride's oldest sister, who is also the maid of honor. How can I put this delicately? She's a fucking disaster."

"That was delicate?"

"Given all the sleepless nights she's caused me—not only because of this wedding, but over my entire lifetime in general—that was positively dainty." He let out a heavy sigh, his brows furrowing in obvious frustration.

"Sounds like a handful."

"I love my cousin, but she has a reputation in my family for bringing nothing but drama. Quite honestly, the bride is convinced her sister will ruin the wedding."

"Will she?" At last, something to divert my attention from the doom and gloom that had been weighing on me. As the saying goes, misery loves company.

"It's possible. Not on purpose," he rushed to add. "She's not mean, just cursed."

"Like me," I added with a wry smile. "I feel her pain."

"She's a tornado in human form," he said with a shake of the head. "Just in the past few months, she's had a car accident and found out her fiancée was cheating on her with a coworker."

"As someone who lived through that last one, all I can say is ouch. Also, I hope your cousin wasn't too badly injured." I massaged the back of my neck, remembering a minor fender bender my first year in Hollywood.

"She only had to wear a neck brace for a few days, although, she's still walking with a cane from what I hear."

"That's awful." But it did make me feel a little better about my own circumstances.

"She's saying she wants to back out of the wedding altogether because of it, but I think it's really that she doesn't want to put up with the ridicule." He sank his teeth into his bottom lip.

"Your family would make fun of her for walking with a cane?" I was horrified. What a cruel thing to do! Mafia families were cold-blooded.

"No, not because of that," he was quick to assure me. "You see, the bride is her youngest sister. They're close, but they're also competitive as hell. She'd really kept this latest relationship under wraps, not wanting to jinx it by oversharing, which is her usual tendency. She wouldn't even tell us the woman's name. Now it's all gone pear-shaped, and my cousin is mortified. She can't admit she ended her engagement right as her sister is having this dream wedding, and it's not like she can conjure up a new woman to take the cheating bitch's place."

"Yeah, that only happens in the movies." I couldn't help thinking that if it would work anywhere, it might be here. I was learning the dynamics in his family were straight out of a soap opera, full of drama and not so hidden rivalries. "Has she actually considered hiring someone? There are enough out-of-work actors right now—"

"She's dead set against actors; believe me."

"Very smart. A woman after my own heart." I pressed my hands to my chest as if struck by cupid's arrow.

"You know what?" Asher got a wicked gleam in his eyes that I knew from experience meant trouble.

"Whatever you're about to say, the answer is no." I raised my hands as if to physically ward off his words, knowing Asher's schemes could be both entertaining and disastrous in equal measure.

"Hear me out."

"No." I stuck my fingers in my ears like the super mature twenty-seven-year-old that I was.

"You need a job."

I blinked at this unexpected swerve in the conversation. "That's your big statement? Tell me something I don't know, buddy."

"I need this wedding to go off without a hitch, or I'll be disowned by my entire extended family."

"You're simply regurgitating facts we've already established. Are you feeling okay?" I pressed a palm to his forehead.

"I'm feeling fine now that I've realized you're the solution to everyone's problems." He gleefully tapped his fingertips together.

"I have no idea what you're talking about, but in order for me to keep up with any of this, I really do need another one of these." Lifting my glass, I caught the eye of a passing server and did that obnoxious thing I hated, that pseudo-sign language motion that signaled I needed another round.

Asher turned to indicate he wanted a fresh one as well.

The woman nodded, doing her best not to seem exasperated. Considering the clientele, she was probably used to far worse. At least I knew we, and by that I meant Asher, would leave a good tip.

"What do you say, my dearest friend in the whole world?" Asher waggled his perfectly trimmed eyebrows.

"Say to what? If you're talking about another cocktail, I think I already made it clear the answer is yes."

Asher clasped his hands together, looking either like a child getting ready to pray or a devious villain about to reveal his master plan.

My money was on option number two.

"What do you say to coming to Hawaii with me as my cousin's fiancée?"

"Me?" I squeaked. "Are you out of your mind? I'm a costumer, not an actor."

"You don't have to be an actor. No one would suspect a person like you of being fake."

"Because I've had zero plastic surgery," I quipped. "I'm surprised they let me get a California driver's license without at least a spray tan and a boob job."

"I'm serious. This could totally work."

"It's preposterous. Your family would figure out I was an imposter immediately."

"I told you no one's ever met the ex. It was all top secret."

"I'm probably not even your cousin's type." I wasn't sure why I said this since I had no way of knowing, but it felt true. Given how much my love life sucked, I was pretty sure I was nobody's type.

"Considering the vast array of men and women my cousin has paraded around in the past, I think it's safe to say she doesn't have a strict type. And you're missing the big picture here. You'll get ten days with me, your bestie, to hang out in paradise. Plus, my cousin's kinda hot, and I know you have a weakness for pretty women." He batted his long lashes, but there was something hidden deep within his eyes. As if I was missing something. Or was that the alcohol and my bad mood talking?

"Sounds lovely, aside from one simple calculation. I. Can't. Afford. To. Go." I tapped my fingers on the table to emphasize each word.

"I thought I made it clear this is a paying gig."

"Come again?"

"My cousin will pay you. Or, she will, once I explain it to her. She's desperate."

"Dude, are you seriously trying to pimp me out to your cousin?" I was starting to rethink that second cocktail, seeing as how the first one must have gone straight to my head. What other explanation was there for what I thought I was hearing right now?

"It's a job."

"So is prostitution."

"Jesus, Margo. You won't have to—you know." He made the kind of repulsed face that could only happen when a gay man tried to contemplate females and sex at the same time. "My cousin is hot, though. Legit. Many people in your shoes would jump at the chance."

"In that case, hire one of them. Things are bad, but not street walker bad." At least I prayed I wasn't on the precipice of that life decision.

"Not sure that's an acceptable term." His nose scrunched. "Escort?"

"No. More like a professional poser. In Hawaii. I don't think you're getting that part. We'll be in paradise, and having you there might keep me from going insane."

"Sorry to break it to you, but I think that ship has sailed. And I've seen enough screwball comedies to know this plan of yours will end in disaster."

"Those movies also always end with romance."

"Which doesn't exist," I pointed out and blew a raspberry. "Hollywood fairytale."

"What if my cousin paid enough to cover your expenses for the next six months? The strike will surely end well before then, and you wouldn't have to return home a failure."

"Six months? No woman in her right mind would agree to pay someone else that much money just to avoid some gentle teasing by her family because of a broken engagement." If his cousin was willing to do so, underworld crime must pay better than I imagined. Exactly who was this woman? No. I didn't need to know. Asking Asher questions would just invite drama into my life. *Hold firm, Margo.*

"My cousin would," he insisted with a crooked smile. "You don't understand how desperate she is to get them off her back about her string of failed relationships."

"You haven't even asked her yet," I pointed out, though why, I wasn't sure. It wasn't like I was seriously considering saying yes, right? I sighed, scrubbing a hand over my face as if that could wipe away the audacity of his suggestion. But I was left with temptation. Mentally, I weighed posing as a fake fiancée to some mafia princess for a short spell against moving back to Minnesota for a lifetime. Which would ding my ego the most?

"Fine. Let's say for a minute I agree to the fake fiancée gig for your cousin in Hawaii. What's in it for me? Other than an obscene amount of money. You've gotta sell this."

God, had I really just agreed, even hypothetically, to this absurd plan? I must have lost my mind. My fingers drummed nervously on the table as I waited for his response, regret already settling in.

"Imagine lounging by the pool, sipping on a cocktail, with nothing to worry about except which sunscreen to use. And let's not forget the beautiful beaches and delicious food. It'll be like a vacation you never knew you needed."

The dimly lit bar suddenly felt too bright as I tried to wrap my head around this bizarre proposition. A paid vacation to Hawaii with some rich, attractive woman pretending to be in love with me?

"You forgot the family wedding and hundreds of people thinking I'm engaged to a stranger. Real relaxing. This sounds like the plot of a bad rom-com, only without the happy ending."

"If this was one of those screwball comedies you love so much, it'd be called *Posing in Paradise*," Asher said with a grin.

"You're such a dork. And so is your cousin," I added, "if she gives this ridiculous scheme even a second of her consideration."

"I know it all sounds a bit unconventional, but I think she'll go for it. And I have faith it'll work. Besides, if you ask me, you don't really have a choice."

"Spoken like a guy who has connections to get me whacked if I refuse. And again, you're making it sound like sex work."

"No sex. I can get that in writing if you need me to." He waggled a finger in my face as the server set down two fresh drinks. "Admit it. You're seriously contemplating it."

"If I am, it's only because I can't afford food, so this booze is going straight to my head." And because the promise of financial security for the next six months was dangling in front of me like a tempting carrot to a starving rabbit. Plus, I'd never been to Hawaii, and I sure could use a vacation after everything that had happened recently.

Shit. Every indication was pointing toward me actually saying yes. Asher knew me too well, damn his meddling ways. I could only pray his cousin would have more sense and would put a stop to this insanity the second she heard about it. But then again, with my luck, she would probably find it amusing and jump at the chance to turn some stranger's life into a chaotic mess.

"While you're at it, we'll have two more of these," Asher told the server, pointing to the fresh drinks. "Keep them coming. And some chicken wings." He winked at me when the server was gone. "I can't have you making a decision like this on an empty stomach."

"Oh my God, fine." I threw my hands up in defeat. "I'll go along with your crazy plan, assuming your cousin is as delightfully unhinged as you are. But mark my words, Asher, if this blows up in our faces, I'm holding you personally responsible."

Asher chuckled, his eyes gleaming with mischief. "Don't worry. It's going to be epic. And who knows? Maybe it will lead to true love."

"Not likely, seeing as how true love doesn't exist." Only suckers fell for it. I'd been a sucker once, but never again.

"That's the spirit. Welcome to the family," Asher said with a smirk. He raised his glass in a mock toast, clinking it against mine. "When you're sipping mai tais on the beach, you won't regret it."

"Too late. I already do." But as I downed another cocktail, my worries did seem to press into me a little less than before. If nothing else, this would be one hell of a ride.

# CHAPTER THREE

The sweet aroma of tropical flowers and salty sea air hit my nose as I followed Asher from the baggage claim area at Kahului airport through a set of sliding doors that led to ground transportation.

"The hotel shuttle is this way," Asher said, pulling his suitcase behind him with ease while my own bag seemed to bump and jostle its way over every crack in the pavement.

I had no idea what was in the damn thing, to be honest. Asher had insisted on packing for me, treating me like a character who needed to be dressed. Which I guess was accurate since I would be playing the role of a rich person's fiancée, and my bank account had me pegged as one step from homeless. He'd even chosen my travel outfit, a pair of loose linen pants and a striped silk blouse with major old money vibes. When I'd suggested I could do it myself, being a costumer and all, he'd just laughed. Considering some of the crap he'd seen me wear because I had neither the time nor the money to do better, I couldn't blame him for doubting me. But it was a little strange to not know what was in my own suitcase.

We approached a gleaming black SUV with the unmistakable Mercedes-Benz logo on the front. I was about to crack a joke about the type of rich asshole who would demand such a fancy ride for a short trip to a hotel when the driver in a dark suit and cap opened the door and greeted us with a warm smile.

"Mr. Donovan?" he said, directing his attention toward Asher before shifting to look at me. "And Ms. Wells?"

Holy shit, Jeeves knew my name.

It was possible my jaw temporarily dislocated from my skull as I tried to formulate a response that wasn't mostly grunts and primitive hand gestures. This was our ride to the hotel?

"That's us," Asher replied, handing over his luggage with an ease that suggested this wasn't the first time he'd been met by a chauffeur at an airport.

"Are you telling me we're taking a private SUV limo to the hotel?" I laughed like I was in on the joke, as opposed to thrown completely off balance by this turn of events. "I mean, I know you said your cousin's wedding was fancy, but this is something else."

"Actually, this is the ride to Maalaea Harbor," Asher said as he slid into the back seat, patting the space next to him for me to follow. "From there we'll take a boat to the hotel."

"A boat?" My brow furrowed as I joined Asher inside the SUV, the driver whisking my bag away to the trunk. "Why a boat?"

"The hotel's on an island owned by a rather idiosyncratic billionaire who prefers having guests arrive by sea for the best view."

"You must be joking. Are you sure we're not secretly in a Bond movie or something? Because I don't remember signing up for any daring spy missions when I agreed to be your cousin's plus one for this wedding."

Asher laughed but didn't exactly deny the possibility. This is when it occurred to me I may not have asked enough questions about what I was getting myself into. Hell, I didn't even know my supposed fiancée's name. Now that I thought about it, Asher had been kind of hush-hush about anything that didn't pertain to my fashion sense.

As we pulled out of the airport and onto the main road, the driver did double duty as a tour guide of sorts, pointing out interesting landmarks and giving us a brief history of the island. But I was too preoccupied with the looming boat ride to a billionaire's private island to fully appreciate his commentary. Was this actually real life? Who was Asher's cousin? For that matter, who was Asher Donovan? My friend was chock full of secrets, it seemed. Maybe they really were a mafia family after all.

When we arrived at the harbor, a sleek boat—I was tempted to call it a yacht, but I knew nothing about boats—was waiting at the dock. Before I could say a word, the driver was already taking our bags onboard, informing us they would be waiting for us in our rooms at the hotel once we checked in. Talk about efficiency.

As we stepped aboard, I couldn't shake the feeling I was in a dream. The boat's luxurious interior, with its polished wood surfaces and plush seating, only heightened the sensation. This was no simple ferry like the one I'd taken with Jenna to Catalina Island our first year in California. Once again, it was more like a movie than real life. I approached the railing, gripping it with both hands as I surveyed the sparkling ocean laid out before us, half convinced it was a product of CGI.

"What do you think?" Asher asked, joining me at the railing and handing me a glass of champagne.

The boat was filling rapidly with passengers, each more

glamorous than the last. Even in my ritzy new clothing, I felt like a mutt let loose at the Westminster Kennel Club. Another minute and I was likely to pee on the railing out of sheer nervousness.

"Holy crap," was all I could think of to say, being nothing if not eloquent in moments of awe. I took a sip of champagne, my nose twitching as the bubbles tickled it.

Unable to hold it back, I let out a sneeze, and Asher chuckled.

"Welcome to the high life." He lifted his glass in salute.

"I think there's something seriously wrong with me," I said as the boat pulled away from the dock.

"Are you seasick?" Concern was etched across Asher's face, replacing the amusement.

"No, just sick. In the head," I added to clarify. "How else can I explain actually going through with this scheme of yours? No one's going to believe for a second that I belong with all these perfect people." I gestured to a group of impeccably dressed guests mingling on the deck, sipping champagne and laughing effortlessly. Not a single one of them had sneezed from inhaling champagne bubbles. I was hopelessly out of my element, and I knew it.

"First, you look amazing, if I do say so myself. And trust me; no one here is perfect. Take the couple down below at one o'clock." Asher whispered behind his hand. "You know what I see? They just got married, and the bride is already contemplating calling a divorce lawyer."

"Why do you think that?"

"She told me at the bar when I was getting us our drinks." Asher shrugged as if it was normal for complete strangers to confide in him like that.

I followed his gaze to the couple he mentioned, and sure enough, the bride had a forced smile plastered on her face while the groom looked more interested in his phone than in her. I wondered if they'd signed a prenup. It looked like they were going to need it.

"You sure do have a way with people, don't you?" I teased. "They just pour their hearts out to you like you're their therapist. Or bartender."

Asher's eyes crinkled as he grinned. "It's a gift. I'm sure by the time this is over, I'll know not only everyone's names, but their deepest, darkest secrets."

"Does everyone confide in you?"

"Absolutely. Two days ago, I was at the store, and the cashier confessed she wanted to try microdosing."

"How did that come up?"

"I asked how she was."

"There's your mistake." I pressed my index finger to his chest. "Never, ever ask people questions. They're likely to answer, and that inevitably leads to uncomfortable situations."

"It wasn't uncomfortable." He laughed as if that was the silliest thing I'd said all day. "I gave her my contact."

"Of course, you have a contact for that." When we'd worked together at the theater, Asher'd had the reputation for being the guy who could get things done. But I'd never realized how far those services extended. Shit. That was one more point in favor of him secretly being a Donovan family crime boss. I really should have asked a few questions of my own before agreeing to this.

"Puppet master, remember?" He lifted his hands and mimed pulling the strings. "To keep productions running smoothly, it helps to have a connection for everything under the sun."

"Do you have a therapist I can Zoom right here and now? Because I'm still convinced I must be nuts to be on this boat."

I turned my head toward the water, and my stomach swirled. Again, it wasn't seasickness. "Oh wow!"

"Who did you see?" Asher glanced around as if expecting Katharine Hepburn to materialize.

I wouldn't have been surprised. It was that kind of crowd, filled with faces that seemed vaguely familiar because I'd probably seen them so often on a movie screen. It felt like the time I'd run into a veteran character actor off set and was certain he was my neighbor. Such an uncanny feeling, and one that never failed to give me a jolt even after years of working in Hollywood. But that wasn't what had me catching my breath.

"It wasn't a person. It was the water. It's so blue. And look." I pointed across the bay, a certain giddiness overtaking me as it truly hit me where I was. "The green over on that island is the kind you dream about."

"Only you're not dreaming." Asher gave me a playful nudge. "You're about to experience one of the most exclusive resorts in the world."

"We may be in paradise, but I'm betting we'll be swarmed by paparazzi," I muttered, certain there was a catch to all this if I looked hard enough. That excitement I was beginning to feel could prove dangerous. It was easier to avoid having your hopes dashed if you didn't have high expectations in the first place.

"Always the optimist. The people who come here do not want their photos taken, and they pay for that privilege. The cost per night is—" He put his fingers to his temples, flicking them outward to convey mind-boggling expensive.

"How is it again that your cousin can afford all this? I know people go all out for weddings, but this is a whole other level." My eyes scanned the well-heeled passengers, my gaze landing on a man with sandy blond hair, his Hawaiian shirt—definitely worn ironically—unbuttoned enough to reveal tanned pecs. "Oh my god, is that George Patrick? He was absolutely divine in that vampire movie ten years ago."

Just because I was a lesbian didn't mean I couldn't appreciate a good-looking man when I saw one. And George Patrick was definitely easy on the eyes. I'd even had a poster of him on my bedroom wall in high school when I was still trying to pretend I was straight.

"That's him," Asher confirmed with a smirk. "But don't get too excited. He'll have his hands full with groomsman duties most of the time we're here, so I doubt he'll be lounging shirtless by the pool."

"George Patrick is invited to your cousin's wedding?" I could barely keep my voice from squeaking. "Next thing, you'll tell me Kermit Gray will be here, too."

"I should hope so. He's the best man."

I stared, my mouth hanging open so wide I could have caught a fish if one had jumped from the water right then. "I feel like I'm missing something here. Your dad's like a stock broker or something, right? Or, like, mafia or something," I gave a half-hearted laugh, not convinced of my own joke. "Why are not one but two of Hollywood's most sought-after actors going to be at this family shindig of yours?"

"Probably because my cousin is marrying Eric Draper."

"*The* Eric Draper," I blurted out, immediately regretting my lack of composure. I tried to mask my outburst by taking a nonchalant sip of champagne, but the burning sensation down my throat only added to my flustered state. I coughed as discreetly as I could to keep the liquid from coming out of my nose.

But who could blame me? It wasn't every day that the entire cast of one of the most formative films of my youth would be sharing a small island with me. George, Kermit, and

Eric were like the young millennial equivalent of the 1980's Brat Pack. This was legendary.

"Careful now. Someone might mistake you for being starstruck. I thought you hated actors."

"I don't hate all of them," I corrected. "Only the ones who get their wardrobe supervisors fired for what was clearly an act of god." And my cheating ex, but that really didn't need to be verbalized since I'm sure the walls I erected around my heart screamed, "Back off!"

Asher chuckled, raising his glass in a mock salute. "Touché."

As I looked around, I realized there were a hell of a lot of famous folks onboard. But I took a certain smug satisfaction in knowing that at least my nemesis wouldn't be one of them. Considering the way the woman had left George at the altar to run off with his best friend, Kermit, to Paris the morning of what was supposed to have been their wedding, Caroline Jacobs would probably rather be chilling in a tree house with a rabid raccoon than show her face among present company.

"Wait a minute. Did you not tell me about this being Eric Draper's wedding because you thought I would say no to attending if I knew how many celebrities were going to be here?" I narrowed my eyes at Asher, whose cheeks colored incriminatingly.

"I might have suspected you'd have a strong opinion about it," Asher admitted sheepishly, scratching the back of his neck. "But honestly, I think you're really going to have a good time if you give it a chance."

"What if I can't do this, though?"

"What? Have fun?" His expression conveyed *get real and look around* as if this was the best thing to ever happen to me.

"No. I mean, what if I can't pull this off? Every school play when I was in elementary school, I was the one moving the sets around. Except one year, I got to be the narrator. Until my teacher replaced me because I kept messing up the lines. Now I need to be a fake fiancée in front of a bunch of famous people, some of whom have won Oscars. This is a disaster waiting to happen." I tried to concentrate on my breathing to avoid passing out.

"Trust me. My cousin will get you through this. It's her thing." Asher looked down at his empty glass with an air of disappointment. "Want another?"

I nodded, handing him my empty glass, but what I really wanted was to travel back in time to that moment in the bar when I had agreed to this whole farce, so I could rethink my life choices.

How had I allowed myself to get roped into posing as a fake fiancée, and for a celebrity wedding of all things? If there was one thing I dreaded more than anything else, it was public humiliation. Considering what I could envision happening in the next few weeks, going back to Minnesota with my tail between my legs felt almost like a hero's welcome by comparison.

Left on my own, I quietly scanned the crowd, quickly realizing it was a literal who's who of Hollywood. And just like when I was physically in Hollywood, I stood awkwardly on the sidelines while the beautiful people flitted around, making it all look so easy. I was about to close my eyes, wanting nothing more at that moment than to block out the whole scene, when a flash of firetruck red caught my eye. Damn, I'd come to hate that color.

Despite my best intentions, my head swiveled toward the source of my retinal irritation. My breath caught in my throat as I recognized Richard Thompson, the male lead on the movie I'd been fired from. At five-foot-seven, he wasn't exactly a towering presence, and to describe his voice as a tenor was being generous.

No wonder I'd been confused as to the gender of my mystery hugger. But in the filtered light of a Hawaiian sunset, all had become clear. This was the guy who had been having an affair with Alex Franklin, Caroline Jacobs' fiancée. Or ex-fiancée, to be more accurate.

My God. With George and Kermit on the boat, and now Richard, too, it was like being aboard a vessel of instant floating karma. I almost wished Caroline was going to be here to be smacked in the face by it.

If that made me a bad person, I didn't want to be good.

Asher returned with our champagne refills and wearing a *cat who ate the canary* grin. "I think I missed my true calling."

With a pang of regret, I dismissed my wild fantasies of Caroline Jacobs getting the comeuppance she deserved and turned my full attention to my friend. "How so?"

"Remember that newlywed who hated her husband? She's madly in love again, thanks to me. I bumped into her on the way back from the bar, and I must've said something right before because she pulled me aside and literally thanked me for saving her marriage." He blew on his fingernails, buffing them against his shirt. "Maybe I can learn to do couples counseling on the side. It'd come in handy in my line of work. Everything boils down to trust." With a sly smile he added, "Or the illusion of it."

I laughed, shaking my head. "I'd like to walk in your shoes for one day so I can experience your confidence."

"I don't think you could handle it." He waggled his brows. "Besides, you are amazing exactly the way you are. You just need to let your light out from that dark cave where you keep it hidden and allow it to shine sometimes."

"You have a therapist's knack for bullshitting." Despite

my cynicism, my cheeks tingled from the unexpected compliment.

We were almost at the dock by this point, and the sight of the hotel rising from behind an oasis of palm trees brought a twinge of foreboding. If this was the stuff of dreams, I was pretty sure it would turn out to be that one where it's the day of the school play, and you find out you're the star but didn't memorize any of the lines.

"Remind me of the plan again," I begged Asher, not because I needed the details but because I hoped he could soothe my nerves with the same magic he'd used on the newlywed with cold feet.

The plan, if it could be called by such a lofty title, was simple. As soon as we disembarked, Asher would introduce me to my fake fiancée, who had arrived at the hotel earlier in the day. We would then have about an hour to learn all we could about one another before heading to the first formal event, a family meet and greet followed by an authentic Hawaiian luau.

Or, I could jump off the side of the boat and swim all the way home to Minnesota.

Sadly, at that moment, the captain turned off the boat's engines. The gangway lowered, and the press of the other passengers moving to disembark shifted me from my spot at the railing. My last opportunity to escape into shark-infested waters was gone.

"Are you ready to meet the woman of your dreams?" Asher crooked his elbow for me to hook my arm through as we walked down the metal ramp.

I raised an eyebrow, studying his arm like it was a snake ready to bite. "I think I was hasty in not looking into a waitressing job. Or a barista. I make a mean latte. I even know how to draw leaves in milk foam."

"You have to trust me."

"I thought you said trust was an illusion. Or was love an illusion?" By this point, my heart was racing, and my palms were starting to sweat. "No, wait. The word I was thinking of is battlefield."

"Not this time," Asher said with a laugh, grabbing my arm and leading me the rest of the way to dry land. "I don't want to brag—"

"Since when?"

"I happen to have some mad matchmaking skills, and I have a feeling about you and my cousin."

"Uh-huh. And you just happen to have never mentioned it before now?" Given that the guy couldn't keep his mouth shut even with total strangers, I had my doubts.

"Hey, for various reasons, I've hesitated to introduce you to this side of my family, but that doesn't mean I didn't think you and Carrie would be perfect for each other."

About halfway through what he was saying, I stopped dead in my tracks, staring ahead at a vision in a tropical print sun dress, her blond hair cascading in loose waves that made my insides flutter. At least until I shut it down, reminding my traitorous body parts that this was the woman who had ruined my life. Or, the most recent one to do so, anyway.

"I can't believe it," I seethed. "That bitch had the nerve to show her face here after all."

"What bitch?" Asher turned around, looking in the completely wrong direction.

"The one who got me fired."

"Hold on a second." Asher blinked as if he'd woken from a trance, the color slowly draining from his face. "Who exactly got you fired?"

"Caroline Fucking Jacobs. That's who." I squealed as

Asher's arm tightened on mine, threatening to cut off the circulation. "What the hell, Asher?"

"Oh God. You never said you were working on that train wreck of a film. I had no idea." He looked like he was experiencing a belated case of seasickness. "I don't know how to tell you this..."

"Tell me what?" I said with urgency as Caroline Jacobs rapidly descended on us, her expression as sunny as a summer day at the beach. Meanwhile, my mood darkened with each approaching step as reality crashed into me with the force of a tidal wave. "What the fuck do you need to tell me, Asher?"

"Uh..." For once, Asher's cool, confident demeanor deserted him as he glanced nervously from Caroline to me. "Uh, Margo, I'd like you to meet my cousin. Carrie, your new fiancée."

## CHAPTER FOUR

"Nope. Nuh-uh." I shook my head so hard I felt something snap between my right ear and shoulder blade. "There is absolutely no way I can do this."

I kept hoping that when I closed my eyes and opened them again, my problem would be gone. But every time my vision cleared, there she was.

Caroline Fucking Jacobs.

Asher gave my ribs a sharp nudge with his elbow.

I shot him a look that clearly communicated how close I was to snapping him in half like a twig. "If you don't stop poking me, I will make sure you regret it for the rest of your natural-born life. You had to have known she was the one who got me fired even if I never told you. And not once did you mention she was your cousin! How did you think this would play out?"

"I swear on my life I had no idea." He swallowed hard, a pleading look registering on his features as his cousin, the fucking bane of my existence, drew closer.

"Your aunt is Vivian Jacobs? I thought you said your aunt was a mafia boss."

"That's insane. I never said anything of the sort. Why would you think that?" He had the nerve to laugh, and I nearly socked him in the mouth.

"I don't know! I swear that's what you told me at the bar. A better question is why would you fail to mention your uncle is married to the most famous woman on the planet?"

To my surprise, Asher's cheeks colored, and his eyes shifted toward the ground. "People have gotten weird about my family, especially theater people. I've learned over the years never to mention it, not even to friends."

He sounded pretty sincere about this, and knowing what I did about the entertainment world, I could only imagine how many people would try to take advantage of the connection if they knew about it. Under other circumstances, I would have felt bad for the guy. Right now, I was too busy fending off a panic attack.

Caroline Fucking Jacobs was less than five feet away and closing in fast.

I became aware that I was blinking an insane amount, which had the effect of making Caroline's rapid approach look like stop motion animation.

"Is there something wrong with your eyes?" Caroline demanded as she stopped in front of us. When I didn't respond, she spun toward Asher. "This can't be the woman you promised me. What's with all the blinking? She looks like a lunatic."

"I'm just... uh, contemplating the mysteries of the universe," I blurted, mentally kicking myself for such a lackluster response.

Caroline's eyebrow arched in disbelief as she crossed her arms over her chest. "Right, because blinking excessively is a well-known side effect of cosmic pondering."

Asher took a step closer to his cousin, as if worried I'd physically attack her.

For the record, I wouldn't have. Not even when her outrageously stunning eyes made me whimper with pain. No one should be this goddamn beautiful while also being such an unpleasant human being. It sends all sorts of mixed messages, and apparently, my libido is not good at sorting through the confusion.

"Maybe my eyes are just allergic to your presence," I retorted, surprising even myself with the quick comeback. Caroline's stunned expression was worth the risk of pushing her buttons.

"Allergic to greatness, huh?" Caroline narrowed her eyes, studying my face. If you think it was intimidating having a world-famous actor scrutinize your every crease and freckle, you'd be right. "Hold on a minute. You look familiar. I know you, don't I? Oh my God, I do. You're the scarf lady." As she belatedly made the connection, Caroline was practically spitting mad. "You could've gotten me killed."

"You blame me?" I shrieked. "I'd be more likely to point fingers at that death trap car that Dennis squeezed you into. Not to mention the wind. I don't control that." If I could, I'd conjure up a gale to blow her right into the nearest volcano. Just why had human sacrifices gone out of style?

"Or that long scarf you wrapped around my neck that nearly blinded me."

"None of which was part of the plan, by the way. But if you think I wanted you dead that day—you have no idea what thoughts are coursing through my mind right now." I pressed my fingers to my temples, but not to soothe a sudden stress headache as it may have appeared. No, it was to physically blot out the dirty thoughts running through my mind. Seriously, this amount of beauty was wasted on a woman as infuriating as Caroline Fucking Jacobs. That should go on her tombstone, which might happen sooner rather than later. If I managed to lure her to the volcano and I accidentally tripped and shoved her. On second thought, that wouldn't require a tombstone. Even better.

"Ladies, ladies, ladies..." Asher stood in the middle of us, his arms held out as if we were ready to hit the ground for a wrestling match. "Let's not lose track of the reason both of you are here right now."

"I couldn't care less about the reasons. I want her gone." Caroline stretched a slender finger toward the boat. "Yesterday."

"You sure about that?" There was a note of caution in Asher's tone. "Don't look now, but your mother's heading this way."

Caroline's eyes widened in panic as she scrambled to compose herself. "Oh God, not now," she muttered under her breath.

For a split second, I almost felt sorry for her. Almost.

But then I turned, and I swear that at the first sight of the legendary Vivian Jacobs walking down the tiki-torch-lit pathway, it was like a choir of heavenly angels began to sing. She was the epitome of elegance, a woman who could command a room with just a look.

As her mother descended upon us like a queen, stopping every few feet to be worshipped by one or more adoring subjects who vied for her attention, the daughter went from being Caroline Jacobs, an intimidating actor in her own right, to just plain Carrie, a mortal being who fidgeted nervously beside me, trying to regain her composure under the prospect of her mother's scrutinizing gaze.

"Fine. I'll do it," Caroline spat this pronouncement out

with all the enthusiasm of someone who'd just agreed to sell a kidney.

"I won't." I crossed my arms.

"You have to," Carrie—she was firmly established as Carrie in my mind now—informed me. "I'm paying you."

"Not enough. I want hazard pay if I have to deal with you," I quipped, meeting her piercing blue eyes with a defiant stare.

"Hazard pay?" Carrie shot back. "That's rich. I'm the one who should probably demand you carry insurance coverage if I have to spend longer than a second with you."

"Insurance for what? The emotional distress I'm likely to suffer?" I scoffed, raising an eyebrow in a way that I was pretty certain made me look suave. "I think I might need a whole therapy package by the end of this trip."

"Ladies, can we save the one-liners for later?" Asher interjected, his face a picture of exasperation. "Your mom's almost here, and I don't think she's in the mood for a comedy routine."

"I think I'd rather get back on the boat and go home," I said, feeling it in every fiber of my being. *Run, Margo, run!* No good was going to come from this.

"I think I get it now," Carrie said accusingly. "This was your plan all along. To connive a way to get more money out of me."

"How does that make any sense? I literally just found out who I'm supposed to be engaged to." I attempted to blow a raspberry, but it ended up sounding more like a horse burping.

Seriously, the idea of spending time trapped on a tropical island and forced to cater to the whims of a woman who insisted on blaming me for her own misfortunes was a fate worse than death in my eyes.

"Bull shit. You had to have known who he was setting you up with. We're his only cousins." Carrie's tone was accusatory

"Nope," I insisted, one eye on Vivian. She'd nearly run out of people to stop and say hello to and do the air-kiss greeting that grated on my nerves. Hollywood types were the worst phonies. "Asher's so tight-lipped about his family. I swear to God, I thought you all were part of a crime syndicate."

Carrie crossed her arms, jutting out her chin. "I'm not buying it."

"Listen, Princess. Not everyone on this planet lives and breathes the Jacobs family. Some of us simply mind our own business. Which is what I'm going to do." I looked around frantically for my luggage, which was nowhere to be seen because the staff here was too efficient.

"Viv's almost here," Asher hissed, watching his aunt with nervous anticipation as she chatted with one final admirer who stood between her and us. "If the two of you keep this up, it'll ruin Cagney's wedding, and then it'll be my head on a platter."

"I need my bags. You know what? Never mind. I'm getting back on that boat while I have a chance." I hitched my thumb over my shoulder and started to walk away, only to be stopped by Carrie's hand on my arm.

"Wait, Margo," she said, her grip surprisingly gentle. Even more surprising was that she'd remembered my name. True that Asher had introduced us not five minutes prior and we had worked together, but I'd rather expected her to call me Wardrobe Girl, if she called me anything at all.

"What?" I asked, unable to keep the hint of annoyance out of my voice. But there was vulnerability in her piercing blue eyes that caught me off guard. Was it possible that beneath her Hollywood glamor, Carrie Jacobs was as afraid of being a disappointment to her parents as I was?

"I'll pay you double," Carrie said, panic clearly evident in her wobbly voice. "Please. I have about thirty seconds before my mom breaks free from her fan club and makes eye contact, after which I will be forced to acknowledge her. I need to introduce her to my new mystery fiancée if I want a moment of peace on this trip."

"I don't like you. I'd rather get eaten by a shark than marry someone like you."

"Triple."

The word hit me like a hurricane, all swirly and confusing. Was she for real? Triple what we'd initially agreed on would mean I wouldn't have to worry about getting a job for well over a year.

"Do we have a deal?" Caroline hissed.

I could only nod because I'd lost the ability to speak. I couldn't believe what was happening. Moments ago, I had been ready to walk away from this whole chaotic situation. And now here I was, agreeing to triple my fee to help out a woman who had caused me nothing but trouble. Had I lost my mind? Or was this the smartest decision I'd ever made? Could both be true?

Triple the pay meant financial security for me, at least for a while. But it also meant being stuck with Carrie Jacobs for the duration of this trip. Stuck on an island resort with my arch-nemesis. Pretending to be in love with her. Clearly, I had made a deal with the devil herself.

"Darlings!" Vivian Jacobs was upon us, a vision in a flowing caftan, her large sunglasses perched on her perfectly coiffed hair.

Faster than I could process what was happening, Carrie looped her arm through mine, flashing a dazzling smile that somehow masked her desperation. I had to admit she was a good actor. It was almost convincing to me, and I knew exactly how fake it was.

Vivian enveloped both Carrie and Asher in a warm hug like a mama hen circling her wings around two small chicks. It was surreal to witness, and I still couldn't believe my friend had never let on about his famous family. But before I could delve deeper into the questions in my mind, Vivian Jacobs was turning her attention to me, and all other thoughts vanished from my head. To say I was starstruck was the understatement of a lifetime.

Her eyes were identical to Carrie's, though slightly softened with age. The resemblance between mother and daughter was striking. The same elegance, the same air of sophistication. Although beneath it, I thought I sensed a warmth in Vivian that her daughter lacked. It was as if she had all the authentic charm that Carrie had somehow missed out on.

Or maybe that was just me projecting my own biases.

As Vivian beamed at us, I plastered on the most genuine smile I could muster. "You're Vivian Jacobs," I said as if this woman who had won seven Oscars needed me to inform her of who she was.

"That's what they keep telling me." She winked at me, but I could tell that beneath the lighthearted gesture, she was busy assessing whether I was actually worthy of her daughter. "And who might you be, darling?"

Carrie interjected smoothly, "Mother, this is Margo. My... fiancée." The hesitation in her voice was barely noticeable. Her tone was steady now, the panic gone. How did she manage it? Inside, I felt like I was about to combust.

"Pleasure to meet you, Mrs. Jacobs," I said, mustering all the charm I could summon. The warmth I'd sensed in the beginning grew cooler as Vivian Jacobs eyed me with a shrewdness that made me feel like a bug under a microscope. Yet she never allowed her pleasant veneer to falter. I could see where Carrie got her acting skills.

"The pleasure is all mine, dear Margo," Vivian purred, her smile not quite reaching her eyes. "Caroline has told me so much about you."

This was absolutely a lie. I had it on good authority from both Asher and now Carrie that no one in the family had a clue about the mystery fiancée, right down to her name. And yet the fabled actor delivered this whopper with such finesse that I almost fell for it.

"Tell me, dear. What have I seen you in?" the woman asked.

I stared like an idiot, uncertain how to answer this question. The seconds dragged on, the weight of Vivian's expectant gaze pressing down on me. I had to think fast. My newly acquired gig, along with a year's worth of pay, was on the line. If I blew it now, I had no doubt Carrie would send me packing without so much as a penny to show for it.

"In a shampoo commercial when I was two," I blurted out finally, mentally kicking myself as soon as the words left my mouth. I had literally recited her daughter's resumé.

*Smooth move, Margo. Real smooth.*

Vivian raised an elegantly arched brow, her amusement thinly veiled. Clearly, she had caught the reference, but perhaps she thought I was teasing. "How delightful! You must have been quite the little star in the making."

Carrie squeezed my arm subtly, a warning, no doubt, against digging myself any deeper into this particular hole.

"Alas, it was her first and last acting role." Carrie shot me a look that clearly said, *Speak and you die.*

But I was way ahead of her. I intended to keep my mouth

shut for the entirety of my time here. Or possibly the rest of my life. At the rate things were going, permanent muteness seemed like the safest bet.

Vivian turned to her daughter with a look of confusion evident on her face, "I could have sworn you said you were engaged to a costar."

"No, Mom. I said we met on set," Carrie corrected with what could only be described as mad improv skills. "Margo was the wardrobe supervisor who had such a keen eye for detail that she became indispensable to the entire production. Her work ethic is unmatched, truly a hidden gem in the industry."

*Laying it on a little thick, don't you think?* Especially considering she regarded me as an attempted murderer by scarf.

Vivian's eyes lingered on me for a moment, as if she were attempting to decipher how much of her daughter's words were the truth and how much was pure fabrication. I held her gaze, trying my best to appear as innocent and competent as Carrie was portraying me to be. After what felt like an eternity, Vivian smiled, genuinely this time.

"It seems I've gone and muddled the details. I do apologize. As you know, my eldest here has had many engagements. It's hard to keep up." She looked at me with a knowing glint in her eyes. "It sounds like you're the person to help keep her grounded, Margo. Lord knows she needs someone to keep her on track."

"Auntie Viv," Asher said, speaking up in time to save me from having to come up with a reply, "I think I'd like to head to my room to freshen up before dinner."

I noticed a key card in his hand and realized that at some point while I'd been frozen under his aunt's scrutiny, someone must have checked him in. I was about to follow him before it dawned on me that I would not be sharing his room. I would be expected to share a room with Carrie. This realization sent a chill down my spine.

"Speaking of rooms, here's your new key, darling." Vivian handed Carrie a small white envelope. "An ocean-view suite in one of the private bungalows, as promised. I'm so sorry for the mix-up with your room earlier, but it's all sorted now."

"The hotel had accidentally switched my reservation with the one for my parents," Carrie explained, taking the key from her mother.

"After that, they tried to claim they were all out of suites and tried to give her two small adjoining rooms in the main building," Vivian added, "but I could tell they were trying to save face by claiming the error was ours. All it took was a little push from someone who knows how to get things done to fix the problem."

I had absolutely no doubt Vivian Jacobs was a woman who knew how to get things done. Probably because people were scared to death of disappointing American royalty.

"I'm sure it will be lovely," I said, and for once, I was speaking the absolute truth. It was hard to go wrong with a private suite in one of the most exclusive resorts in the world, after all. Even if I did have to share it with someone I loathed.

"Now, you ladies can freshen up and relax before dinner," Vivian announced, flashing a smile as if she had orchestrated a brilliant performance.

As soon as she left, Carrie turned to me with a sardonic grin. "You're Vivian Jacobs," she mocked in a voice that was clearly meant to be mine even if it sounded nothing like me. "I thought you didn't give a fuck about my family, but there you go, gushing like a starstruck teenager."

"It was Vivian Jacobs. She's a living legend," I offered in my defense.

"I'm well aware of who my mother is. Everyone always reacts like that." It was difficult to tell if she was proud, annoyed, or simply resigned to the fact.

"Now what do we do?" I asked, turning my attention to the much more important issue of how to make our fake engagement believable to her entire family at dinner. "We have to make sure we get our story straight before we walk into that lion's den."

Caroline ran a hand through her hair. "We'll stick to the facts as much as we can."

"Sure. It was hate at first sight."

If I was totally honest, it hadn't been hate at all. I'd secretly believed Caroline Jacobs was a goddess before she'd had me fired, and if I remembered correctly, the first time she said more than two words to me, it had involved stripping me naked and having her way with me. Well, with the fiancée she'd mistaken me for, but regardless, who cared about accuracy when you had a chance to fire off a good zinger?

I sneezed, causing her to step back.

"Are you getting sick? Do you need a doctor for that?"

"For allergies? Um... no."

Caroline studied the key card in her hand as if it were molten lava. "Follow my lead at dinner tonight. Smile and nod. Think you can handle that?"

I gave her a wide grin and nodded like a fool. "Less lunatic. More normal person."

She turned her back to me and began climbing the steps toward the resort. The soft glow of torches illuminated the path, casting dancing shadows on the lush foliage that surrounded us. I followed closely, trying to match her graceful strides with my own less elegant ones, enjoying the sight of her tense shoulders as she led the way. At least I knew I wasn't the only one who was nervous beyond belief at the charade we were about to enact.

A gentle evening breeze teased my nostrils with the mingled scents of plumeria and night jasmine. Despite my nervousness, I was blown away by the manicured perfection of this tropical paradise. Everything, from the twinkling lights on the trunks of the palm trees to the way the moonlight reflected off a swimming pool that looked like a natural lagoon, only added to the surreal feeling that tonight was a dream I hadn't yet woken up from.

As we approached a private bungalow that looked like a secret jungle hideaway, complete with a thatched roof and a flowering hibiscus beside the door, Carrie stopped abruptly, causing me to almost run into her.

"Just remember, whatever your feelings about this arrangement may be—and trust me, I have my own list of reservations nearly as long as that scarf you tried to strangle me with—when we walk out this door for dinner tonight, we are the perfect love story."

"What a pity we're already engaged, or you could have popped the question in front of the whole crowd at the luau. Girls love an excruciatingly public grand gesture." Sarcasm dripped from my words, and I was surprised to see Carrie's expression take on a hint of embarrassment. "No. Please tell me you didn't pop the question to Alex that way."

"I don't want to discuss it." By which, she definitely meant yes.

"Does your family know? Am I going to have to pretend to be the type of woman who falls for that kind of shit?"

"I wouldn't dream of taxing your limited acting skills like that. Clearly, you're not a normal girl who appreciates romance the way I do."

"News flash, princess. I'm as normal as they come. If you

actually go in for that grand gesture bullshit, it's only because you're a spoiled—"

Carrie pressed a finger to my lip, instantly cutting off my airway, stopping my words, and sending a wave of confusion through me as I realized how much this simple touch turned me on. "I wouldn't complete that sentence if I were you," she warned. "I may not be a crime boss like you thought, but you still probably don't want to find out firsthand how many people I have to help me bury bodies."

With that, Carrie opened the door, and I was struck breathless for an entirely different reason.

The interior of the suite exuded refined luxury, with natural grass wallpaper and deep teak accents. The decor gave off a vaguely Asian-inspired feel without crossing the line of being campy or cliché. One entire wall was made of sliding doors and glass, opening to a private lanai with an unobstructed view of the ocean, where the final rays from the setting sun painted the waves in shades of pink and gold.

Sometimes, while eating ramen in my shitty apartment, I'd wondered how the other half lived. Now I knew, and I won't lie. It was glorious.

"I'm going to go change." Carrie headed past the dining area and living room, disappearing through a door that I assumed led to one of the bedrooms.

"What about me?" I asked, trailing after her like a lost puppy.

She stepped back out into the hallway. "What about you?"

"Where are my bags?"

"I assume they're in your room."

"Which would be where?" My eyes scanned the suite, quickly locating another door off the living area. "Oh. Never mind. I think I found it."

I went to the door and opened it, only to find it was a closet. The next revealed a half bath. What type of hotel room had a half bath? I couldn't even imagine why anyone would need that.

I was beginning to despair when I spotted a third door, so well camouflaged I would have overlooked it if not for the sleek handle that caught the light. I headed toward it with high hopes of a room to call my own for the night. I turned the handle and swung the door open, revealing not a bedroom but a small office with a desk, a plush armchair, and a large window overlooking the resort's lush gardens. It was a cozy and intimate space, but it did not contain a bed. Or even my wayward luggage.

At this point, I seemed to have run out of doors.

"Um, Carrie?" I called out, my voice echoing in the massive suite. "I think I need some help."

She stepped out of her room wrapped in a fluffy bathrobe, and my traitorous brain took that opportunity to remind me that all it would take was a simple untying of the belt to send it cascading to the floor. I shook my head vigorously, trying to banish the inappropriate image that invaded my mind.

"What's wrong? You look like you're trying to dislodge a bug from your ear."

My face went up in flames. "Uh, there doesn't seem to be a second bedroom."

"There has to be one." Carrie waltzed to the first door I had tried, and I let her see for herself because I had a feeling nothing I could say would stop her.

The woman thought I was a moron, and okay, I hadn't been brilliant when meeting her mother, but even I could spot the difference between a closet, a bathroom, and a bedroom. Nevertheless, she tried every door I had already checked. Twice.

"This is my mother's doing," she announced when she reached the same conclusion I'd already come to several minutes before. "She was so insistent on getting me a suite, she failed to realize I'd requested two bedrooms for a reason. No wonder your luggage is in my room."

"We are supposed to be engaged," I pointed out with a dry smile, enjoying the way she huffed as she paced back and forth across the living room.

"I get the bed."

"Why's that?" I crossed my arms, daring her to hit me with her most entitled explanation. She didn't disappoint.

"Because I'm paying for the room, and I'm paying for you to be here. A ridiculous amount, I might add."

I sucked in a deep breath, indignation burning through me, but honestly, what could I say? I wanted the bed, but she kind of had a point. Damn her. "What am I supposed to do? Sleep on the desk?"

Caroline went to the couch. "This has to pull out."

Sadly, she was correct.

I wanted to battle her because I was willing to bet the real bed was the type fit for royalty, while the couch mattress would be lumpy and miserable. But one look at her expression told me there would be no winning.

## CHAPTER FIVE

"*A*re you almost ready, my love?" In addition to choking on the word *love*, there was no disguising the sarcasm in Carrie's voice as she called out to me through the bathroom door.

"Better practice your lines, sweetheart," I replied, taking one last look at myself in the mirror before braving her scrutiny.

I'd been pleasantly surprised by the choices Asher had packed for me, all very chic and old money in style, but that didn't make me any more comfortable wearing something other than my usual ultra-casual clothing. The dress I'd chosen for tonight's luau was a soft coral color that looked surprisingly good against my olive skin, even if the flowy fabric made me feel like I was playing dress-up in a much more sophisticated woman's closet.

I cringed at the mess I'd left in our shared bathroom, certain Carrie would not appreciate the scattered garments and beauty products strewn across the counter. She'd already claimed the bedroom for her own, and if I wasn't careful, I might find myself banished to the half-bath for the rest of the trip. But we were already running late, and there wasn't a spare moment to tidy up.

When I emerged from the bathroom, Carrie was lounging on the bed, looking every bit the Hollywood starlet in a slinky teal dress that clung to her curves like a second skin.

"Took you long enough," she drawled, but as she turned to face me, her icy blue eyes scanning me with an inscrutable gaze that felt as sharp as a blade against my skin.

"What's wrong?" I wrapped my arms around my boobs, certain I was being judged unfavorably. "Is one of my nipples showing?"

"Huh?" Carrie blinked a few times, and I could've sworn I saw the color in her cheeks darken slightly. Had I misinterpreted the message in her demeanor? "No, you're fine. Caught me off guard is all. You look... nice."

The slight tremor in her voice was at odds with the casualness of her words. I tried to search her expression for a clue to what this meant, but she averted her gaze, suddenly very interested in something on the nightstand.

I raised an eyebrow, uncertain what to make of all this. "Nice?"

Carrie cleared her throat, sitting up a little straighter on the bed. "Yes, well, you know... It's a change from those grungy T-shirts you wore on set that made you look like you've wandered away from a nearby homeless encampment."

"Gee, thanks for the glowing praise," I said with a snort, realizing I should've expected a backhanded compliment. Not to mention exaggeration. I never looked that bad at work, did I? Maybe I did. "I'll have to let Asher know you approve of his costume choice for this event."

"Asher picked out your clothes?" Carrie's eyes trailed over my body as if trying to decipher hidden clues. "Interesting..."

"I'm great at dressing others, but when it comes to myself, I can't be bothered. You know, it's like a Michelin star chef eating cheese from a can in the privacy of their own home." I studied her face, my belly tightening as I tried and failed to make sense of the neutral expression that cloaked her features. "What's wrong? Do I need to change?"

"No. You look fantastic."

Apparently, in the span of a minute, I'd been upgraded from nice to fantastic, and without the slightest trace of a barb hidden in her words. Did this mean Carrie actually meant what she said, or was she just getting better at delivering her lines?

"We should get going, or Mom will give me a demerit for tardiness." Carrie put her arm out for me to loop my own arm through. It was an unexpected gesture, and not particularly welcome, but I had to play the part if I was going to keep up my end of the bargain.

As I slid my arm behind her elbow, my hand made contact with the exposed skin along the low-cut back of her dress, sending a jolt of awareness through me. I quickly withdrew, trying to ignore the tingling sensation that lingered on my fingertips. The touch was innocent, accidental even, but it sparked an unexpected heat, a surge of excitement that pulsed through my body and awakened every nerve.

"Lead the way, Princess." I chuckled in an effort to mask the sudden rush of attraction that threatened to light me on fire.

Carrie shot me a quizzical glance, perhaps catching the slight tremor in my voice. "Princess, huh? I'm not sure how I feel about this choice of nickname."

She held out her arm again, more insistent this time, and I had no choice but to entwine my arm with hers. This time, I was exceedingly careful not to let my fingers wander. The last thing I wanted was to set off any more unexpected sparks that could potentially burst into flames.

I needed to have a serious conversation with my libido. This was hardly the appropriate moment for it to act so rebelliously. No good would come from giving in to temptation, not even in the smallest of ways. It was much too risky to let myself be swayed by the woman's intoxicating proximity. She was an actor, and this was all fake. I would do well to remember that.

We traveled the path up to the main building of the resort, tropical paradise flanking us on both sides. For a moment, I was distracted by the lush vegetation, the distant sound of waves crashing against the shore, and the subtle fragrance of exotic flowers that filled the air. It was almost enough to drown out the nearness of Carrie's warmth and the scent of her perfume, but not quite.

"This is going to take some getting used to," I said.

"What is?" Carrie whispered, her voice light and teasing as if she knew the effect she had on me. God, I sure hoped that was all in my mind.

"Everywhere I look is picture-perfect." Instead of the lush landscape I'd intended to reference, my eyes drifted to her cleavage, and my clit instantly stood at attention as if begging for me to ditch the idea of doing anything to quash my libido.

"It takes my breath away each time." Thankfully, her gaze was fixed on the path ahead and not on me, or it would have been impossible to hide the heat spreading across my face faster than a lava flow.

"You've been here before?" I asked, feigning interest in polite conversation to cover my embarrassment.

"Yes, many times. Ever since I was a kid."

"Huh. We went on a road trip to the Wisconsin Dells for a family vacation when I was a kid. Not quite the same."

"When your mother is the most famous woman in the world, you don't get to go to the same places as everyone else." It was hard to tell from her tone if this was something that made her happy or sad. "A private resort like this is the only place I've ever been able to relax without having to worry about an unflattering photo being plastered on the internet."

As we reached the courtyard where the tables had been set for the luau, Carrie slowed her steps. The glow of tiki torches illuminated the space, casting dancing shadows on the ground, while the scent of roasting pig was enough to make me want to race to find a table.

But Carrie seemed less eager to join in the festivities than I had expected. Her eyes scanned the crowd, her expression guarded.

"What's wrong?" I asked, noticing the tension in her posture.

Carrie's grip on my arm tightened imperceptibly. "I think I saw someone I know."

I couldn't help but let out a soft laugh. "I imagine so. Isn't your whole family here?"

"That wasn't what I... oh, never mind."

Her eyes seemed to follow a flash of red that almost instantly blended into the crowd. My insides tightened. I was beginning to hate the color red. But Carrie shook off whatever had been troubling her, and the next moment, a smile as bright as the midday sun lit up her face. "Ready to meet my dad?"

"S-sure," I choked out, feeling about as prepared as a fledgling bird getting kicked out of the nest for its inaugural flight.

"Wait. You need to put this on first."

A moment later, I felt a warm metal band sliding onto my left ring finger. When I looked down, a flash of more diamonds than I could count caught the torchlight. "Holy shit. Is this thing real?"

"What do you think? That I'd risk having you wear a fake in a crowd like this?"

I swallowed, suddenly aware of the weight of my left hand. "What if I lose it or something?"

"Why? Is it the wrong size? I told Asher to make certain."

"No, it fits just fine." Perfectly, in fact, not that my heart needed to flutter quite so much at the realization. "But it must be worth a fortune."

"Don't worry. With all my broken engagements, I get a bulk discount at my jeweler. Buy one more, and I'll get one free." There was a lightness to her tone, but it didn't come across naturally.

Leaving me to digest this bit of raw humor, Carrie waved excitedly toward a slightly built man with silver hair standing near the center of the courtyard. "Daddy!"

He turned to face us, and I could see that while the blond hair and Amazonian stature was all Carrie's mother's influence, her father had the same easy smile that could charm anyone in a heartbeat.

Not me, of course. But lots of people seemed to fall for that kind of thing.

He'd been chatting with a group of distinguished-looking guests, but as soon as he spotted Carrie, his face broke into a wide grin. He excused himself from the conversation immediately and made his way over to us.

"There's my princess!" The man enveloped her in a warm hug while I felt vindicated to discover I was not the only one who thought the royal nickname suited her.

"Dad, I'd like you to meet Margo, my fiancée."

I had to hand it to her, this time she nailed her lines to the point I nearly believed them myself. My heart fluttered a little, despite my better judgment, as I extended my hand to shake his.

Her father's grip was firm and warm, and his eyes held a spark of curiosity as he looked me over. I wondered exactly how many times he'd had similar introductions to other people his daughter had been convinced she was going to marry.

He tilted his head, a smile spreading across his tanned face. "It's a pleasure to meet you, Margo."

"Likewise, Mr. Jacobs."

Carrie's grip tightened around my arm to the point of blocking the circulation. I knew I'd done something wrong, though I had no idea what.

"It's Mr. Blythe," Carrie said through clenched teeth. "Thomas Blythe."

Oh, shit. That was definitely something a real fiancée should have known. "I'm so sorry, Mr. Blythe," I stammered, feeling the heat rise to my cheeks.

"Call me Tom. And I get that all the time. Hazard of being married to the most famous woman on the planet." He laughed, but I detected a hint of melancholy beneath the easy-breezy facade and a tightening of the crinkles around his eyes.

Poor guy. Just how much of his life was overshadowed by his wife's illustrious career? I wondered if he was always in her shadow, constantly overlooked or called by the wrong name. I found myself feeling a pang of sympathy for the man, even though I barely knew him. Standing next to Carrie right now like a plain moth beside a gorgeous butterfly, I had a keen sense of what it must feel like to be him.

"Please tell your mother the champagne will start flowing

at ten," Tom told Carrie, after which he dipped his head goodbye.

I watched him head away, coming within mere inches of his wife. Why had he asked Carrie to deliver the message instead of telling her himself? I wanted to ask, but I knew I'd already made a mess of things with the name thing, and I didn't want to dig myself in any deeper.

"I'm sorry about getting your dad's name wrong," I said to Carrie as soon as Tom was out of earshot.

She shot me a withering look before sighing dramatically. "It's fine. I mean, a quick look on my Wikipedia would've told you everything you needed to know. But it's... whatever."

"I really am sorry. If Asher had told me ahead of time who you were, I would have come better prepared." In truth, if he'd told me everything, I would've been back in LA right now, packing for my move home to Minnesota. But that was a minor detail.

"It's a sore point between us sometimes. My legal name is Blythe. All my siblings use his name professionally, too. But I started acting when I was a toddler, and my mom chose my stage name. It is what it is."

She looked away, and I had to wonder if that was the full truth or a story she'd latched on to. Her career had certainly benefited from the association with her mother, to a degree that even I had heard the whispered accusations of nepotism more than once where Carrie was concerned. Not that she didn't have talent. She certainly did. But her illustrious family name cast a long shadow over her achievements.

Leading me through the growing crowd, Carrie whispered, "We're about to meet the bride-to-be. Her name's Cagney. And the groom is—"

"Erik Draper. I know."

She whipped her head to meet my gaze, her eyebrows

shooting upward. "I thought you didn't follow celebrity news."

"Asher explained that much to me on the boat." I hesitated, biting my lip as I contemplated what else I had learned on the ride over. "Um, you know George Patrick and Kermit Gray are both here, right?"

"You don't know my legal name, but you know about that embarrassing incident from my past?" Carrie's lips thinned into a tight line.

"I don't live under a rock," I pointed out in my own defense. "Anyone who stood in a grocery store checkout line ten years ago knows what happened."

Carrie forced a tight smile at my comment, clearly uncomfortable with the reminder of her past. "To answer your question, yes. I know they're both here. It's water under the bridge."

Gracefully navigating the sea of guests, Carrie led me to a spot near where hula dancers were beginning to assemble for the evening's entertainment.

"Cagney!" Carrie went up to a woman who could have been her ten years ago. "Don't you look picture-perfect tonight."

"Is this the new flavor?" Cagney eyed me and let out a boisterous laugh.

"This is Margo." Carrie's fingers dug into my arm again, making me regret that Asher had not packed me something with long sleeves because I was going to be bruised beyond belief if this kept up. "My future wife."

I nearly choked on my own tongue at this introduction. Of course, being called a fiancée implies that you'll eventually be a wife, but to hear it in so many words came as a shock. What the hell were we playing at?

"Of course," Cagney said, though her tone seemed to

imply she'd believe it when she saw it. "How lovely to meet you."

"The pleasure is mine," I ventured to say, not liking the glint in Cagney's eyes. Like she suspected something was amiss. I didn't want to say anything that would contribute to those thoughts. Why did she look so familiar, aside from being Carrie's sister? I could almost picture the movie poster with her image, but it fizzled at the edges, making it impossible to conjure the title.

"Here's the lady of the hour." Erik Draper swooped in, and a little part of me that was still a middle school girl with the actor's posters on my bedroom wall swooned. He lifted his bride-to-be's fingertips to his lips. "My Juliet."

Surely, he wasn't referencing the Shakespearean play. Did he not know how that one ended? I was only a costumer, but even I knew it didn't go well. You'd think an actor would be up on these things.

Cagney giggled like a girl who had been invited to sit at the popular table in the cafeteria. "You always know how to make an entrance," she purred. "Have you met Carrie's new, uh…"

"Fiancée," I supplied, clenching my jaw slightly. I knew this was a charade, but if I'd actually been engaged to this woman's sister, I would have had every right to be livid by now. It was no wonder Carrie had dreaded her family finding out about her breakup.

"Yes, that's right." Cagney laughed it off like she'd done nothing wrong. "Margie, was it?"

"Margo." This time it was Carrie whose jaw looked ready to crack in two from the pressure of gritting her teeth.

Erik turned his attention to me, and the starstruck teen in me sobered up fast at the almost lascivious look in his eyes. "It's a good thing I'm engaged because—" He finished the statement by making a lewd sound followed by biting into his bottom lip.

"Oh, Erik. You're impossible." Cagney swatted his hand, dragging her groom away.

"Well." I sniffed loudly once they were gone. "He's charming."

"They're perfect for each other."

I took this to mean Carrie didn't have a high opinion of either one of them. I was going to ask her to elaborate, but when I turned to speak, Carrie's gaze was fixed on something in the distance, her face ashen.

"Sandra?" Carrie blinked, her eyes wide with shock. Without breaking her gaze, she whispered, "It can't be."

"Who's Sandra?" I swiveled my head but couldn't for the life of me figure out who in this gathering of the beautiful and elite could have elicited such a reaction.

"Sandra is my ex."

All at once, an overwhelming need to laugh bubbled up inside me, and I barely managed to cover the response with a well-timed cough. "Let me see if I'm keeping up. The other two members of your love triangle are somewhere on this island tonight, and now we've introduced a third player into the mix?"

Carrie nodded, looking grim. My God, this evening had more drama than a telenovela.

As a woman in a stunning red dress approached us, her eyes locked on Carrie, my jaw dropped. Was there anyone in Carrie's romantic past who wasn't a perfect ten? Sandra, at least I assumed that was who it was from the sudden stiffness of Carrie's demeanor, was beyond stunning. I was also fairly sure her dress was the source of that flash of red earlier. No wonder Carrie had been so rattled.

There was a tension in the air as Sandra drew closer, her

gaze fixed on Carrie with an intensity that made my skin prickle. I mentally prepared for whatever was about to happen, which could range from another round of awkward introductions to someone ending up with a cocktail fork to the eye.

Why hadn't Asher packed me an eye patch? I'd at least have one intact eye after this trip.

"Carrie." Sandra's voice was like honey, sweet and alluring. "It's been a while."

"Sandra." Carrie's voice held warmth, despite her skin feeling cool to touch. "I didn't know you were going to be here."

"I'm here with Kermit."

Carrie nearly sputtered, and it was a blessing we'd yet to make it to the bar for a drink, or it would probably have ended up all down Sandra's front. "You're Kermit's plus one?"

"A bit more than that." Sandra extended her left hand to display a rock the size of a golf ball glittering on her ring finger. "We're engaged, actually."

Carrie's mouth fell open for a moment before she caught herself, the corners of her lips twitching slightly. "Engaged? Wow, that's... something."

"We're engaged, too," I heard myself say. Now both of them were staring at me like I'd announced I was from outer space looking for suggestions for a nice place for a snack.

"That's right," Carrie confirmed once she'd managed to snap her jaw back into place. "Margo and I are engaged as well. To each other." She grabbed my left hand and shoved it under Sandra's nose, my own massive diamond ring nearly slicing into one of the woman's nostrils.

And to think I'd worried I would be the one to screw up on the acting front tonight.

"Engaged?" Sandra's perfectly plucked eyebrows shot up, and for a second, I swore I saw a flicker of jealousy cross her face before she composed herself. "What a small world."

"It really is," Carrie said, hooking her arm around my waist and pulling my body against hers with a force that nearly knocked the wind out of me.

"You know George is here." It may have been my imagination, but it seemed that Sandra was taking a great deal of pleasure in that reveal. "Kermie and I are getting together with him tomorrow for brunch. You should join us. Both of you."

Kermie? I was pretty sure I was going to puke. But she had to be joking about brunch.

"Now, isn't that an idea?" Carrie's demeanor didn't show whether or not she liked this particular idea, but I was guessing not. Because it was ridiculous. Sharing a meal with three of her exes. Personally, I would rather sit down with velociraptors. At least with them, you knew they weren't the cuddly types and could prepare ahead of time.

"You know me. I'm full of ideas." Sandra's eyes never left Carrie's, and I was definitely getting some weird unfinished lesbian love affair vibes. This spelled trouble.

"That sounds lovely." Carrie glanced down, her eyes locking on mine like a heat-seeking missile. "Don't you think, Go?"

I was about to ask "go where?" until I realized she was referring to me. *Go?* That was the nickname she'd come up with on the spot? I never thought I'd prefer Cagney's choice of Margie, but I most certainly did. Hell, even Kermie was a better option, and that was something that made me think of a pig talking to a frog.

I smiled and nodded because if I attempted to speak, I'd tell them both where they could *go*.

Despite it being the worst idea ever, plans for brunch were

swiftly settled. As soon as she could manage it, Carrie whisked me away from the crowd.

"Are you insane?" I blabbed when it was safe to speak my mind.

"More and more each second." Carrie laughed in that nervous way that brought to mind padded walls and straitjackets.

I placed my hands on my hips. "This is a very bad idea."

"You think I don't know that?" she spat back. "But I don't see a way out of it."

"Food poisoning," I said, blurting out the first escape plan that came to mind.

"Seriously? That's the worst excuse ever. They'll see right through it."

"Then I will find something to eat at the luau tonight that will literally poison me, because I can't go to this brunch. No way will I be able to pull that off. Not with all of your exes at one table." Who were all perfect specimens, by the way. How could I ever compare?

"You have to."

"I don't think you understand. I won't be able to pull it off. I didn't even know your real name until fifteen minutes ago." Which seemed like another lifetime given this turn of events.

"We'll spend every second of the day tomorrow getting to know each other."

When she put it like that, the prospect wasn't terrible.

Wait! No, it was terrible. Of course, it was!

Dammit, libido. I mentally shook a fist.

I really needed to have a stern word with my raging hormones, pronto. I was right on the verge of swooning at the chance to spend the day getting to know Caroline Fucking Jacobs. I had officially lost the plot.

Carrie's eyes narrowed. "Need I remind you I'm literally paying you to go?"

My daydreams vanished, and commonsense returned just like that. Along with a healthy dose of anger. "To pretend to be the love of your life, not to be tossed into the viper's den. What's this all about, anyway? Was Sandra the one who got away?"

"Don't be ridiculous." Carrie's gaze shifted to the horizon, telling me I'd hit a bull's-eye with that one.

"Seriously," I urged. "Reconsider the food poisoning angle. I volunteer to barf at the table in front of everyone if it will help sell it."

"Not going to happen." Carrie crossed her arms. "What will it take to get you to go with me to this brunch?"

"The bed."

"What?"

"You heard me. I get to sleep in the bed. You get the pull-out couch."

For a moment, I thought she might refuse and storm off, but instead, Carrie sighed in defeat. "You're going to be the death of me, but fine. We have a deal."

## CHAPTER SIX

"How do you live like this?" Opening the bedroom door, Carrie used her cane to clear a path through the clothes I'd discarded haphazardly all over the floor. "It's like a hurricane hit Neiman Marcus in here." She wrinkled her nose at the mess, giving me a pointed look.

"Apparently, when I'm stressed, all semblance of organization flies out the window." I had finally settled on a creamy linen shirt dress and pair of strappy sandals after trying on half my options. Now it was time for accessories. I inserted an earring, changed my mind, and took it out again.

"I'm just surprised, considering how often you lectured everyone on set about the proper care of our costumes." Finally making her way to a chair, Carrie eased herself into it, wincing slightly as she straightened her injured knee in front of her.

"I wasn't that bad," I insisted, even as I hastily scooped up a pile of assorted garments and tossed them into a nearby drawer.

"You practically had a conniption every time you caught

so much as a sock lying around. The other actors called you the Wardrobe Warden behind your back."

"At least I was good at my job. Until I got fired." I chose a different earring and poked it through my lower hole, studying the result in the mirror and letting out a soft groan. "Damn it. This one doesn't work, either."

"You need to relax," Carrie suggested, leaning back in her chair and propping her uninjured leg up on the bed. "It's not healthy to be wound up like this over a silly piece of costume jewelry."

"I can't help it that I'm a stress ball."

"Go with the coral ones. It's a good color on you, and they kind of have a 1930s flair."

"You think so?"

She wasn't wrong. The pair she'd pointed out happened to be my own and not ones Asher had packed for me. They were authentic vintage coral drop earrings from exactly that era, and I'd paid a pretty penny for them, too. I was just surprised she'd noticed a detail like that, perhaps having assumed that she wouldn't have the same interest in fashion history that I did.

"That's one of my favorite eras, for clothing as well as movies," I said as I held one of the earrings up to the light.

"Mine, too. What's your favorite movie from that decade?" There was a sharpness to her gaze, almost like this question was a pop quiz with do or die consequences.

"*Bringing up Baby*," I replied, for once not caring if I passed or failed. When it came to that question, there was only one correct answer, and I was willing to fight anyone who said otherwise.

"Well, obviously." The lines in Carrie's face softened, her whole demeanor growing more relaxed. "Katherine Hepburn and Cary Grant were unbeatable."

"A dynamic duo, for sure," I agreed, surprised at this spark of connection from such an unlikely source.

"Why are you so stressed today? If you don't mind my asking." Instead of sounding annoyed, Carrie almost seemed sincere.

"You're kidding, right?" I shoved the suggested earring into my earlobe. It was the perfect choice, which kind of annoyed me. Considering my line of work, I should have been able to spot it myself instead of relying on some actor to suggest it. "We were supposed to go over our cover stories this morning, but we both overslept. Now we're rushing to get ready before having brunch with three of your exes, who presumably know you a lot better than I do."

"I'm not sure about the last part." Carrie moved to stand and winced again.

"Is your knee okay? I couldn't help noticing the cane. Mostly because I thought you might be coming in here to bludgeon me with it for being late."

"Knee's fine." Carrie spoke through gritted teeth, and there was no question she was lying.

"I told you not to join in on that hula lesson last night at the luau."

"Cagney was doing it." She stated it as if that was explanation enough.

"Cagney's like ten years younger than you. Why didn't you have your cane with you then?"

"Now who's kidding? One rule about Hollywood you need to remember. It's a den of vipers, and actors are the worst kind of gossips. Always whispering behind your back while commiserating about the treachery of the latest humiliating detail circulating in the tabloids." She mimed whispering behind a hand, before finishing with, "Nine times out of ten, they were the ones who leaked it."

"You don't have to tell me that. I've had enough interactions with actors to know they suck."

"Does that include me?" Carrie batted her eyelashes while she popped two ibuprofens into her mouth, chasing them with a swig of water.

"Time will tell."

Carrie laughed. Honest to God laughed like she found it funny. It was something I was starting to appreciate; her evil sense of humor. "You know, most people tiptoe around me, trying not to upset my delicate sensibilities for fear of getting blacklisted. But not you."

"What's the point? You already had me fired."

"That's the second time you've mentioned that this morning. I'm beginning to think you're holding a grudge."

"What I'm holding," I said, giving my reflection in the mirror a final once-over, "is a tenuous grasp on my sanity."

"If this is still about the brunch, don't let it worry you too much. Neither George nor Kermit ever listened to a word I said while I was with them. I don't expect them to have changed much. I was more a trophy than anything." Her lips thinned into a disapproving line.

I noticed she left Sandra off that list, once again making me believe without her saying it that Sandra was the one who got away. I remembered the tabloid coverage of that relationship, too. They'd had a field day with it, of course, painting Carrie as a diva who went through relationships like rolls of toilet paper. But the more I got to know her, the more I suspected there was a depth to Carrie that the tabloids could never capture. Why else would she be going to such great lengths to hide her most recent failure from the world?

"You ready?" I asked, grabbing the room key card from the dresser and putting it in the soft leather handbag that matched my sandals.

Carrie's eyes narrowed. "I need to talk to my cousin about your clothes."

"I know matching your purse to your shoes is a little outdated, but give the guy a break. Considering he had to round up a completely new wardrobe for me, he's basically a miracle worker." Especially considering he was dressing me, a plain Jane if there ever was one.

"I don't disagree. I've seen what you wear to work, remember? If he can make you look this good—"

"You think I look good?" I'll admit I was surprised by the compliment, even if it was veiled in sarcasm. I was even more surprised by how flustered Carrie became when I called her out on it.

"You're not a complete disaster," she confirmed, refusing to make eye contact and fiddling with a pair of sunglasses on the dresser. "Don't let that go to your head or anything."

"Not a chance." But I'd be lying if I said I didn't feel a warm flush of pleasure from our exchange. Which probably just meant I was a total idiot. I knew better than to believe a Hollywood diva.

She leaned the cane in the corner with a look of determination. "Okay. Let's roll."

When Carrie offered her arm this time, I willingly took it. Not only did I enjoy being close to her more than was probably wise given this was going to go up in flames because my life always did, but now I understood something I hadn't the night before. I was her cane.

When we stepped outside, I was truly in awe. It was the first time I'd seen the resort in broad daylight, and it made me wish the sun never set. The water in the distance sparkled like gemstones, while the palm trees swayed gently in the warm breeze. It was a picture-perfect day, and I couldn't help but smile at the beauty of it all.

Carrie glanced over at me as we ambled down the pathway, a soft smile playing on her lips. "Not too shabby, huh?"

I gasped as a yellow and black bird flew past so fast I barely caught a glimpse of it. "Wow, that was incredible," I said, my eyes following the bird until it disappeared out of sight.

"That's a white-rumped shama."

"You're making that up."

"I swear to you I am not."

"I only saw yellow and black. Where's the white?" I squinted, but the bird was nowhere to be seen.

"Under the tail feathers. Do you not know what a rump is?" Her teasing had a husky quality, and I hated to admit it, but it worked on levels she probably never intended.

"I've seen a few rumps in my day." I retorted, feeling a touch indignant. "I just wasn't aware you had a habit of looking up birds' skirts to catch a glimpse of their bare bottoms."

"Now you've learned something new. The white-rumped shama is a songbird. They aren't indigenous, though. They were introduced from Malaysia about a hundred years ago."

"Can you imagine what it must have looked like here back then?" I gave Carrie a sideways glance, making a note of the way her eyes had lit up with excitement as she talked about the birds.

"Considering none of the vegetation on the resort is original to the island, it was probably a lot less glamorous than it is now," Carrie observed, her eyes scanning the horizon.

"Is that true?" I could hardly believe the lush greenery, the vibrant flowers, all carefully curated and tended to, weren't native to the island.

"This particular island is naturally more mountainous in terrain. Think pine trees, not palm trees. There's actually a second resort on the island that's more like a mountain lodge. The place has charm, though it's not as popular with the A-list crowd."

"How the heck do you even know any of that?"

Carrie shrugged. "Some kids went to 4-H camp in the summers. I came here and learned about fauna and flora from the hotel maintenance crew while my mother signed autographs and posed for photos with guests."

Our conversation halted as we stopped in front of a building with classic Polynesian architecture and a roof made of thatched palm leaves. The door opened as a couple made their way out, and as soon as they did, the salty sea air was replaced by the aroma of bacon.

My stomach rumbled.

Carrie chuckled, and I was mortified as I realized she'd heard the sound.

"Alright, alright, let's get you fed before you start chewing your own arm," she teased, holding the door open for me.

The interior was just as charming as the exterior, with wooden beams crisscrossing the ceiling and woven straw mats covering the floor. Carrie made her way toward a table where two men were already seated. George and Kermit, apparently BFFs again now that unfortunate love triangle unpleasantness was well behind them. Hollywood was nothing if not weird that way.

The table was next to a window overlooking the crystal-clear waters of the Pacific Ocean. The waves were so close I could hear them crashing, and I could vividly picture Carrie taking me out and drowning me under them if I screwed up this brunch.

"There's the happy couple." George stood as soon as he spotted us, rushing to pull out a chair for Carrie. After some momentary confusion, Kermit did the same for me, though I gathered his manners weren't quite as baked in as his friend's. Two empty chairs remained.

"Where are the others?" Carrie settled into her chair with only the slightest trace of pain on her face as she situated her knee.

"Sandra's back in the room, probably trying to decide on a pair of shoes." The way Kermit said it, it was clear he found Sandra's indecisiveness endearing.

Carrie responded with a tight smile that I was certain was hiding pain, though not from her knee this time. It may not have been obvious to the men, but I had no doubt she'd been carrying a torch for Sandra long after their break-up. I regretted not having the chance to get all the details earlier today, and not only for research purposes. I was genuinely curious what had happened between them to end a relationship Carrie still clearly held onto in her heart.

Carrie turned her attention to George. "What about your date?"

"She broke up with me about a month ago." George's grin was sheepish, tinged with regret. "Not even the promise of a couple weeks in Hawaii was enough to keep her hanging on."

"Oh, no, George!" Carrie's laugh over his self-deprecating joke was filled with sympathy. "I'm really sorry. If it makes you feel better, I totally understand. None of my relationships have lasted, either."

"Except for ours," I felt compelled to say. Had she already forgotten the existence of her fake fiancée? Or maybe finding out one of her exes was back on the market was enough to make her regret the charade. Even if George was definitely not the one she would have chosen of the three. We had that in common. I was sure I wouldn't have been her first choice, either, if Asher had bothered to ask her opinion before our arrival.

Carrie ordered a Bloody Mary from the waiter discretely milling near the table, and I ordered one as well. My stomach rumbled again, and I cursed the social niceties that demanded we wait for our whole party to be present before diving into the buffet.

Just when I thought I would pass out from starvation, Sandra swanned in, stopping at the other tables to say hello to people as if she was on the way to the stage to accept an Oscar.

"Am I very late?" Sandra's smile was blinding, and it was obvious she didn't give a damn that she had inconvenienced us.

"Not at all." George winked at me, strengthening my feeling of kinship with him. I regretted putting his poster below both Erik's and Kermit's when I was younger. Clearly, I'd been a bad judge of character.

After placing her drink order, Sandra folded her hands on the table and eyed me like a wolf sizing up a juicy rabbit. "I'm dying to know how you two met."

The interrogation had commenced. My eyes darted to the window, wishing I could hurtle onto the beach and start swimming.

"We met on set." Carrie swept up the drink that had just been set down in front of her.

"A workplace romance between actors? Scandalous."

I thought that rich considering they all had worked together. And slept together. Not all at the same time, probably. Although, now that the image was in my head, I couldn't shake it off. Heat was rising to my cheeks, and I nearly snatched the drink from the server's hands to help put out the flames.

Carrie laughed, either not noticing my awkward behavior or choosing to ignore it. "No, nothing like that. Margo worked in the wardrobe department."

"Tell me more. Was it love at first sight?" Sandra wasn't going to let it go, and I couldn't determine if she really wanted the details or if she was absolutely convinced Carrie would not be with such a plain Jane.

"Hardly," Carrie said, and at least, this much was true.

"It was more like a workplace animosity than a romance in the beginning," I offered. "The film was set in the 1940s—sadly not the 1930s, as we both love that era more."

"Do you?" Sandra asked, and I nearly did a fist pump under the table at this revelation of her ignorance. "But why the animosity between you?"

"Because I had to make two identical copies of every outfit due to a certain someone's nacho-flavored Doritos addiction. Orange fingerprints everywhere." Though it had irked me at the time, I chuckled over the memory now.

"I thought I heard somewhere you were doing Keto, Carrie." Sandra's eyes glimmered with the pleasure of knowing this tasty morsel, and I suddenly understood why Carrie had been so keen to hide her cane.

"Modified Keto," Carrie corrected, whatever the hell that meant. "But I'm sure I wouldn't have eaten nacho Doritos."

"Au contraire." I kind of enjoyed the way Carrie bristled as I contradicted her. "I would recognize the smell of them anywhere, considering they happen to be my favorite guilty pleasure."

"In Carrie's defense"—George cleared his throat—"I'm also a stress eater on set."

"And I seem to recall Sandra here hammering down Hershey Kisses like they were life-saving medication." Carrie spoke innocently, but her eyes conveyed if you tell my secrets, I'll blab yours.

"You do!" Kermit laughed, and I realized it was the first time he'd spoken in ages. From the withering look it earned him from his fiancée, I didn't think he'd venture to speak again anytime soon. But to be fair, if Sandra's eye-daggers could actually kill, every last one of us at this table would be dead.

"You still haven't told me how you went from enemies to lovers," Sandra prompted, causing Carrie to squirm a little in her chair.

"Ah, yes. That." Carrie took a long, slow sip of her drink. Probably to buy herself some time to come up with a reply. "You see, one day, Dennis wanted me in this outfit that was truly hideous, but Go here stood up to him. I ended up in this killer skirt that did things to my legs that are probably illegal in five states. After that, I kind of looked at her a different way. I've always had a thing for feisty brunettes."

This would have been kind of a weak story except for two things. First, it had actually happened. I couldn't believe she remembered this exchange, because we'd never even spoken to one another at that point, and I never witnessed her paying attention to me at all. And second, now that I had an image in my head of her wearing that skirt, I would struggle to concentrate on anything else for the rest of the day.

"If I could interject, I'm pretty sure it was illegal in at least twelve states." I flashed a grin at Sandra, relishing the pure, cold hatred Sandra sent my way. "After that, I just had to get over my rule never to date an actor who didn't know how to put clothing back on a hanger, and the rest was history."

"You're one to talk," Carrie nearly roared. "You should see our suite right now. All of Go's sexy dresses are strewn around like confetti. I swear it's like wading through a department store dressing room on a sale day."

Was it weird I was starting to warm up to her nickname for me? The more she said it, the more it suited me. No one had ever called me that before. And, did she really think my dresses were sexy?

"You two sound like an old, married couple." Sandra spoke the statement as a dig, but I could see the relief in Carrie's loosened shoulders. It was only in that moment I finally let out my breath.

Once we finally all made it up to the buffet, the rest of the meal passed in a blur as Kermit and George regaled the others about their recent bro-trip to Botswana.

"Did you see any lilac-breasted rollers?" Carrie asked, keenly interested.

"We did!" George shared a story, but I couldn't focus on the details.

I was too blown away by a startling revelation. The white-butted-what's-it wasn't a one-off. Carrie truly liked birds. As in, she was full out nerdy for them.

Out of all the possible hobbies, birding would have been the last one I would have picked for her. It wasn't glamorous, aside from traveling the world to see it. But I imagined most of the places were more remote, away from crowds. Perhaps that was part of the appeal.

Before I knew it, we were wishing everyone adieu and heading back to our room.

"Nice job with the 1930s reference," Carrie whispered, patting my hand where it was looped through her bent elbow.

"Sorry about the Doritos dig," I said in return.

Carrie's expression filled with chagrin. "Did you really need spare outfits because of that?"

"Uh, well... yes." I felt bad, but I think I would have felt worse lying to her. Which seemed weird. Why did I care? She was my enemy, even if she was pretending to be madly in love with me. None of this was real.

"Why didn't you say something?"

"You do know who you are, right? I needed a paycheck too much to tell the star to lay off the cheesy orange Doritos."

Carrie put her free hand to her forehead. "I wish someone had said something because I do it every time I film. I feel awful to create more work for people."

I was struck speechless—though not by this statement, surprising as it was. It was because, turning onto the same path and heading right for us, was Jenna. My ex. The last person on the planet I wanted to run into in paradise or anywhere else.

"I'm about to do something reprehensible, and please know I'm not looking forward to it, but I need you to go with it. Okay?" I gulped as a stunned Carrie nodded.

The next second, my lips landed on hers.

A shockwave zipped through me, my heart racing. I could feel the heat of her lips, soft and pliant against mine. For a moment, time seemed to stand still, and the world around us disappeared. Somehow, I forgot all about Jenna approaching us, about the tension and animosity that had been brewing between Carrie and me since the second we'd arrived on the island. All I cared about was never letting this feeling end.

For her part, Carrie let out a confused squeak but deepened the kiss almost instantly. Mental note, if you ever need a fake fiancée, choose a really good actor. She got right into the scene with a kiss that had my toes curling in all the best ways.

From the end of a long tunnel, I vaguely heard someone calling my name.

"Margo?" It was louder this time, but it was clear the person speaking no longer sounded convinced it was me.

I broke away from Carrie with great reluctance and what was certain to be a goofy grin spreading from ear to ear. "Jenna! What a small world!" Considering I may have threatened to claw her eyes out the next time I saw her, my cheerful greeting was probably over doing it.

"It is. What are you doing here?"

"We're here for my sister's wedding." Carrie wrapped an arm around me.

"You're Caroline Jacobs." It was almost exactly what I'd said to Carrie's mom the night before, and seeing the stupid expression on Jenna's face right now, I really hoped I hadn't come across that way. How embarrassing.

"I'm sorry. Margo hasn't mentioned you. Did she work on one of your movies, too? That's how we met. And fell in love." Carrie squeezed me. "Isn't that right, darling?"

"No. We moved to California together." Jenna stared as if she were imagining the scene before her.

"Wait." Carrie shook her head in disbelief. "You two dated? Go never told me that."

While it was the truth, it was also a delightful zinger. *Take that, Jenna!*

"This is Luke Abbott," Jenna introduced the man who had strolled up behind her, clutching his arm like a lifeline. For his part, the director my ex had left me for looked excited enough to pee his pants.

"I'm a huge fan, Ms. Jacobs." He shook Carrie's hand like she was royalty. "I heard a rumor your family was on the island, but I didn't think I'd be lucky enough to bump into you."

"We're staying at the other resort," Jenna said in what was a desperate attempt to insert herself back into the conversation. "The mountain one. It's more remote. To give us more privacy. Isn't that right, Abbie?"

Or because it was the best they could do as a solid C-list actor and a director with almost zero name recognition. But what do I know?

"You know, Ms. Jacobs," Luke said, ignoring Jenna entirely, "I have this new film project—"

Jenna pulled on his arm like she intended to remove it from its socket. "We better get going for our scuba lesson, dear."

Left alone, Carrie boosted her eyebrows at me. "So that was your ex."

"It was ages ago." I made a pshaw noise.

"Still, I actually did recognize her from her last film, even if I pretended not to. You're keeping me on my toes." She didn't say it like it was a bad thing, which left me more confused than anything.

"Don't let the shock keep you up at night," I huffed.

"I won't. I'm going to sleep like a baby tonight." Carrie's eyes sparkled with mischief, and my stomach tightened.

"Why's that?"

"Because, after that little unscripted make-out stunt you pulled, obviously, I get the bed."

## CHAPTER SEVEN

I sat at the edge of the pool, dipping my feet into its coolness as the sun beat down, turning the surface of the water into a sparkling mosaic of light. I gave a discreet tug at my bikini top, unaccustomed to wearing something quite so low cut and revealing. Leave it to Asher to choose the sexiest one he could find. I was eternally grateful for the cover-up I'd draped over my shoulders.

I was starting to wonder if it was really just about projecting the right image for a fake fiancée, or if he secretly was trying to get his cousin to fall for me for real. Not like there was a chance of that happening. I mean, I didn't look half bad in the thing, even if my skin was a little pasty and my boobs kept trying to escape. But this resort was filled with movie stars. Carrie wouldn't look twice at normal ol' me with so many more beautiful people to catch her eye.

Not that it was even an issue right now. Carrie was off with Cagney doing some sort of super important bridesmaid stuff. For the moment, I was alone. I'd come to the pool for some time to myself to process. And after brunch this morning, there was a lot to mull over.

"There you are!" Asher waved from the other side of the pool. A second later, he did a cannonball into the water, splashing me and earning disapproving looks from some of the other swimmers in the adults-only pool.

"You're such a child sometimes," I chided. "Lucky for you, it's hot out, so I don't mind."

"I've never understood people who go to a pool but get angry if they get water on them." He shook his hair vigorously, sending water droplets all over me as if to hammer home his point.

I laughed even though I knew he probably didn't need the encouragement.

Hefting himself onto the smooth stone edge of the pool, he settled beside me, though he continued kicking his feet like a kid on a sugar rush. "How's everything going with you and my cousin?"

"It's been..." After searching my vocabulary for the right word, I settled on, "interesting."

"Interesting good? Or bad?"

"To be determined. Do you know what we did this morning? Brunch—"

"Lucky duck," he chimed in before I could finish my thought. "The only thing I've had a chance to eat today is a pack of peanuts I took from the plane. I'm telling you, this director's strike is a crock. The people who should really be striking are wedding planners. It's inhumane."

"I take it Cagney is a bit of a bridezilla?" I hadn't quite figured out what I thought of Carrie's youngest sister, or her husband-to-be, for that matter. The first impressions had been less than stellar, but I was trying to keep an open mind.

Instead of answering my question, Asher acted out zipping his lips shut. I hated it when he did that because he was one of the few people I knew who could actually resist spilling secrets if he'd specifically sworn not to. Good news if it was my own business he was keeping, not so good when I wanted intel on someone else.

"Fine. Be that way." I crossed my arms, pretending to be madder than I was. "Before you rudely interrupted, I was about to tell you we had brunch with not one, but three of your cousin's ex-fiancés. Talk about being thrown into the deep end. With rabid sharks."

"George and Kermit?" His quizzical expression claimed he didn't buy that.

"No, George seemed nice, and Kermit, it was hard to tell. But I mostly was referring to Sandra."

"Yeah. She's…" Asher shuddered.

"Cutthroat?" It was the best word I could think of to describe her. "What's the story between Carrie and Sandra, anyway? She's supposedly madly in love with Kermit, but I swear the woman kept staring at me like she wanted to rip my heart out with her bare hands and eat it."

Asher shrugged, looking over his shoulder at a couple passing behind us to avoid making eye contact.

"Come off it. I can't believe you have any interest in keeping Sandra Harris's secrets. Don't pretend like you aren't one of the biggest gossip whores when you want to be."

"Hey now. Language." He laughed, knowing full well he used worse language in his sleep. "My impression of Sandra has always been she's the type to think everyone else's toys are better than hers."

I leaned close, whispering, "Did she cheat on Carrie? Is that why they split up?"

"No idea, but I wouldn't be surprised."

"What do you mean by no idea? I get it if you promised not to say, but surely your cousin told you."

"Nope. Not a word. Carrie has spilled the beans on all of her other relationships but not that one."

I studied the sunlight on the water for a moment, not sure what to make of this revelation. "Don't you find that curious?"

"Very. But Carrie isn't the type who likes to be pushed on details. And while I may be willing to talk out of turn about a lot of the actors in the biz, Carrie isn't one of them."

"Because you love and respect her?" I guessed, secretly admiring his noble streak.

"Exactly. Plus, she scares the crap out of me." His fearful expression seemed convincing enough.

"Oh, sure. Now you tell me." I jabbed my elbow into his side. "Can I run something past you from earlier today?"

"Sure."

"At brunch, I was kinda floored when Carrie shared stories about times we interacted on set."

"Bad stories? Scandalous stories? Did you not so accidentally cup her breasts during a fitting?" Asher waggled his eyebrows, and I rolled my eyes as I elbowed him again.

"No. Just true stories. Which was bizarre. I would have sworn on a stack of Bibles all the way to the moon that she had never noticed me on set until the day she had me fired."

"That's something to mull over." He nodded, his expression thoughtful. "One thing you should know about my cousin, she has perfected the art of affecting a dead-eye stare when in fact, she's paying attention to everything going on around her."

"Hey there!" Carrie popped up out of the water, and I nearly jumped out of my skin. "What are you two talking about?"

No wonder Asher found her scary. She was like a silent assassin with the way she could sneak up on a person.

"You, sweetheart." Asher blew her a kiss, before hopping to his feet and dashing off, leaving me to fend for myself.

"What was that all about?" she asked, bewildered.

What was meant to be a quick glance in Carrie's direction became a full-fledged stare as whatever answer I'd been about to give died on my lips at the sight of her bosom rising up from the water. My heart pounded like it was attempting a drum solo as water streamed over her bronzed shoulders. She shook her long blond hair, and I swear it was like a scene ripped from a movie. Or possibly from one of my dreams last night, one I would never admit to, no matter how much I was bribed.

Carrie rested her arms on the side of the pool, not moving to get any further out of the water. "I think I'm ready for a drink."

"I can get it. I'm already out." I started to get up, but she placed a hand on my leg, the warmth of her touch searing through me like a hot poker.

"No, hop in and join me. There's a swim-up bar." She hesitated a moment before adding, "Being in the water is easier."

From the way she said it, I guessed she was referring to her knee. But I could tell from the initial reluctance that she didn't really want to make a big deal of it. So, I simply shrugged. "Sure, why not? When in Hawaii and all that."

I have never felt as self-conscious in my life as I did removing my cover-up. I've never claimed to be an expert on chopped liver, but I sure knew how it must feel to be in the deli case next to all of those sexier lunch meats. That was basically me as I slid into a pool with at least a dozen members of Hollywood's A-list beauties looking on because whenever Carrie was around, all eyes gravitated toward her.

Quickly, I fully submerged my body in the water, wanting

to hide as many of my flaws as possible from view. As I surfaced, I was confused to find Carrie watching me with an intensity that made my throat go dry. Was she judging me on my awkward entrance, or was there something else in those piercing blue eyes? Probably regret she hadn't quizzed Asher about the mystery woman he was bringing.

"I feel like a drowned rat," I told her, wearing a sheepish smile as I peeled away the strands of hair that were plastered to my face.

"If that's the case, you're the most glamorous drowned rat I've ever seen," she quipped, her tone teasing. She held out a hand. "Ready, my love?"

I took hold of her hand, not knowing what to think as I let her pull me through the water toward a squatty tiki hut at the far end of the pool. Had she really meant to say I was glamorous? I couldn't imagine how, unless she'd temporarily forgotten the meaning of the word.

We found two seats on one side that were unoccupied, and we ordered mai tais, saying it at the exact same time and dissolving into laughter on the spot.

The bartender, a friendly man with a thick Hawaiian accent, grinned and started preparing our drinks.

Carrie leaned in closer, her lips almost brushing against my ear. "You know, Margo," she began in a low voice, "I have to admit this is the highlight of my day so far."

"I'm not sure that speaks highly of your sister's company," I told her, fighting back a giggle at the tickle that traveled from my earlobe to the base of my spine. "Day drinking is usually considered a silent cry for help."

"Day drinking? Oh, hmm..." It almost seemed like she'd been thinking of something other than the trip to the bar as the highlight of her day, but I couldn't imagine what. Maybe taking a dip in the swimming pool.

"What's Cagney up to, anyway?" I asked.

"Our other sister, Camilla, got in from New York last night. She's been doing a show on Broadway. Anyway, Cam took Cagney off my hands for a bit. Which was good because I hear it's bad luck to kill the bride before the wedding."

"Possibly criminal depending on the reasons," I cracked. "Seems like the two of you don't get along."

Carrie lifted the freshly made drink to her lips as if she needed liquid courage to broach the subject.

But the silence dragged on a second longer, so I assumed she wasn't going to say anything. Maybe Cagney and Sandra were both off-limits where topics of conversation were concerned.

But when about half her drink was gone, Carrie started to speak again. "Cagney and I used to be really close. She's my baby sister, you know? I'm not proud of this, but the past couple of years have been difficult between the two of us, and it's basically my fault."

"What happened?"

"Hollywood bullshit. That's what always gets in the way of every relationship." There was no mistaking the bitterness in her tone.

I frowned. "What do you mean?"

"You know the role Cagney has won every single award on the planet for this past year?"

"What movie was it again?" I didn't want to outright admit I had no clue who her sister was. Even though I worked in Hollywood, I wouldn't call myself a movie buff. Not for contemporary ones at least.

"Lovers and Thieves. It was her debut performance, and she received rave reviews and accolades."

"That's it! I can picture the movie poster now." Cagney

had been practically naked on it, so I was surprised I'd forgotten.

"Originally, I was the one they were going to cast in that role. But the project changed directors, and the new guy wanted someone younger. So he hired my little sister. He literally told me to my face that my best years were behind me."

"J-Jesus," I spluttered.

"It's why I don't want anyone to see me hobbling around on my cane while this stupid knee injury heals. I already feel way past my prime. I don't really need to round out the image." She made a circle in the air with her index fingers, and I couldn't stop staring at how slender and perfect they were.

"Does Cagney know what happened between you and the director?"

"I'm not sure." Carrie took another hefty dose of liquid courage, draining the last of her mai tai and signaling the bartender for another. "I hate myself for it, but I'm jealous as hell of her. It was her first movie. She wasn't sure she wanted to follow in our mom's and my footsteps, you see. Now everyone's treating her like some prodigy. I've been busting my butt since I was a toddler for this career, and she waltzes in front of a camera and wins everything on the first go. This business is emotionally exhausting sometimes, and it messes with your head."

"I kinda get where you're coming from," I said softly.

To my surprise, Carrie pushed her new drink aside and turned her focus on me. The intensity of her gaze made me feel like I was suddenly under a spotlight, but I also sensed she truly wanted to hear whatever story I was going to share.

"When I was growing up in Minnesota, I thought I would go into my family's business, too. Dry cleaning," I added in response to Carrie's slight head tilt. She chuckled, and I laughed along, aware of what a far cry my current life was compared to what I'd once imagined. "I know. Glamorous, right? But my grandparents started Busy Bee Cleaners back in the 1950s, and it's been a part of my life for as long as I can remember. My mom and grandma taught me everything about tailoring, alterations, and customer service. I was set to take over the business one day."

"What changed?"

"I got a job doing costumes at a local dinner theater, where I met and fell in love with Jenna. Like an idiot, I followed her to LA. It was rough at first. I found a job at a theater, which is where I met your cousin. But Jenna wasn't getting roles, and she couldn't hold a job because she needed so much time off to go to auditions. So I eventually moved into doing wardrobe for a small studio, networking for her as I worked my way up. I was responsible for getting her first big break, and she repaid me by dumping me for her director."

"The guy we met earlier?"

"The very one." My cheeks burned as I recalled the run-up to that meeting, the way I'd grabbed Carrie and kissed her like my life had depended on it. Was Carrie thinking of it, too? I didn't dare turn my head to see her expression, staring instead at my barely touched drink.

"If it makes you feel better, she didn't trade up with that move, no matter what she told you or how she made you feel."

Gobsmacked by those words, I did what I always did when offered a compliment: I changed the subject. "Are you really as into birding as it seems?"

"Yes. Does that surprise you?"

"Very much so. What's the appeal?" I tried to convey an honest interest, and I could tell by how her eyes crinkled that she'd taken it the right way.

"It's hard to explain." There was a joy reflected from the

depths of Carrie's eyes of a type that few other topics sparked in her. "I've been surrounded by beautiful people all my life, but it's all so fake. I find birds to be so gorgeous and real. Also, they live in the most unspoiled places on the planet. Do you know"—she turned on her seat in the water—"honesty is a core value among birders?"

"How so?"

"More often than not, there's no time to get a photo to prove you've seen a rare bird. Instead, we record it in a journal. It's all about trust and honesty. I think that's what pulls me in." She took a sip of her drink, but not a gulp as she had before, seeming more relaxed. "I'm so sick of bullshitting. Like your ex's director. It took me less than a second to suss out he's here to get someone to star in his next film."

"He was pretty transparent about it," I agreed. "Do you think that's why they came here? I don't know how widely known it is that your family is here right now, but it wouldn't surprise me if that's why they suddenly decided to visit Hawaii."

"It wouldn't be the first time someone tried to cozy up to the Jacobs name for their own gain." Carrie's jaw was tight. "The fact your ex finds that type of person attractive, though? Count your blessings she's out of your life."

It was the most personal conversation we'd ever had, and I was starting to wonder how many cocktails she'd imbibed between brunch and now. But there was a sharpness to her expression that made me believe she was fairly sober. I wasn't sure what to make of that.

"About tomorrow," Carrie said, letting out a deep sigh. "My sister has booked us all to go zip lining. I tried getting out of it, but... well, you know the women in my family."

"Will your knee be okay?"

She shrugged. "Sure. Probably. Anyway, plan to be up early so we can get to the hotel's shuttle in time."

"I'm going?" I squeaked.

"Naturally. I may not need the cane, but with all my siblings and my parents there, I will need the moral support." She quickly added, "It'd be noticeable if I didn't bring my doting fiancée." She batted her lashes in a mocking way, effectively stomping any hope that we were connecting.

But I had a bigger problem to contend with.

"Doting, huh? You always ask the impossible." I swallowed, trying to sound calm even as my heart threatened to beat its way out of my chest. "How high will we be?"

"Kinda high." Carrie's eyes narrowed. "Why? Please don't tell me you're afraid of heights."

"Of course not." It technically wasn't a lie because I wasn't merely afraid. I was petrified. "Sounds fun."

## CHAPTER EIGHT

"Why do mornings have to start so early?" Sitting on a barstool in the suite's kitchenette, I massaged my pounding head. "Mai tais—so beautiful, so deadly."

"The same can be said of so many of the people in my past." Carrie chuckled over the rim of her coffee cup, looking as refreshed as if she'd had a full night's sleep and a spa treatment instead of rolling out of bed at the crack of dawn.

"How are you looking so perky while I feel like a piece of gristle someone's relentlessly chewed up before spitting out?"

"Wow. There's an image."

"I noticed you didn't answer my question." I would have stared daggers at her if it didn't cause my head to hurt more. "Is it some sort of drugs only Hollywood doctors can prescribe?"

"Hydration. In between every mai tai, I chugged two glasses of water. That's the key to not feeling like roadkill after a night of unlimited cocktails."

"Now you tell me."

"If I remember correctly, I tried telling you last night. I

think your exact response was, 'Why drink water when I can drink a liquid sunset?' You only have yourself to blame."

"You're enjoying my misery."

"It's refreshing to be around someone who doesn't hold back how they feel." She set her coffee cup down and checked the time on her phone. "Chop-chop. We need to meet the rest of the group in twenty minutes."

"Don't worry. I'll rally. I just need..." My voice trailed off as I failed to think of anything that would cure me from my stupidity. Honestly, it felt like the story of my life. My tombstone would probably read: *Here lies stupid*.

"Hold on. I'll get you a sandwich. It's my world famous, time-tested hangover cure. It'll help soak up the extra booze like a sponge in a spill. You'll be right as rain in no time."

"Oh—" I had intended to argue, but as the words belatedly formed a coherent sentence in my foggy brain, I realized she might be onto something. "Actually, that'd be great. I'm going to take a quick shower."

If I was lucky, I'd drown while staring at the showerhead, too out of it to remember to put my head down. I would give anything to be put out of my misery and avoid having to go on the zip line. Just the thought of being up so high made me queasier that I already was.

I stumbled toward the bathroom, the bright light stabbing into my skull with the sharpness of a knife. As the shower heated up, I splashed cold water from the sink on my face, willing myself to snap out of it. The previous night's debauchery was catching up with me in the most unforgiving way, and Carrie's so-called hangover cure sounded like my only salvation at that moment. Life couldn't get much worse.

Stepping into the steaming cascade of water, I let out a sigh as the heat worked its magic, washing away the remnants of the alcohol haze that clouded my mind. As the water cascaded down my weary body, I couldn't help but replay snippets of the previous night's revelry. The loud music, the clinking of glasses, and Carrie's infectious laughter kept echoing in my head.

Had I just called my nemesis's laughter infectious? That wasn't necessarily a compliment. Chicken pox was infectious, too. But on the off chance that sandwich cure actually worked, I didn't see the benefit in clinging to our ongoing, if mostly one-sided, feud. At least not this early in the morning. I'd accept her sandwich offering with as much grace and dignity as I could.

By the time I emerged from the shower and threw on some clothing, feeling marginally more human, I was met with the sight of Carrie standing in the doorway. She held a paper sack in one hand and one of those trendy thermal tumblers that cost more than my weekly grocery budget in the other.

"Here's some coconut water." She handed me the tumbler. "Hydration is key."

"I thought the sandwich was the magical cure."

"It is, but the coconut water keeps it from sticking in your throat. I'll have you know my sandwich cure has fixed the hangovers of more celebrities than you can imagine."

I cocked my head to the side, eyeing Carrie warily. It was hard to believe she was capable of kindness, especially after the way she had orchestrated my dismissal from the set. "Why are you being so nice to me? It's not like anyone's here to witness it."

"I guess you'll have to tell everyone all about it later today." There was a tightness to her smile, like I should have figured this part out on my own.

"Got it." At least I could rest assured that my initial judgment of Carrie's character hadn't been misguided after all.

Her helpfulness was transactional. That was something I could understand. "I may get the hang of being a fiancée by the time this ordeal is over."

"Ordeal? That's a strong word." She fitted her shades to the top of her head where they would be waiting for that moment in the far-off future when the sun finally came up. "Ready?"

"To willingly plunge off a volcano to my death? Sure."

"That's the spirit. Don't forget to drink. Lots of water."

When we met the rest of our group at the tour bus, I was vindicated to discover I was not the only one incapable of more than mumbling or grunting good morning. Aside from Vivian, who looked like she was ready for the red carpet. It should be illegal to always be so put together. Like mother, like daughter. I suspected I was right about the special Hollywood drugs. I was pretty sure both Vivian and Carrie had a secret supply. If so, I wondered if Vivian could hook me up because I was definitely going to need whatever magic potion she was using to survive this day without collapsing.

"The two seats on the rear left side are reserved for a couple of passengers we'll be picking up at the lodge," the driver told us before opening the door. "Otherwise, take your pick."

As we climbed onboard, I was struck by two things. First, while the mini-bus had all the basics, it wasn't exactly luxury at its finest. It almost made me believe the rich traveled like the rest of us. At least it would have if I hadn't known our immediate destination was a private charter flight that would take us to the Big Island.

Second, Carrie's parents didn't sit together. Instead, they opted for both aisle seats in the same row, right in front. This had the potential to make things awkward as nearly everyone was paired up with a significant other.

George, one of only two of the singles on this excursion, squeezed in beside Tom. Meanwhile Cam, Carrie's other sister, whom I had only a vague recollection of meeting the previous night, edged past her mom to take the final seat by the window. Considering Tom and Vivian were known as one of Hollywood's few true love stories, I had to wonder if there was trouble in paradise.

"Where's Asher?" I asked as I completed a quick headcount and realized my friend was not part of the group.

"He's got a full day of wedding planning duties," Cagney explained as Erik rolled his eyes. It was pretty clear the groom-to-be was up to his eyeballs in wedding talk and hated every second of it.

Carrie and I sat together all the way at the back of the bus, with two rows separating us from Cagney and Erik on one side of the aisle and Sandra and Kermit on the other. The amazing thing, neither Carrie nor I had communicated that we wanted to be as far apart from everyone else as possible. It made sense, though, since the less intrusion on the facade of our relationship, the better. Still, it was weird to be on the same wavelength as her. Which was happening more often than not.

When the bus fired up, I leaned in close enough to Carrie's ear that I wouldn't be overheard by anyone else. "What's up with your parents? I thought they were madly in love."

"They used to be." The way she said it, tinged with sadness, made me pause.

"What happened?"

"*Desert Melodies.*"

"Your mom's last movie?"

Carrie nodded, her lips pressed into a thin line. "Mom wasn't around much when I was young. Dad gave up a promising career as an artist to raise the four of us. About three years ago, they'd agreed Mom was finally going to retire so they could travel the world together. Then mom got the script for *Desert Melodies*, and she said she couldn't turn it down. She was convinced it was her comeback role."

"What on earth did your mother need to come back from? She's a household name on seven continents." I thought for a moment, recalling the film in question. "Didn't that movie sweep the Razzies?"

"Worst picture, worst screen writing, and worst actress." Carrie's lips twisted upward before she got her expression under control. "Let's just say, *Ishtar* is a classic compared to that stinker."

"Ouch."

"Dad was devastated. Not that the movie sucked, to be clear. They had a deal, and she broke it. So he stopped talking to her, and it took her such a long time to notice that it kind of stuck. He feels like he doesn't matter." She added with a shrug, "He has a point."

I don't know why, but it shocked me that Carrie had sided with her father on this one. I suppose I had assumed that, as a fellow actor, she would have been more likely to see things her mother's way.

"Whose side are you really on?" I asked in a tone I hoped came across as teasing.

"You're devious this morning." Carrie offered up a wicked grin that did things to me I probably should have tried harder to stop. "Growing up, I spent more time with Dad, but I see both of their sides. It's hard, ya know? Mom's been at the top of the acting world for so long. It'd be a challenge to walk away from all that for good. But Dad spent so many years waiting for her, living in her shadow. And it's a fucking big shadow." She recoiled slightly in her seat.

"I can only imagine. I will say I thought it was classy of your mom to show up to the ceremony to accept her Golden Raspberry in person." I could picture the smile Vivian had worn as she gave her self-mocking acceptance speech.

"I was proud of her for that," Carrie agreed. "It was a bold decision. Of course, the next night, Mom won an Oscar for a different film. That movie was made way before *Desert Melodies*, but the delays in the release benefited her." Carrie's tone implied that was always the case. "That eased the blow and allowed her to play the good sport."

"Play?"

"She's Vivian Jacobs. She's always playing a role, even right now. I just wish she'd decide to play the role of a wife who realizes how much she hurt my father and apologizes for it."

"Your mom has done some amazing apology scenes," I said, thinking back over some of Vivian's best performances. "Like the one in *Redemption's Embrace*, where she delivered that heart-wrenching monologue to her on-screen husband in the rain. She could really make you feel every ounce of emotion with just a single tear."

"Or the one from *Unspoken Truths* where she confessed to her on-screen daughter about the affair she'd had with her best friend's husband. That scene was gut-wrenching, and you could see the pain in every line on her face," Carrie added, a hint of admiration in her voice. "Any one of those would be better than trying to impersonate Kathleen Turner and Michael Douglas in the final scene of *The War of the Roses*."

I shivered. "Didn't they end up falling to their deaths, crushed by a chandelier?"

"Memorable, right? The last thing I want is to drop in on them one day and find two lifeless bodies on the floor."

The bus rocked from side to side as it took a corner,

making my stomach lurch. I grabbed onto the seat in front of me to steady myself, feeling Carrie's hand brush against mine as she did the same. Our eyes met for a brief moment, and I saw a flicker of something in her gaze that made my heart skip a beat.

"Look at this town," I said by way of distraction, pointing out the window to the small collection of palm-thatched buildings we were coming up on. "It's so cute."

Carrie pressed against me to get a better look out the window, foiling my plan to forget all about the way my tummy had gone from lurching to fluttering a moment ago. "This island has one post office, one grocery store, and a single bank. Can you imagine?"

We both chimed in simultaneously, "That sounds delightful."

My cheeks flushed.

"Are you like your mom?" I asked, mulling over the statement she'd made about Vivian earlier. When Carrie gave me an odd look, I clarified, "Always playing a role."

Carrie furrowed her brow, contemplating the question for a moment before answering with a wry smile. "Maybe. Acting is in my blood, after all. But I like to think I'm more authentic than my mother. She takes it to a whole new level. Sometimes I think she forgets how to be herself when she's not in front of a camera. Like she's played so many roles she's forgotten reality."

"Do you want your parents to stay together?" I wasn't sure why I asked. It was intrusive and not really any of my business, even if I was her fake fiancée.

As if to prove I'd gone too far, Carrie's smile faltered for the briefest moment. She turned her gaze back out the window. The picturesque scenery outside seemed to fade into the background as she considered my question. I was almost convinced she was going to give me the silent treatment like her dad did to her mom when she finally spoke.

"I want them to be happy. They've been playing this game for years. Living separate lives under the same roof. It's like a never-ending stage play with no audience but me and my siblings. Sometimes I wonder if they even remember why they fell in love in the first place." She looked at me, her blue eyes searching mine for understanding. "It's complicated, you know?"

I nodded, feeling a pang of sympathy for everyone involved. Before I could say anything else, the bus jerked to a sudden stop, nearly causing me to slide off my seat.

"You're looking a little green." Carrie pointed to the paper sack we'd brought along. "Try the sandwich."

I reached into the bag and pulled out a peanut butter and jelly sandwich. That was her fool-proof hangover cure? It seemed more effective for managing a hungry toddler.

Two rows up, Sandra half stood and announced, "I smell PB&J. Is someone hungover?" She shot me a gleeful glare filled with poisoned arrows, and I could tell the woman was just hoping I would incriminate myself by puking all over the back of the bus.

"Yeah, me." To my surprise, Carrie took the sandwich from my hand and took a big bite, forcing it down. "Poor Go-Go had to put up with me moaning and groaning all night."

"To be fair, I don't usually mind it when she moans," I added, struggling to hold in a grin as Sandra's jaw visibly tightened.

Carrie nearly choked on the sandwich, her face turning a lovely shade of pink as she coughed and sputtered. Seeing her riled up like this was almost worth the risk of being stabbed by Sandra's dagger eyes.

Sandra gave a two-finger salute and turned back around. I

was probably lucky it hadn't been a one-finger salute, which I kind of deserved for my sassiness. The truth was, I hated that Carrie had probably made more than one of her famous hangover cures for Sandra. But it made me feel all warm and fuzzy inside that Carrie hadn't ratted out my poor alcohol tolerance to her ex.

With Sandra no longer paying attention, Carrie returned the sandwich to me, but not before taking another bite. "I always forget how good these are. My dad used to make them for us when we were sad."

Another shock. Carrie was sharing something from her childhood with me. Something that made her happy. My head was spinning from all of these personal revelations.

The bus stopped outside of the mountain resort. When Jenna and her director beau stepped on board, my brain spluttered. It took a second to remember this was where they were staying. Just my luck that they were the final members of our tour group.

When Jenna spied the row next to us was open, she squealed with delight and made a beeline for Carrie and me. My only explanation for this was that in a past life, I'd been a terrible person and was now paying retribution seven-fold.

"Isn't this a surprise, Abbie?" Jenna shoved Abbie—what a stupid nickname for a grown man—to the window seat before taking the aisle. After settling in, she looked at us. "I still can't believe you two are engaged."

Carrie tossed an arm over my shoulder, giving me a squeeze. "And yet, it's true."

"But how? I haven't heard anything about it, and Margo isn't the type to jump into things. Wait!" Jenna hunched forward to meet my eyes. "Are you going zip lining with the rest of us? You'll die of fright."

"Maybe you have the wrong Margo in mind because, last

month, we went skydiving. At night." Carrie paused a second, her facial expressions selling the lie like it was one of her mother's award-winning performances. "It's when I knew she was the one for me. Someone willing to dive head first into the most amazing experience of our lives—that's who I want by my side until the day I die."

She said it with such conviction I nearly believed her. Aside from the simple fact that none of it had happened.

"Is it scary?" Abbie stretched his neck to peer over Jenna. "Zip lining, I mean. No way would I go skydiving."

Jenna rolled her eyes. "You need to live a little."

This was bold of her because no way would the Jenna I knew go skydiving. She was the type to get sick on a roller coaster. Which raised the question, why were they on the bus with us? Had they heard through the grapevine that all the Jacobs were going? It would be just like Jenna, ever the social climber, to try to engineer an "accidental" encounter. In my mind, I made vicious air quotes.

I wished that was the worst of my problems at the moment, but we had just arrived at the tiny airport for the flight to the main island, where I would be strapped to a thin cable and pushed off a platform, most likely to plummet to my death the next instant.

I couldn't ride in a glass elevator without the world turning upside down. How was I going to do this?

For the next hour or so, I'm pretty sure I went through an out-of-body experience. I remember nothing of the plane ride, nor of the tram that had taken us from the base camp to the zip lining course. I was like a zombie, shuffling along, my thoughts consumed with the impending doom that awaited me.

When I finally came to my senses, I was standing in a harness and helmet at the top of the first platform.

"Getting nervous?" Jenna displayed the wickedest smile I'd ever seen. It made me want to slap the expression right off her face, except that I would have had to move my arms to do that, and right now, I was too busy clinging to the platform's railing to take that risk.

"Not at all," Carrie answered on my behalf, her body shielding me from Jenna's scrutinizing gaze. "You?"

I peeked at the line and whispered into Carrie's ear, "Please don't hate me, but I can't do this, and Jenna's going to figure out our relationship is a fraud."

## CHAPTER NINE

"Why did you lie to me when I asked if you were afraid of heights?" Carrie hissed into my ear. She'd moved in closer to avoid being heard, so I took advantage of the opportunity to cling to her arm like a cat getting ready to climb a tree to escape a predator.

"Is this the time to parse that?" I demanded in an equally hoarse whisper. It was a weak argument because, really, I didn't have a leg to stand on. In fact, both my legs were buckling with fear.

Carrie wrapped her arms around me, pressing me to her chest. To a casual observer, it may have seemed we were in a passionate embrace, but in reality, I was holding on for dear life.

"Everything okay over there?" Jenna called out, and I could tell by her tone that her suspicious mind was going into overdrive.

"If Margo prefers to stay behind, we can go down together." Sandra's predatory gaze ignited a rage within me for two reasons. First, Carrie was my fake fiancée, damn it. No way was I going to let Sandra swoop in for the kill. Second, how close had she been to overhear our conversation. The woman had no decency.

Summoning all the courage I had left, I straightened up and plastered a smile on my face, hoping it looked confident and not like a grimace of terror.

"I am absolutely fine, thank you." I projected my voice for Jenna's benefit as well as Sandra's, making sure they both heard me loud and clear.

"Come on, Sandra." Kermit tugged on her arm, the expression on his face clearly indicating he didn't enjoy playing second fiddle to their mutual ex.

Sandra yanked her arm away with a scowl. "Go without me. I might be needed here to—"

"To what? Margo said everything's fine. We're going together." There was no denying the anger in Kermit's voice, and I wondered if he had picked up on the fact that Sandra was doing her best to get Carrie alone.

As alone as two people could get zipping down a volcano on side-by-side cable lines, anyway. I wasn't sure what Sandra's endgame was, but Asher had said she was the type who always found things more desirable as soon as someone else had them.

"Yes, let's all get going." The authority in Vivian's voice as she clapped her hands twice in rapid succession suggested it would be best for all of us not to disregard the order.

I wasn't sure if she did this out of sympathy for my predicament or annoyance that she wasn't the center of attention.

"We'll be right there," I called out as cheerily as I could manage, tossing in a carefree wave with my right hand while I continued to cling to Carrie with my left. "You all go ahead."

As the rest of our group got in line to be hooked up for their turn on the zip line, Jenna turned back and shot me the kind of look that turned my insides cold. She knew I was up to something, and I knew her well enough to guess that if she ever figured out what was really going on, she would be the first to use it to her own advantage. Blackmail, maybe. But she was more the type to position herself professionally than to outright demand money. She'd want to secure her future.

Carrie turned to me with a furrowed brow. "What's the plan? Is this going to happen, or are you staying behind?"

I shook my head, a small smirk tugging at the corner of my lips. "No, I'll be fine. I just—Oh, God!"

At that moment, Vivian and Tom flew down the lines, making my heart rate skyrocket. I dug my fingers into Carrie's arm, no doubt leaving crescent-shaped marks behind.

"Sure you will. If you don't make it down this thing, Jenna will know I was lying about the skydiving," Carrie pointed out as if it was my fault she'd invented such a preposterous story.

As if to reinforce Carrie's concerns, Jenna flicked her fingers in my direction, an unmistakable taunt, before she and Abbie hopped off the platform and went careening down the line, Abbie screeching like a banshee the whole way.

By now, the only others left besides the guy whose job it was to make sure we were properly secured and didn't die, were Cagney and Erik. The two of them were whispering to each other, and while I didn't know either of them very well, it didn't look like a loving exchange. But soon they were off as well, and then it was only Carrie and me.

I swallowed hard, wishing I had stayed in bed. Although, I had wished for death several times since landing in Hawaii. I just didn't know anyone had been listening and decided to put me out of my misery.

Carrie gazed at me, a pleading in her eyes that was hard to miss. It was such a stupid way for us to get caught, but I feared as much as she did that if a single lie unraveled, our whole story would fall apart.

Carrie turned to the attendant on the platform. "Is there a way we could go together? Not side by side, but maybe with me holding onto her?"

The guy rolled his eyes, and I could tell he thought the request was romantically motivated as opposed to the sheer terror that was the real cause.

"How much do you weigh?" he asked in a bored drawl.

"Excuse me?" Carrie bristled, taking a step back.

"Those cables can only support so much weight at a time. I need to know your combined weights to see if it will work. Didn't they do a weigh-in at base camp?"

"I was one thirty-eight-point two," I supplied, immediately seeing the wisdom of giving the precise number, right down to the decimal point.

Carrie stayed mute.

"Are you going or not?" The guy was losing his patience.

"Carrie?" I prodded.

"There are three things everyone wants to know about an actor," Carrie said, a tinge of bitterness in her tone. "How much they weigh, how much they earn, and who they're dating. I can only really control the first one, by never ever saying the number out loud."

"I doubt he's got connections at the *National Enquirer*." I jerked my head in the guide's direction.

"One fifteen." Carrie lifted her chin defiantly as if daring him to argue.

He gave her a get real expression in response.

"Now who's lying?" I said with a snort. "I'm sorry, but my fourteen-year-old niece who's three inches shorter than you weighs more than that. I know you don't want the tabloids to get a hold of the info, but I really don't want to plummet to my death. I'm going to give it to you straight. Jenna is a conniving bitch. If we don't make it down, she's going to figure out everything and make both of us pay."

"Fine," she growled. "One twenty-seven."

"Okay, then." The guide motioned for us to get ready.

"How close are we to the limit?" I asked, holding back.

"You've got about ten pounds to spare," the guide responded.

I grabbed Carrie's shoulder, my fingers like a vice. "You'd better not be lying."

"We're fine," she said, and I thought I detected a look of relief in her eyes that suggested she may have lied a little, but not ten pounds' worth.

The guide sorted through a tangle of hooks and rope. "Who wants to be in the back, and who's in front?"

"I'll go in the back." Carrie didn't even give me a chance to decide, not that I would've chosen differently. Something about the prospect of Carrie being behind me made me feel safer.

I took a deep breath, trying to calm my nerves as the guide secured our harnesses and ropes.

"Brace yourself," the guide said, "because this is going to be fast."

"What?" I squeaked, my knuckles turning white as I gripped the rope in front of me.

"More weight means faster—" Carrie's words disappeared into the whipping wind as we flew off the platform and down the line.

I screamed and pinched my eyes shut.

She wrapped her arms around me.

I leaned into it, telling myself it was only because I didn't want to die.

But as we zipped through the air, the rush of adrenaline

and fear morphed into an unexpected exhilaration. The wind roared in my ears, drowning out my screams, and Carrie's arms held me tightly, almost protectively. It was a sensation unlike any other I had experienced, and despite the initial terror, I couldn't help but feel a strange thrill coursing through me.

Maybe half of it, tops, had anything to do with zip lining.

By the time we reached the end of the first run, I was hooked. I mean, there were worse ways to spend a day, right? Cage-free shark diving, perhaps? I'd take zip lining any day over that.

"That was awesome!" George high-fived each of us before making his way down the platform to start the short hike to the next line.

"I didn't know we could go together," Cagney said with a pout, though her eyes were glued to her phone. "I'm going to kill Asher."

She hurried to catch up with Erik, who whipped around and screamed, "Enough!" slicing both hands in the air, before storming off ahead, leaving Cagney alone on the trail.

I couldn't help noticing Jenna picking up her speed to join him. I didn't know whether to feel relieved that she was no longer focusing on Carrie and me, or sorry for Abbie, who would no doubt learn the same lesson about Jenna that I had a few years ago.

"What's that about?" Carrie whispered to Cam, pulling her sister aside and motioning toward Cagney, who was walking several yards ahead of us in a huff.

"Seashells," Cam answered.

"What about them?" Carrie pressed.

"Cagney wants to glue seashells to the menu cards, but Asher can't find the right kind in any of the island shops."

"Why am I getting the feeling this isn't the last of this

particular crisis?" Carrie let out a breath, reaching for my hand.

Did she need my support, or was she just acting the role of girlfriend for her sister's benefit?

"Once Cagney sets her mind on something, she won't settle for anything else." Cam released a *shoot me now* sigh, and I had to stop myself from informing her someone was listening to those pleas, so she should be careful.

"This is such a beautiful spot," I inserted, mostly to get Carrie to stop squeezing the life out of my hand.

We'd reached a bridge that spanned a rushing waterfall, the sun casting a prism of rainbows in the mist. The air was thick with the scent of exotic flowers, and the sound of chirping birds filled the lush greenery surrounding us. It was a scene straight out of a postcard.

"I've always loved it." Carrie paused to lean against the bridge's railing. She gazed out at the waterfall, her eyes distant, lost in thought. "Did you know I filmed my first scene as the star of a major motion picture right over there?"

"The dinosaur one?" I asked, recalling that Carrie had been in a summer blockbuster about a prehistoric science camp at a fairly young age.

"Yep. I was fourteen." Carrie laughed. "And, I thought I was the queen of the world in my little khaki shorts, tank top, and hiking boots."

"You looked hot in that," Sandra said, coming up behind us. There was no sign of Kermit. Sandra flashed Carrie a smile that riled me. "Over on that beach is where we had our first kiss."

I plastered on a fake smile. "First movie kiss?"

*Please, say yes.*

"Not that kind of movie." Sandra winked, and I experienced the sudden urge to push her off the bridge. "We've known each other all of our lives, and we keep finding our way back to each other. Don't we, Carrie?"

Carrie's response was a grunt, but it didn't really put my mind at ease. Did it mean she liked this stroll down kissing lane, or was she annoyed Sandra was being so obvious?

"I think we'd better hurry to catch up with the others," I interjected, eager to put an end to Sandra's flirtatious advances toward Carrie.

Whatever it was Carrie was thinking, my feelings on the matter were crystal clear. I desired nothing more than the opportunity to personally feed Sandra to a ravenous pod of killer whales.

---

THE SUN WAS low in the sky as the shuttle pulled up in front of the resort, and it was all I could do to keep my eyes open after a long day of activity and travel. We were the last to exit the vehicle, but when we reached the steps, Carrie motioned for me to go in front of her, a peculiar expression on her face.

I'd barely set foot on the pavement when Carrie wrapped both arms around my shoulders, forcing me to support all of her weight on my back.

"Knee. Bad. Laugh," Carrie whispered into my ear, the pain evident in each strained syllable.

I quickly adjusted my stance to accommodate her, feeling the strain in my own muscles as I tittered like a mad woman.

"I just love you so much, Go-Go," Carrie exclaimed as though this whole escapade was nothing more than an oddly timed public display of affection.

"Look at the love birds." Vivian pressed her hands

together. Was she praying her daughter's latest engagement would finally stick?

Sandra's gaze lingered on us a moment too long, before Kermit steered her away.

Soon enough, it was just the two of us, still standing in the middle of the circular driveway with Carrie gripping me tightly.

"Can you make it back to the room," I asked her, "or should I flag down someone and get a wheelchair?"

"Not if you want to continue living."

"Pretty sure I could outrun you right now." I eased her weight to one side, wrapping my arm around her waist to support her. Carrie let out a soft chuckle at my remark, despite the discomfort etched on her face.

"I think it's recovering. I might be able to take a step on my own now. It does this sometimes, ever since the accident."

"We shouldn't have gone zip lining," I scolded. "You were seriously injured a few months ago. This isn't the time to act—"

"It's always the time to act. Or have you forgotten what family I come from?" With a look of defiance, Carrie stood on both feet, though not without some wobbling.

"How could I forget the great and illustrious Jacobs acting dynasty?" I replied, feigning a melodramatic tone. I couldn't help but shake my head in exasperation, knowing all too well that Carrie's determination often bordered on reckless.

Carrie took a step forward, not letting go of me just in case, but I could see the strain around her eyes was lessening. "You see? I'm a hundred percent better."

Right then, her knee buckled, but I was expecting it this time and caught her almost before she, let alone any onlookers who might have taken an interest, realized it was happening.

"Yeah. You should head to the beach for a rousing game of volleyball with Sandra and Kermit." Even as I said it, I had to question why I'd mentioned that viper's name. All I knew was if Carrie had been my actual fiancée with Sandra sniffing around her like she had been all day, she might not have lived to see tomorrow. Something about that woman set my teeth on edge.

Carrie shook her head, making it clear she'd rather pass on my suggestion. "Hot tub. My knee does better with heat."

"You want to go to the one by the pool?"

"No, the one on our lanai. I've had enough people for one day."

Once again, I was surprised to discover that Carrie and I were completely on the same page.

Slowly, we made our way down the pathway to our suite. I was almost convinced that Carrie's knee was back to normal, but as soon as we entered the room, she let out a gasp and reached for her cane.

"That settles it. From now on, we're not leaving without that," I informed her, pointing to the cane. "And before you argue, remember, I'm a costumer. I can jazz that thing up so everyone will want one."

"Sadly, my family members aren't idiots. Life would be so much easier if they were." Carrie stretched out her leg, wincing slightly as she moved her knee. "I'm going to change into my swimsuit. You joining me in the tub?"

"S-sure," I stuttered, taken aback by the prospect of wearing so little clothing around a woman who had been named one of the world's most beautiful people. Twice.

"What's wrong?"

"Honestly? Learning I'm more than ten pounds heavier

than you hasn't exactly done wonders for my self-esteem." I'm not sure what possessed me to admit this, other than I was too tired to come up with a convincing lie, but it was true.

"Don't be ridiculous. I lied, obviously. It's not even eight pounds. And it looks good on you." With that, Carrie limped to the bedroom, leaving me alone with my racing mind.

Looks good on me? What did she mean by that?

And why had that simple phrase sent a jolt of electricity down my spine?

Shaking off my confusion, I quickly changed into my swimsuit in the half-bath, opting for a one-piece while thanking my lucky stars Asher had thought to pack at least one option that was made from more than string and fairy dust.

I was on the lanai and settled into the hot tub before Carrie emerged in a striking blue bikini that left me momentarily breathless. Instantly, I turned my head away, trying to act casual as I pretended to focus on the crashing waves.

"Enjoying the view?" It was possible this was an innocent question, but an impishness in her tone suggested otherwise.

"I've seen better," I retorted, trying to play it cool despite the rapid thumping of my heart. Carrie chuckled, but as she took a step onto the lanai, her pronounced limp had me jumping up from the water and offering her my hand for support. "Do you need help getting in?"

"Nah," she said but took my hand anyway. Gingerly, she eased into the water.

"How's the knee?" I squinted into the water, trying to see for myself.

"Swollen." She sucked in a breath, the pain evident on her face. "My entire body aches. Next time you try to kill me, make sure you finish the job."

"I didn't—"

"Kidding," she said with a forced smile. "It's frustrating how the pain comes and goes."

I hesitated for a moment before deciding to take a chance. "Let me see."

"Why? Do you have medical training I'm unaware of?"

"No, but I earned a first aid badge in Girl Scouts, which is the next best thing." Trying not to overthink it, I lifted her leg onto my lap, gently digging my fingers into the flesh just above her knee. "Does this help?"

"You have no idea." Carrie rested her head against the lip of the tub, closing her eyes.

I continued to massage the area around her knee, feeling a sense of satisfaction as I noticed her muscles relaxing under my touch. Unexpectedly, the tension between us seemed to dissipate with each stroke of my fingers, and for a moment, it felt like the only thing that existed was the sound of the waves crashing against the shore.

Finally, I felt brave enough to ask about something that had been plaguing me all day. "What's the deal with Sandra?"

Carrie flinched at the mention of her ex's name but didn't open her eyes. "What do you mean?"

"It's pretty clear she wants you back."

Carrie blew out a raspberry, not missing a beat. "Doubtful. More than likely, she's trying to get under Kermit's skin to get her way about something."

"You think she's that manipulative?" I had no doubt that was the case, but I didn't think Carrie was seeing the situation clearly.

"She's a complicated woman."

From where I was sitting, Sandra wasn't the only one. "Would you want her back if that was her goal, not riling Kermit?"

For a moment, Carrie didn't answer.

"I get it," I said to fill the silence, prompting Carrie to let out a long, tortured sigh.

"It's... complicated."

"You've used that word already. It's starting to sound like a theme." I wanted to come across as teasing, but there was an edge to my voice I couldn't quite hide.

Carrie finally opened her eyes, her gaze meeting mine. "I don't know how to explain it, but when you aren't the one to end things... My feelings since seeing her again are topsy-turvy."

I nodded, exuding an air of calm understanding even though I felt a pain like a dagger being plunged into my belly at this frank, unvarnished response.

Unresolved feelings were the most dangerous kind.

I'd be wise to remember that in the future, like the next time Carrie threw her arms around me or told me I looked good. We were playing roles, nothing more. None of this was real. She was a star, and she belonged with someone who was the same. Someone like Sandra.

Which was totally fine, because I'd never liked Caroline Fucking Jacobs anyway. Not one bit.

# CHAPTER TEN

Sitting at a small table on a patio overlooking the beach, I clutched my coffee mug like it held the secrets to life, the universe, and everything in between. Across from me, Carrie sat, glassy eyed and quiet, staring out at the waves as she took a sip from her own mug.

I assumed it had been a rough night for her with her knee, as I'd heard her up and moving around in the bedroom well past the time I'd retired. She'd still had a slight limp today, but she'd stubbornly refused my offer of help to make it from our suite to the restaurant. Fair enough. If she didn't want sympathy, I wasn't about to give it to her.

"Do I look as tired as you do?" I asked, causing her to snap her gaze back to me, her blue eyes piercing through me.

"You know that GIF from the cartoon Tom and Jerry, where Tom is taping his red eyes open?"

"Yes." My eyes narrowed. I wasn't sure where she was going with this.

"If they held an audition for the role of Tom right this second, you would definitely get the part."

"Gee, thanks. I have to say I'm surprised you're so familiar with GIFs." I adjusted my swimsuit tie beneath my sundress, more than ready for a day relaxing at the pool.

"Why's that?"

"I assumed the only thing movie stars cared about on social media was themselves." I offered a sweet smile.

Much to my annoyance, Carrie darted her eyes toward the sky at the dig. She'd developed the habit of laughing off my mocking of celebrities, like she wasn't one of them. It made me grit my teeth a little harder every time she did it. Another week of this and I was going to need a trip to the dentist.

"I'm sorry, Margo. Did my stardom blind you with jealousy?" she teased, her tone light yet with a hint of challenge.

"Hardly." I took a sip of my coffee, relishing the way the liquid burned its way down my throat. "You seem testy this morning. What's the matter? Sad you can't get me fired again?"

"Pretty sure it's easier for me to fire you now than before." She boosted those perfectly proportioned eyebrows, and my traitorous stomach did this loopy thing I wished I could blame on the coffee. Alas, while my brain may not have warmed to Caroline Jacobs, my body had apparently missed the memo.

"There you are!" Asher pulled a chair from a nearby table and squeezed in between us. "You can try to hide, but I'll always track you down. Now, here's today's agenda." He pulled out a lilac-colored paper that was covered in delicate calligraphy.

"Let me see that." I snatched the paper from him and held it close to my eyes. "Is this handwritten? It doesn't look like it came from a printer."

"Didn't my cousin ever tell you how he won the penmanship contest in elementary school?" Carrie asked.

I dropped the paper to the table and raised my eyebrow at

Asher. "Are you telling me you wrote this whole thing out by hand?"

"All thirty of them." The look on Asher's face was part pride and part what I could only imagine a prisoner would look like at the end of a day spent breaking up rocks with a pick. "Thank goodness only close family and friends are here right now to need a list of the pre-wedding events." He rolled his wrist as if he'd never regain full use of it.

"Whatever my sister is paying you, it's not nearly enough." Carrie leaned back for the server to place her egg-white omelet down in front of her.

"Pay?" Asher blinked, the word sounding unfamiliar on his lips. "That's rich. This is a labor of love. Or possibly insanity. Jury's still out."

As the server set my French toast and fresh berries on the table, I nearly squealed with delight. The zip lining adventure the day before had left me both physically and emotionally drained as well as completely famished.

"Hula dancing?" Carrie had grabbed the agenda from the table and was reading through it with an expression of mounting horror. "I sense my mother's input on this. She's crazy for family games. Beach ball hockey. I mean I can't even picture it. And a Hawaiian outfit race. What the hell is that?" She took a bite of her omelet as she continued to scowl at the sheet.

"Contestants run from one station to the next, selecting Hawaiian shirts at one, grass skirts at another..." Asher motioned etcetera, grinning at what he clearly found to be a clever game idea.

"Sounds... very active." Carrie's face paled, and I could tell she was thinking about how this would impact her already worn-out knee. This day would not go well for me. She'd made it clear she blamed me for the accident, and despite knowing it wasn't really my fault, I would no doubt bear the brunt of her frustration.

"Be glad you get to have fun," Asher said with a forlorn look at the agenda. "Darling Cagney is sending me on a mission to retrieve seashells from a beach all the way on the other side of the island. It's going to take me an entire day."

"Are you allowed to take the shells?" Carrie asked, leaving me somewhat amazed. I would have thought a spoiled Hollywood brat would think she could take anything she wanted.

"Shells yes as long as no one takes the menu cards home with them. They need to remain on the island out of respect. Taking sand from the beach is illegal," Asher added. "And no lava, obviously, unless you want to be cursed."

"What's this?" I asked. He'd said it so matter-of-factly that I wasn't sure if he was joking, but both his and Carrie's expressions remained serious.

"Pele's curse," he said, not at all helpfully.

"Legend has it that taking lava rocks from the islands brings bad luck," Carrie explained before turning her attention back to her cousin. "Will Cagney kill you if you don't run this errand yourself, or can you delegate?"

"What do you have in mind?" Asher crossed his arms as if afraid he was being duped.

"I'm peopled out and desperate for an escape. It's exhausting pretending to be madly in love all day."

"You should try being me. Isn't pretending literally the top item on your job description?" I demanded while my mind pondered if in a former life, I'd swiped some of the cursed lava, and this Pele hadn't forgotten. Hence why I was stuck in paradise hell with the woman who seriously thought I'd tried to kill her.

"Sounds like we're in agreement," Carrie said, ignoring

me. "We'll go shell collecting, and you can participate in the Jacobs family Olympics."

"You two wouldn't mind?" Asher perked up in his seat.

"You already missed zip lining. It seems only fair to spread the misery," Carrie told him.

"You'll need a 4×4 to get to the beach," he said. "It's the one with the shipwreck. I'll have the concierge put the rental in your name."

"No way." I raised my fork in the air to object, a drop of syrup splattering back onto the plate. "Put it in my name. I'm driving."

"What? No." Carrie's rebuttal was instant.

I knew Carrie's knee was still tender from all the activity yesterday, but I had no desire for her to know my reason, and I wanted to avoid another confrontation about the role she thought I played in the accident. Instead, I said, "Out of the two of us, I'm the one who hasn't wrapped a car around a tree."

"Good thinking, Margo. And if you get done early, the concierge promised to leave the map to this hidden waterfall in the car for me. I didn't think this island had any waterfalls, but apparently, it's something only the locals know about." Asher got to his feet. "I really owe you."

Considering he'd just doomed me to a day alone running errands with his cousin instead of lounging by the pool, he sure did. But he took off so fast there was no chance for me to shake him down for loose change.

The first thing I noticed when we got to the Jeep Asher had arranged for us was the stick shift. No way could Carrie, with her bad knee acting up, have managed to operate the clutch, especially on bumpy back roads. As I slid into the driver's seat, Carrie shot me a skeptical glance from the passenger side, clearly not sold on the idea.

As we left the hotel grounds, Carrie cleared her throat. "Last night, I said something I shouldn't have."

"Oh, really?" I would be lying if I said I wasn't dying to know which thing she meant. Could it have been the way she'd implied she'd get back together with Sandra in a heartbeat? Because if I were her, that was the one I would regret most.

"Yeah. I put all the blame on you for my accident. That was out of line."

I briefly took my eyes off the road to look at her. "You admit I had nothing to do with it?"

"I didn't say that. But you weren't entirely to blame. I was the one behind the wheel, which means ultimately it was my responsibility to handle the car. Even if I did have a damn scarf wrapped around my face."

"Caroline Jacobs is admitting fault? Mark today's date on the calendar, folks," I teased, unable to resist a smirk.

Carrie narrowed her eyes, but a small smile tugged at the corners of her lips. "Don't get used to it. I just wanted to clear the air."

"Air cleared," I replied. "Although, I wasn't the one who chose the scarf. In fact, when I showed them to the director, I specifically said for him not to choose the one he did."

Carrie said nothing as she gazed out the window at the passing scenery, a thoughtful expression on her face. With the top off the Jeep, the warm breeze tousled her blond hair. Somehow, it managed to look perfect on her, even while my own hair was probably sticking out in all directions. There was no doubt which of us was the former star of a shampoo commercial.

Asher hadn't been lying about how remote our destination was. Just driving to the beach took well over an hour, most of the time on roads that were little more than sand and rock. Finally, we arrived, and I could instantly see why it was referred to as Shipwreck Beach. The hulking remains of a rusted oil tanker from the 1940s sat beached some distance from shore, looking like a ghost ship that time had forgotten.

Carrie stepped out of the Jeep, quickly followed by a sharp cry that could only mean her knee had stiffened up during the long, bumpy drive.

"Are you okay?" I asked, concern lacing my voice as I helped her steady herself.

Carrie waved me off, flashing a reassuring smile. "I'm fine. Just need a minute to stretch it out. Being tall has its disadvantages."

"I wouldn't know," I joked. "I'm perfectly average in every way."

"Hmm," she began but chose not to elaborate.

We'd been given a couple of beach pails by the concierge, and I grabbed them from the back of the vehicle. "Baby Yoda or Sponge Bob?" I asked with a grin, wiggling the pails in each hand.

"His name is Grogu," she corrected as she grabbed the Baby Yoda pail. "I've always had a soft spot for that little guy."

I was going to express my shock that she had a soft spot for anything, but somehow the dig didn't quite make it to my lips. Perhaps because, despite my compulsive need to keep up a facade of annoyance around Carrie, it wasn't really true.

Carrie looked ridiculously adorable gripping the plastic pail, like she was ready for a day of building sandcastles with a group of kindergarteners. "What do these fuckers look like?" she asked. Her choice of language was another matter.

I pulled up an image on my phone that Asher had forwarded to me as a guide for what kind of shells we were supposed to bring back. Carrie moved closer, bending down to see the screen, accidentally giving me more than a glimpse of her cleavage in her bikini, her tank top billowing out.

It took more willpower than I'd known I possessed to navigate my eyes elsewhere. Who could blame me? She was Caroline Fucking Jacobs after all. Few people in my position wouldn't have been tempted to gawk.

"Okay. Let's get this done." Carrie lowered her sunglasses into place.

We walked along the beach, picking up shells when we found them amidst the rocks and bits of debris.

"I never intended to get you fired," Carrie said, seemingly out of nowhere. "Just so you know."

"Excuse me?" I straightened up from where I'd been crouching, digging through a section of sand with a stick.

Carrie shrugged. "I mean, sure, I was mad about the whole scarf in my face incident, but I didn't ask for you to be fired because of it. That was all the production team trying to cover their own asses."

I focused my eyes on the sand underfoot, not fully buying her explanation. "So, what? You figured it was better to stand by and watch me take the fall for something you knew I didn't do?"

"I wasn't in the best frame of mind at the time. My relationship with Alex had ended moments before I got behind the wheel, and after the crash, I was in a lot of pain." Carrie swallowed, her expression tinged with guilt. "It's not a great excuse for not trying to intervene, but it's the truth. I let my emotions cloud my judgment. I'm truly sorry you got caught up in all of that mess."

"More caught up than I realized until it was too late," I said. "It's occurred to me that if I hadn't been mistaken for Alex twice that day, first by her lover and then by you, maybe none of it would have come out, and you never would've crashed."

"Yeah, maybe." Carrie gave an angry chuckle. "To this day, I still don't know who she was cheating on me with. Not that it matters, I guess."

I knelt down to pluck a seashell from the sand, dropping it into my bucket and wondering if I should say anything about what I'd discovered on that front. Maybe it was better to keep the culprit's identity to myself. "Why doesn't it matter?"

"I didn't have time to dwell on it after the accident. With my injuries, the only thing on my mind was healing." She let out a sigh. "Sometimes I don't know what's wrong with me."

"In what way?" I asked, too interested in her answer to even attempt to make a snide comment despite her leaving me the perfect opening.

"When it comes to relationships, I have a nasty habit of falling hard and fast, going all in. When it ends though, it's almost like it didn't happen. Alex and I broke things off over two months ago, and I've barely given her a thought." Carrie tapped the side of her head. "Something's not right with me."

"Maybe you haven't found your person. Once you do, you'll know."

Her sapphire eyes bored into mine, making me squirm like a child standing in front of the high school principal, being accused of something I didn't do but couldn't prove I hadn't.

"Hmm." It was the second time she'd offered this response. A moment later, the fury in her eyes bleached out, and she went in a different direction, hunting for more shells.

It was my job to fake being in love with her in front of her family, not to be her fucking therapist. If she didn't like the way her relationships played out, she could... not have them. Simple as that. It's what I had done after Jenna. It wasn't that hard. All you had to do was get rid of any lingering emotions, put up your walls, and focus on other things. Like collecting seashells.

"Do you think we have enough?" I asked, showing Carrie the contents of my bucket. The bottom of the pail was now covered, so we were at least making some progress.

"I hope so because I never want to see another seashell in my life." Carrie set her bucket down next to mine in the sand, rubbing a hand into her lower back with a grimace.

"How's your knee?" I asked.

"My entire body hurts," she admitted. "I was trying to avoid it, but I think I may need to take a couple of the pain pills my doctor prescribed. I've got them back in the car. I should warn you, though. They make me a little loopy."

"Oh?"

"Yes, last time I took one, I ended up serenading a flock of pigeons with show tunes. Quite the spectacle."

"I might pay to see that."

As we got back into the Jeep, I spotted the map the concierge had given us with the directions to the secret waterfall marked in black ink. "What do you think about a quick dip in the lagoon?"

"It might be exactly what the doctor ordered," Carrie agreed, popping two pills into her mouth and chasing them with a swig of water.

I started the engine, and we made our way down the winding road leading to the hidden waterfall. The lush greenery and the sound of the Jeep's tires crunching on gravel created a serene atmosphere, a stark contrast to the tension that usually simmered between Carrie and me.

As we arrived at the entrance to the trail leading to the

waterfall, I parked the Jeep and gave Carrie's knee a questioning look.

"The rest of the way is by foot. Do you think you can make it?"

"Woo, yeah!" she exclaimed with a thumbs-up, her eyes slightly unfocused. If I'd been concerned the medication wouldn't kick in, it appeared my worries had been misplaced.

I chuckled, shaking my head. "Alright, let's go, Show Tunes. I mean, Carrie."

"You're a riot, Go-Go," Carrie informed me with a sloppy grin.

We embarked on the trail, the canopy of trees casting dappled sunlight along our path. Carrie was surprisingly nimble despite her earlier complaints. After a short walk, we heard the distant sound of rushing water and glimpsed a shimmering cascade through the trees.

As we got closer, the air became cooler, and mist from the waterfall lightly kissed our skin. The sound grew louder, mixing with the chirping of birds and rustling of leaves.

"Wow, this is incredible," I began, but Carrie was already ahead of me, stripping off her tank top as she went. She dropped her barely there shorts at the edge of the lagoon and strode into the water without a moment of hesitation.

"You coming?" she called, splashing water playfully in my direction.

Her eyes seemed glued to me as I stripped down to my swimsuit, causing my heart rate to kick up a notch. Why was she looking at me like that? I tried to brush off the feeling, but there was an intensity to her gaze that made my skin prickle with awareness.

I nearly gasped as my foot hit water so cold that it stole the breath from my lungs. Even so, I didn't wait to adjust, submerging myself to my neck in an instant to avoid her eyes on my curves.

She did the same, our heads bobbing in the water.

"I feel like there's something I should tell you," I said, unsure if this was wise, but it'd been bugging me all day. "I think I know who Alex was cheating with."

"You do?" It was difficult to decipher her tone, as everything she said seemed to come out in a singsong voice thanks to her happy pills.

"On the boat," I began hesitantly, uncertain how she would take what I had to say, "I caught a glimpse of red. The man who put his arms around me in Alex's trailer was wearing that exact same shade."

"You're basing your guess on a color?" She didn't seem sold on this piece of information.

"No, not exactly. I'm basing it on the fact that the person on the boat, when I took a closer look after noticing the red, turned out to be Richard Thompson."

"Richard Thompson, my costar? That Richard Thompson?" The melodic tone had faded from Carrie's voice, replaced with an edge that had me holding my breath.

"Yes, that Richard Thompson," I confirmed, treading water a few feet away from her, unsure of how this revelation might change things between us.

"You're telling me Alex was fucking Richard Thompson behind my back on the set of my own goddamn movie?"

"Uh, I'm not one hundred percent certain about that," I backtracked. "But my gut says probably yes."

She burst into laughter. The maniacal kind. "That sneaky little weasel. And if he was on the boat, that means he's probably still on the island. Maybe even staying at the same hotel."

"I shouldn't have told you." I paddled backward in the water, trying to put some distance between us in case she developed a taste for murders. "You aren't going to track him down and make a big scene are you?"

"On the contrary. You wanna know something weird?" Carrie's words were slightly slurred, and one look at her dilated pupils told me she was higher than a kite. "I feel nothing."

"Yeah, that would be those magic pills your doctor gave you."

"No, I mean I feel no anger at this news. None at all." Carrie paused, blinking as if trying to focus. "I think... I think I'm done with all of it. The drama, the heartbreak, the constant need for validation from people who don't really care about me."

"That's quite a breakthrough," I mused, cautiously moving closer to her in the water.

"Right? I mean, I feel a little sick to my stomach. Richard Thompson is kind of gross. Did you know he ate an entire loaf of garlic bread right before filming our sex scene?"

"Ew, seriously?" I wrinkled my nose in disgust, but secretly, I was grateful for the shift in Carrie's demeanor.

"I know, right? And he kept burping throughout the whole scene. Forget the car wreck. I should've gotten hazard pay for *that*." Carrie let out a genuine laugh, the sound echoing through the secluded cove. "Hey, wanna go see what it's like behind the waterfall?"

"So you can murder me without any witnesses?"

Carrie swam in a circle around me, making me think of a hungry shark. "We're all alone here. I could murder you any time if I really wanted to. Although, you're more the murdering type." Her grin oozed sex appeal.

Ignoring the heat surging through me because of that grin, I lamely said, "Asher knows I'm with you."

"He's family. He wouldn't rat me out." She winked, and

I'm embarrassed to admit, I was more turned on than terrified.

"Sure," I said, my stomach tightening even as I agreed. "I've never seen the backside of water before."

"You really are funny, Go-Go." Her eyes swept over me, the corners of her mouth quirking into a smile that made me think she was admiring more than my quick wit.

But why?

This was Caroline Jacobs, after all. The woman who could probably have anyone she wanted with a smile and a flutter of her long lashes. With her Hollywood charm and effortless beauty, no way could she possibly be interested in someone like me.

She swam ahead of me, making her way to the side of the falls, getting out on the rocks. I followed suit, careful not to slip on the wet stones.

As I reached the waterfall, Carrie turned to face me, her blond hair slicked back against her head.

"I think the backside of the water is about the same as the front. Wanna see?" She held out her hand, pulling me into a small alcove behind the falls.

We stood behind the roaring cascade of water plunging down from above. The air was thick with a fine mist that danced in the sunlight, forming rainbows in every direction.

If she did intend to murder me, it was a good place to die. That thought made me smile.

Carrie stepped closer, pulling me further into her orbit.

"Thank you," she said.

"For?" I gulped, my heart hammering in my chest, unsure of where this was going.

"For being honest about Alex." Her voice was low, almost a whisper, and I could feel her breath against my skin.

"Sure." How was that for a response.

"There's something about you, Margo."

"Just one thing?" I laughed at my own joke.

Carrie didn't. Instead, she closed the gap between us, and before I knew what was happening, her lips were on mine.

Caroline Fucking Jacobs was kissing me. Me, Margo Wells, the daughter of dry cleaners from Minnesota. A Hollywood star who had gotten me fired from my job—though that may not have been intentional, apparently—had her mouth all over mine.

And you know what? I frigging loved it.

Her lips were soft. Inviting. They felt like they were meant for mine, like two puzzle pieces finally fitting together after a long nearly hopeless search.

The roar of the waterfall faded into the background, replaced by the rushing pulse of my own blood in my ears. Time seemed to slow down, my heart pounding, our breath mingling. My hands hovered in the air, unsure whether to push her away or pull her closer. But as her fingers gently tilted my chin upward, deepening the kiss, I let myself succumb to the moment.

If I'd had my wits about me, I might have pondered what game Carrie was playing.

Instead, I sank into the kiss with reckless abandon.

# CHAPTER ELEVEN

On the way back to the hotel, I steered the jeep around a massive pothole but couldn't manage to miss it entirely. Wincing at the violent jolt, I shot a glance at Carrie, who was out cold in the passenger seat. She hadn't so much as stirred since we left the lagoon.

How in the world was she sleeping through this? The jeep juddered and bounced with each new obstacle, but Carrie's head merely lolled to the side, wisps of blond hair obscuring her face. I sighed, resigned to my fate of having to navigate the treacherous road back to the hotel on my own as Sleeping Beauty's personal chauffeur.

Whatever meds she was on, I wished I could have some. My brain hadn't shut up for a single second since our lips had parted after that waterfall kiss.

What the hell had that been about?

It had to be the drugs. Or maybe the drugs combined with what had been an undeniably romantic location. Or maybe on some small level, she was actually attracted to me.

Yeah, I know. That last possibility was laughable.

The entire drive, as the sun dipped lower and lower into

the sky, the questions ran through my head on a loop. I could only come up with one conclusion: Who the fuck knew?

Would Carrie even know why she'd done it once she roused from this pain-killer-induced coma? I wasn't even certain she'd remember it happening. But I would never forget.

"Welcome back," said the valet when we arrived at the resort entrance.

"Thank you." I glanced at Carrie. "Can you help me get her out?"

"Of course." If he found the request unusual or at all unreasonable, he didn't show it. Maybe he was used to it from all the rich tourists who partied too hard.

But as he lifted Carrie out of the jeep with practiced ease, his eyes widened a fraction in surprise. Maybe he recognized her from one of her movies or from the tabloids that feasted on her personal life like vultures.

"What's happening?" Carrie stirred when the man placed her feet on the ground. She flashed him a million-watt smile. "You're so handsome. I love you."

"And I love you, Ms. Jacobs." He spoke as if this wasn't the first time he'd been showered with affection by a barely conscious celebrity. Maybe he was used to this, too. I gave him a tight smile, murmuring my thanks as I slipped a generous tip, procured from Carrie's wallet, into his hand.

As we made our way to our private bungalow, she proceeded to give every staff member we bumped into a hug.

"You're all so amazing! This place is like heaven on earth," she exclaimed, her voice groggy.

I followed close behind, feeling like an awkward shadow in her wake. It was a bizarre sight, watching Carrie, usually so guarded and composed, acting so freely and openly under the influence of painkillers. It was as if her charm and charisma flowed effortlessly, even in her medicated state.

Her behavior pretty much answered my questions about the kiss, though. It had meant nothing to her. She was high as a kite, ready to declare her love for anyone within arm's reach. And I had most certainly been within easy reach at the lagoon.

Case closed.

Inside the suite, I was able to get Carrie as far as the bed before she flopped down ungracefully, arms spread wide, giggling to herself like a child. I watched her indulgently, feeling a reluctant smile tugging at my lips. Despite everything, she was undeniably charming in her own peculiar way.

"I'll be right back," I told her when my desperate need to pee couldn't be put off a moment longer. "You should change into your pajamas, okay?"

Carrie nodded, and I made a dash for the half bath.

I returned a few minutes later wearing a T-shirt and sleep shorts, grateful to have finally changed out of my still-damp suit. I found Carrie sitting up where I'd left her, still in her clothing. She hadn't budged an inch while I was gone, and I wasn't convinced she was actually awake.

"You need to change out of your wet swimsuit," I chastised, speaking loudly enough to wake her from her daze. Carrie blinked slowly, as if trying to focus on my words. After a moment, she raised her arms in the air, like a child ready for their parent to undress them.

"Why don't you help me with that, Wardrobe Supervisor?" Her voice was low and husky, laced with sarcasm as she gave me a sly, if somewhat lopsided, grin.

I arched an eyebrow, caught off guard by her sudden shift in demeanor. A rush of heat crept up my neck. "You want my help?"

Carrie nodded, her eyes half-closed. It wasn't like I hadn't seen a hundred stars naked before. It was all part of being a costumer.

So why did it feel so different now?

Perhaps because I wasn't as experienced removing wet Lycra off a semi-comatose actor. One whose tongue had been in my mouth hours earlier. I hesitated for a moment, trying to shake off the memory of our heated kiss by the lagoon.

But Carrie didn't give me much time to dwell on it. Pouting with impatience, she reached for the edge of her bikini top, attempting to peel it off herself. The fabric clung stubbornly to her damp skin, and she huffed in frustration.

My professional instincts getting the better of my common sense, I stepped forward, my fingers deftly reaching to unhook the bikini top. "Don't strain yourself now. We wouldn't want you to pull a muscle," I teased, trying to mask the flutter in my chest at the close proximity. As the fabric came loose, Carrie let out a sigh, her eyes meeting mine in a moment of unexpected intimacy as the bikini top slid off her shoulders, leaving her breasts exposed.

I turned my head away quickly, averting my gaze. "I think you can manage the bottoms yourself. Where are your pajamas?"

"What pajamas?"

"The ones you sleep in," I replied. "You should change into something dry before you catch a cold."

"But I always sleep like this," she insisted, standing up.

Out of the corner of my eye, I caught a bleary-eyed Carrie gesturing to her very naked body. I nearly choked on my own breath. What the hell was wrong with me?

I needed to start acting like a professional.

"Then you're ready to be tucked in," I said airily.

Approaching the bed with my eyes anywhere but on her, I peeled the covers back. "Get in."

I stared at a seashell painting on the far wall while she climbed in.

Safely covered, I said, "Good night, Carrie."

"Where are you going?" She popped up from the mattress, her exposed boobs standing at attention.

"To the couch," I groaned, no longer able to keep my eyes off her chest. "I'm wrecked and need sleep."

"So, sleep here."

"Don't you remember? I lost our little bet. You get the bed. I get the couch." It hadn't really been a bet, but it was hard to concentrate on choosing appropriate words with Carrie's boobs in full view. No one should be allowed to have such beautiful tits. And given the way they bobbed around, I was quite certain they were one hundred percent real.

"I can't sleep without my Go-Go Bear," she muttered, pouting like a child denied a treat.

Despite the situation, I had to stifle a laugh. Go-Go Bear? Seriously, what kind of drugs was she on?

"We can talk about that in the morning."

"No. Now." Like a wildcat going in for the kill, Carrie wrapped an arm around me, pulling me onto the bed with surprising strength. "You're so cuddly, like a teddy bear."

And just like that, I was pinned to the bed with Carrie snuggling up to me like I was her favorite stuffed animal.

"This is even better than I imagined," she whispered as she nuzzled her face into the crook of my neck.

My heart pounded as I processed what she had said. She'd imagined what I would feel like in her bed?

That couldn't be right. It was just the meds talking, those same magic pills that had prompted her to profess her love for half the staff. This wasn't the real Carrie.

But real or not, she was surprisingly strong. Was that a side effect of the medication, too? Because no matter how I wiggled, there was no escape.

"Stop fidgeting," she scolded. "We need to sleep."

And I needed her to stop confusing me. What happened to the woman who hated my guts? That was much easier for me to manage than this.

Carrie's warm breath tickled my skin as she nestled even closer, her fingers tracing lazy patterns on my back. Despite my racing thoughts, the gentle touch was oddly soothing, and against my better judgment, I found myself relaxing into her embrace. Her scent, a mix of lavender and something uniquely her own, enveloped me as I found myself beginning to drift off.

The last thing I heard was a whisper against my ear. "Sweet dreams, Go-Go Bear."

---

I ROLLED ONTO MY SIDE, crashing into an unexpected foreign object in my bed. Only this wasn't my bed.

It took me several blinks of my eyes to restart my brain enough to process the fact I was in bed with Caroline Fucking Jacobs. But no matter how hard I tried, I couldn't come up with a rational explanation for why she wasn't wearing clothes. Thank God I was.

Snippets of the previous day flashed through my head. The seashells. Carrie's knee and the pain pills.

Wait. Did we kiss behind a waterfall? Or had that been a dream?

The more I strained my brain to remember, the more I became fairly certain that had been real. And I had to admit it sure beat my first kiss with Jenna at a drive-in movie on a hot and buggy summer night back in Minnesota.

I was also positive nothing had happened between us during the night, despite my ending up in Carrie's bed. Unless you counted snuggling, which we definitely had done. Or, more accurately, she had snuggled, and I had been trapped like an old stuffed bear.

Oh, dear God. Had she called me Go-Go Bear?

I tried to disentangle myself from the sheets and make my escape, but Carrie pulled me back into her arms. It was clear, however, given the tiny bit of drool and the hair plastered to her face, she was still dead to the world.

And kind of adorable.

What time was it? I checked the Fitbit on my wrist. It was after ten in the morning. I hadn't slept that late since high school.

It had to be the mattress. This was some ritzy bedding, too. A million thread count, at least. The combination must've knocked me out cold. There was no other explanation for it. Certainly, it hadn't been the company.

My stomach growled, and I couldn't remember eating dinner the night before.

Carefully slipping my body from Carrie's arms, I snuck out of bed with one mission in mind. Breakfast.

The restaurant by the pool was blessedly deserted, and the server from the day before brought me a cup of coffee before I had the chance to beg for it.

"French toast?" she asked.

"You know me so well. Yes, thank you." My mouth watered over the prospect.

"Will Ms. Jacobs be joining you?"

I had a mental image of Carrie's comatose body sprawled

out naked in bed and couldn't hold back a smirk. "I don't think so. Can you box up an omelet for her when I finish?"

"Of course."

I nursed the scalding hot coffee while waiting for my food. It arrived promptly, reminding me yet again that this really was as close as a person could get to paradise on earth. Taking my first bite, I let out a satisfied moan. I could get used to living like this.

"Hello, dear."

Startled, I glanced up to find Vivian Jacobs staring down at me. Had she heard me moan?

"Mind if I join you?" she asked, already pulling out the chair opposite me.

"Please. Carrie is sleeping in. She wasn't feeling that well last night. Don't worry, though. I'm bringing her an omelet when I finish." I had no idea why I was spilling all of these details to the woman who was supposed to be my future mother-in-law. Other than the fact she was the most famous woman on the planet, and she intimidated the crap out of me.

She offered me a mysterious smile. "You're so different from the others."

"Excuse me?" I took another bite of my food, more and more convinced I was going to need the energy to make it through this conversation.

"The previous fiancées in Carrie's life." Her nose wrinkled as she spoke, and I got the impression none of the others had earned the Vivian Jacobs seal of approval. "I can tell you're the caring type. And you two were so cute together, zip lining the other day. Enjoy these moments now, while you're still happy together." As she looked away, I could detect a wistfulness in her eyes, and she released the type of long, heavy sigh that begged to be addressed.

"I hope you don't mind me mentioning this, but Carrie

may have let on that things have been difficult between you and Tom."

"Did she?" Her smile was tight, but I got the impression this was not unwelcome news, like maybe she'd been waiting for someone outside of the family to talk to. "It was sudden. One day, we were madly in love, and the next, he stopped talking to me."

"Have you asked him why he did that?" I asked politely, not letting on that I had a few theories on the topic.

She stared at me blankly as if she hadn't considered that option. "Maybe he's having an affair," she mused, her voice laced with a hint of bitterness.

"Or, maybe asking him would be a more reliable way to find out what's going on," I said carefully. "I've found sometimes couples can overlook that all-important first step of asking how the other feels."

"Why doesn't he ask me?" When Vivian pouted she bore an uncanny resemblance to her eldest daughter.

"He might not know how," I offered. "Men, you know."

Not that I had any clue about men, but it seemed the kind of thing that women who were into men usually liked to hear.

Vivian bit down on her lower lip, looking surprisingly uncertain for a woman who usually oozed confidence. "Do you think it's that simple?"

"You don't know until you try."

"I'll think about it." She got to her feet. "I almost forgot why I stopped to chat. I booked you and Carrie for a sunset cruise tonight, just the two of you."

"You didn't have to do that," I argued, a desperate feeling clawing at my throat as I realized I was about to be stuck on a boat at sunset with the woman I'd woken up next to in bed. Naked. Her. Not me.

"But I did. You two went above and beyond with Cagney's ridiculous seashell quest—yes, I heard all about it from my nephew Asher. And you haven't been able to enjoy much time together on the island as a newly engaged couple."

*Except for a kiss we'd shared behind a waterfall.*

Vivian patted me on the shoulder. "Remember to embrace these days."

"I will," I promised to her retreating back.

"There you are," Carrie approached from behind me, apparently not seeing her mother rounding the corner. "I'm starving."

I caught the server's eye, who nodded when she spied Carrie.

"Your coffee and omelet will be here soon."

"Perfect." She took a seat, looking surprisingly relaxed for someone who had been blitzed out of her mind on pain meds most of the previous day. "What'd I miss?"

Was this her way of fishing for details about the kiss and sleeping in the same bed? Or did Carrie have zero memories of any of it?

I should follow my own advice, like I'd told Vivian to do, and ask Carrie, but I was a lot better at telling people what to do than heeding my own wisdom.

"Your mom has booked us on a sunset dinner cruise."

"More family time," Carrie groaned.

"Not tonight. It's for the two of us."

Carrie's eyes widened. "Just us?"

I nodded, a rush of nerves hitting me as her gaze locked with mine. "Just us," I confirmed, suddenly acutely aware of how close we were sitting.

A smile crept onto Carrie's face, a genuine one that made

her eyes light up. "In that case, I suppose I can tolerate a romantic sunset cruise with you."

I raised an eyebrow. "Tolerate, huh? That's a relief. I'd hate to think you were actually looking forward to spending time alone with me."

Carrie chuckled, her laughter musical in the open-air restaurant. "Believe it or not, you're not the worst company."

I scoffed in disbelief, trying to hide the smile that tugged at my lips. I could have said the same about her. But no way was I going to.

## CHAPTER TWELVE

"Welcome, ladies." A man in a crisp white shirt and black trousers put a hand out, helping Carrie onto the boat. "My name is Kai, and my top priority this evening is to ensure you have a wonderful experience."

"Nice to meet you, Kai," I said, accepting his hand as I boarded the boat.

Carrie tilted her head, smiling at me in a way that made me wonder what she was thinking. Then again, there were plenty of things about this woman that made me wonder. Her smile could be as dazzling as a spotlight, but her eyes often held shadows of a different story, secrets known only to her.

Somehow, the more time we'd spent together, I'd gone from wanting nothing more than to get away from her to wanting to unravel every mystery she held. It was a truth that left me feeling unsteady in her presence. Or maybe it was my complete lack of sea legs making me feel that way.

"Your table is at the bow of the ship," Kai said.

I turned in one direction, Carrie quickly catching me by the elbow and turning me the other way. As a typical member of the middle class, I hadn't spent much time on yachts. I couldn't tell the difference between the bow, stern, or even the anchor. But it seemed that Carrie was an expert. And why wouldn't she be? She'd been raised around luxury her entire life.

We're from different worlds, I told myself, in case I needed another reminder for why we would never work in real life. How was my brain even entertaining that thought? It was impossible to deny the pull I felt toward her, but it didn't mean anything. We were too mismatched.

Carrie lived in such a different reality with her fame and fortune, while I was trying to make ends meet. She was a star adored by millions. I was a bit above average with a sewing needle. What did we even have in common?

It was a strong argument against developing feelings for the woman. One of my best efforts, in fact. But as Carrie guided me to our table, her touch was warm and familiar. No amount of careful reasoning could stand in the face of such undeniable chemistry. In short, I was doomed.

As we settled at a table for two at the narrow, pointier end of the boat—going to assume this was the bow—Carrie leaned back in her seat, crossing her legs with a relaxed grace that made my heart flutter despite my attempts to remain grounded. She looked at me with an intensity that seemed to pierce through all my doubts and reservations. How did she manage that without uttering a single word?

"Would you two like to start off with something refreshing to drink?" Kai asked, seeming to appear out of nowhere once we were seated.

"What would you recommend?" Carrie asked, her smile as effortless as it was dazzling, though no more than surface deep. I doubted Kai would know the difference. Most people wouldn't. Slipping into a role, whether on stage or in real life, was second nature to her. But once you'd seen a genuine smile in an unguarded moment, as I had, it was impossible not to see the difference.

Sure enough, Kai's ears turned slightly pink as his face flushed from Carrie's attention. "In Hawaii, you're never far from a mango tree. Might I suggest our signature mango martini?"

Carrie arched one eyebrow, indicating she wanted my input.

"If it has alcohol in it, I'm in." Instantly, I regretted my phrasing. I sounded like a lush.

But before I could backtrack, Carrie threw her head back, letting out a melodic laugh that was as infectious as it was disarming.

"Two mango martinis, please," she said to Kai.

"Excellent. If you need anything, don't hesitate to ask." He disappeared as quickly as he'd come, leaving us to enjoy the view of sparkling water and deep blue sky.

"I've never been on a boat in the middle of the ocean before." I glanced down as I said this, fidgeting with the edge of a thick cloth napkin I'd placed in my lap. My nerves were starting to get the best of me now that we were alone, and I hoped Carrie wouldn't notice.

"Minnesota, right?"

"What?" It was a simple question, but it left me stunned, wondering how she knew where I was from.

"That's where you grew up." Carrie tossed one arm on the back of her chair, completely at ease. Then again, what did she have to be nervous about? It wasn't like I was the type to inspire intimidation.

"Yes, right," I muttered, realizing I had to have mentioned it once before. "I'm surprised you remembered."

"Because I'm a spoiled celebrity who never listens or

cares?" Her smile—a most genuine one this time—was doing things to my insides that shouldn't be happening.

"It's funny. A little birdie told me you do listen intently, all the while pretending not to care."

"Remind me to kick Asher in the shins when we get back," Carrie said with the most adorable pout.

I cocked my head, a grin playing at the corners of my lips. "Why do you think Asher's my source?"

"He's the only person who really knows me." There was a hint of sadness in her words, and I wondered if she really believed this was true. "In fact, only Asher has my real phone number."

I quirked an eyebrow.

"A girl has to have more than one phone."

"Is your real phone like the Batman signal in the sky so you know shit's about to get real?" I joked, not really buying this story about two phones. I could barely keep track of one.

"Kinda," she said in all seriousness.

"Here you go, ladies." Returning with all the silence of a ninja, Kai set down our drinks. "Your meals will be ready soon."

I nodded a thank you as he left.

Holding my cocktail up to the light, I tilted my head in careful consideration. "This might be too beautiful to drink. So far, all the drinks we've had here have looked and felt like drinking the sunset."

"The sunset colors certainly sell it." Carrie took a drink, her expression morphing into something just shy of total ecstasy. "Oh my God. This is delicious. You have to stop admiring it and take a drink."

Floored by her insistence, I sampled the cocktail and was immediately transported to a state of pure bliss. "Jesus. If we were actually engaged, I would totally insist on naming our first child Mango. Is that weird?"

Carrie nearly choked on her drink, a moment of completely unscripted shock, before making a quick recovery. "Mango Blythe-Jacobs does have a certain ring to it. Our child would grow up with an exotic flair."

"Blythe-Jacobs?" I gave her a stern look. "Where does Wells figure in? It seems like you're already planning on cutting me out of this imaginary marriage."

"Seriously?" She playfully rolled her eyes "Mango Wells-Blythe-Jacobs sounds like a law firm."

I took another sip of the cocktail, feeling the alcohol warm my insides. "If you think I'm going to carry this pretend baby of ours for nine months and have you swoop in at the end to take all the glory, you've got another thing coming."

"Who says you would be the one carrying the baby anyway?" Carrie countered, her tone issuing a challenge I couldn't help but accept.

I arched an eyebrow. "Really? You'd willingly give up your red-carpet events and luxurious lifestyle to waddle around for nine months like a pregnant penguin?"

"Penguins lay eggs, darling," Carrie informed me, doing an uncanny impression of her mother. "Besides, I have excellent childbearing hips. I would make the whole pregnancy thing look effortlessly chic."

All at once, an image of Carrie standing on a red carpet, cradling a baby bump in a designer gown flashed through my mind. Surprisingly, the mental image didn't repulse me as much as I thought it should have. Quite the opposite, actually. The sudden rush of emotion caught me completely off guard. I quickly set my glass down on the table to hide my unsteady hands.

"I suppose you do have a point about those hips of yours," I told her, "but let's not get ahead of ourselves. Making it through your sister's wedding is the priority right now."

"Ugh. Don't remind me." Carrie sucked in a deep breath. "The closer we get to the wedding, the more irrational Cagney gets. And, I don't know if this is a thing, but Mom is turning into a mother-of-the-bridezilla. Everything has to be absolutely perfect. She even sorted through the shells we got, sending George back to find fifteen more because that was how many had chips in them."

My mind flitted back to that moment after we'd spent the day beachcombing, when she'd kissed me behind the waterfall. It had been more than twenty-four hours, and I still hadn't asked Carrie about it. Did she even remember what she'd done?

"With more guests arriving tomorrow, I'm scared. Terrified, really." She leaned over the table, the V in her dress giving me a bird's eye view of those perfect tits. I could swear she did it on purpose. Was there another set of breasts that could compare to hers on the planet? If there were, I had never come across them. And in my line of work, I'd seen a lot of breasts.

"Margo?"

Her voice snapped me out of the inappropriate fantasy.

"Yes?" I asked, trying my best to focus my attention on the conversation and my eyes on any point north of her neck.

"Are you okay? You seem distracted."

"Not at all," I lied, hoping she wouldn't notice the tremor in my voice. "Terrified of what, exactly?"

Carrie sat back in her chair, a pensive look clouding her carefree expression. "When people want perfection, it usually guarantees one thing."

"Which is?"

"Disaster. In all caps. Can you believe Mom hasn't learned that lesson yet, in all of her years?"

"Maybe she thinks perfection is the only way to control the chaos of life," I offered, surprising myself with my own insight.

"All that money spent on psychoanalysis, and she could have simply asked you," Carrie quipped, but I was fairly certain she'd been impressed, too. "You won't believe what else she did. She wants me to sit down with Dad to have a heart-to-heart about why he stopped talking to her."

I laughed with gusto at this, thinking Vivian had gotten my advice half-right.

Carrie laughed with me. "How am I supposed to start that conversation? Dad, Mom truly cares about you, so she's sent me as her emissary? I swear, each day she gets more and more out of touch with normal humans. What will she be like in ten years?"

Before I could answer, Kai returned. "Here are some traditional Hawaiian meatballs with a Polynesian-inspired pineapple sauce. Enjoy."

Before I could turn to thank him, Kai was already gone. "That's spooky."

"The meatballs?" Carrie's eyebrows nearly met in the middle as she gave me a quizzical look.

"Not the meatballs, you dork," I retorted, smiling despite myself. "Kai's silent ninja skills. How does he do that?"

"I imagine that's part of the allure of this romantic escapade. Kai seems nice and all, but I'm betting not many passengers want to spend their time chitchatting with him. Most of them are probably too busy rushing for the dessert." She emphasized the last word, making me swallow hard. It was clear she wasn't talking about something sweet that could be ordered from the menu.

"You don't think people..." Words failed me as I contemplated all the shenanigans other passengers might have gotten up to on this ship. "But there's not even a bedroom."

"Who says you need a bedroom? There are plenty of hidden alcoves on a boat this size, and the crew is paid to be discreet." Carrie chuckled at my flustered expression. "Desperation is the mother of invention, darling."

I felt a blush creeping up my neck at the implication of what she was suggesting. "That's a bit scandalous, even for a tabloid queen like you."

"Scandal is my middle name." She leaned in closer, lowering her voice to a conspiratorial whisper. "And if there's one thing I've learned in this industry, it's that scandal sells."

"Luckily for you, scandal seems to follow wherever you go. Almost like it's a tailored role you've perfected." I'd meant my comment to be teasing, but the way her eyes flickered with something unreadable made me wonder if I might have stumbled on a kernel of truth.

Carrie's facade of nonchalance slipped for a moment before she recovered with a smirk. Lifting a toothpick, she speared one of the meatballs on the plate Kai had brought us. "Try one."

I thought she was going to hand it to me, so I reached out to take it. Instead, she bypassed my hand and brought the meatball to my mouth. I couldn't help the sharp inhale of surprise as I realized she was feeding it to me, like a real lover might do.

Caroline Fucking Jacobs was... what? Trying to seduce me on this boat? Angling for a little after dinner dessert?

No, she was acting. That was what she did best.

As I bit into the meatball, the savory flavor exploded on

my taste buds, momentarily distracting me from the intimacy of her gesture. Carrie's eyes held a mischievous glint as she watched me savor the bite.

"Well?" she prompted, her voice light and slightly breathy.

I swallowed before answering. "It's divine."

Now that we were fully focused on the food, the rest of the meal went off without a hitch. I found myself drawn into a conversation with Carrie that was surprisingly easy and peppered with witty banter. She shared stories of growing up amidst the glamor of old Hollywood, painting vivid pictures with her words that drew me in despite my initial reservations about her and her world.

The more I listened, the more I started to see the woman behind the tabloid headlines and scandalous relationships. She spoke of her family with a mix of fondness and exasperation, like I did about mine when I recounted stories of my years growing up at Busy Bee Cleaners. Time and again, she laughed at my anecdotes, almost as if she was really fascinated by the world of dry cleaning.

Was this the real Carrie Jacobs, or was it another role she was playing, this time for an audience of one? Surely, I was imagining things. There was no way Carrie found me intriguing enough to seduce, right?

As the sun started to set, Kai reappeared to announce that it was time for us to move to the viewing area at the stern of the ship. By process of elimination, I worked out that this was the not-pointy end on the opposite side from where we were.

"We're not watching it from here?" I inquired. As far as I was concerned, we had the best spot already. We were literally on a boat, bobbing along the water with nothing between us and a horizon already glowing with all the colors of a tropical sunset.

"If I may," Kai said deferentially, "I believe you'll find the viewing area much more comfortable. It's a bit more private."

With a knowing look, Carrie took my hand, threading our fingers together as she rose from her seat, pulling me gently along. The touch sent a spark through me, the warmth of her hand fitting perfectly against mine.

As we made our way to the other end of the boat, I couldn't help but steal glances at this woman who fascinated so many millions of fans. In the fading evening light, her features softened even more, and the excitement in her eyes seemed genuine, unguarded.

We arrived at a curtained space at the stern that reminded me of what the inside of a genie's lamp might look like. Curtains shielded the space from prying eyes while still offering an unobstructed view of the setting sun. Inside was a cozy seating area with pillows on the floor in the Turkish style. On a small table sat a bucket of ice with a bottle of what I was certain was premium champagne.

I turned to thank Kai, but he'd already gone. Was I imagining the man's existence?

"Would you like a glass?" Carrie lifted the bottle.

Suddenly hit with the romance of our current setting, I hesitated, recalling what had happened at the waterfall. "I'm not sure if we should."

"I hadn't pegged you for a watch-the-sunset-without-a-drink type of woman."

"It's just..." I stumbled over my words as the awkwardness of the moment enveloped me. "Um, have you taken any of those pain pills today?"

Carrie's smile faltered for a moment before she replied, "I may have conveniently forgotten. I hear I might not have behaved completely appropriately last time. In fact, two staff members informed me I declared my undying love for them."

"Only two? The others had more restraint," I teased.

"There were more?" Carrie looked horrified. "I don't think I'll be taking any more of those pills any time soon. Fortunately, my knee is doing much better today."

"I'm glad to hear it."

She poured herself a glass of champagne, tilting the bottle questioningly in my direction. "Are you sure you won't join me? It's Louis Roederer Cristal Brut from 2009."

I knew even less about champagne than I did about boats, but I assumed it was outrageously expensive by the way Carrie said it. I hesitated for a moment before giving in to the allure of the setting.

"Alright, just this once," I said as she poured me a glass.

We clinked our glasses together, and the fizzy liquid tickled my nose as I took a sip. After that, we settled on the plush pillows to watch the sunset. The atmosphere was so full of romance that I found myself letting my guard down more than I intended, letting my imagination run wild. It felt like a scene from one of Carrie's movies, except this time, there was no script to follow.

This was real life. And as such, I needed to remind myself that despite the picturesque setting and the shared champagne, we were not a newly engaged couple. We were two near-strangers who found ourselves caught in a moment of unexpected intimacy. Again.

"Do you remember the waterfall?" I blurted out, unable to stop the words from slipping past my lips.

Carrie took a sip of champagne, her eyes on mine. "Yes. Do you?"

"Why wouldn't I? I wasn't the one blitzed out of my mind on pain pills." Since I didn't think Carrie was going to say more, I pressed. "Do you remember the kiss?"

There was another sip, and I swear I could see the liquid travel down her long, sensuous throat before she said, "I do."

Frustration over her vague responses bubbled up in me like the fizz in my champagne glass. I wanted clarity. I wanted honesty. But most of all, I wanted to understand what fueled that fleeting moment at the waterfall, whether it was the pills, the pain, or something more profound.

"I swear I can't decide who you take after more, your mom or dad."

She had the decency to laugh. "It's awkward, isn't it?"

My heart sank at what her words implied, but I put on a happy face. If it had been nothing to her, then it was nothing to me. "It really is. I'm glad we're on the same page."

"Are we?" Carrie's chest heaved up and down in a surprising way for someone who was so nonchalant about the situation.

I nodded, staring at the last rays of the setting sun, wishing we were close enough that it's heat would disintegrate me right then and there. I had been a fool to think for even a moment that the kiss had meant anything, or that Carrie would reciprocate any deeper feelings I might have been developing. It was clear now that the waterfall kiss was nothing but a passing moment, a blip in our lives that didn't hold the same weight for her as it apparently, devastatingly, did for me.

"I also remember you sleeping in my bed while I was naked," she remarked in a husky tone.

I whipped my head toward her, my eyes wide with shock and embarrassment. "What are you accusing me of? Because that's not how it played out. You pulled me into bed."

"Why did you stay?" Her head moved closer to mine, her tone questioning and provocative. I could feel the warmth of her breath on my skin, sending shivers down my spine as I tried to gather my thoughts.

"You had a tight grip," I answered lamely.

"Even after I fell asleep? It must have been torture for you." Carrie's gaze locked with mine as if daring me to look away. Every fiber of my being was acutely aware of her proximity, the way her presence seemed to fill the space between us with an unspoken tension. "Given the way you think I'm a spoiled brat who only cares about myself and always gets my way."

"I never said that." I brushed a stray strand of hair from my eyes, twirling it nervously around my finger. "I may have thought it a few times, but I've never said it out loud." Had I?

Carrie laughed. "You know how they say actions speak louder than words? Your actions that night..." She let her words trail off suggestively.

Heat rose to my cheeks as I tried to come up with a witty retort. "It's possible I don't find you completely hideous and unbearable all of the time."

"Is that so?" Carrie inched closer to me. "How do you feel about me right now?"

"Confused."

"I love that about you."

"That I'm easily befuddled?"

"No, That you're honest. You don't ever play a part, do you?"

"I've actually been pretending to be your fiancée for almost a week now. Or is this your way of telling me I suck at it and I'm getting fired again?" I tried to sound confident, as if I didn't care either way.

"What if I kissed you right now? What would you do?" Carrie's eyes searched mine for any sign of resistance or reciprocation.

"You're the actor here. Tell me how that scene would play out," I teased, trying to mask my racing thoughts with humor. "I mean, here we are on this magnificent boat, in what could only be described as the canoodling section, with the frigging sun setting, sipping what must be ungodly expensive champagne. It couldn't get more romantic than that."

"Is it romantic for you?" Carrie paused. "Or are you waiting for the right moment to push me overboard?"

"What exactly are you asking?"

She leaned in closer, her lips a breath away from mine. "No one is here, Margo. You don't have to kiss me to play the part. What I want to know is if you want to kiss me anyway."

"No one was at the waterfall, either," I argued because, of course, I did. I couldn't see a good thing if it slapped me across the face.

"No. No one could see us at the waterfall," Carrie confirmed slowly, deliberately. "Which is why it should be obvious that it meant something to me."

"It did?" I asked, my voice barely above a whisper, searching her eyes for any hint of insincerity.

"Yes."

"Yes," I responded in turn.

"I'm sorry?" She didn't seem to understand.

"Yes, I want to kiss you," I confessed, my heart beating wildly in my chest as the boat gently rocked beneath us. "More than you could possibly know."

## CHAPTER THIRTEEN

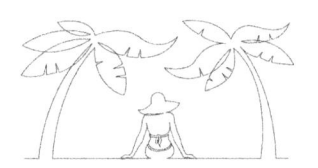

Carrie's eyes widened at my confession, a mixture of surprise and desire swirling in their depths. A flicker of vulnerability crossed her face, quickly replaced by a mischievous smile. She leaned in closer, the scent of her perfume enveloping me in a dizzying haze. "Well, Margo," she drawled, her voice soft and teasing, "what are you waiting for?"

Before I could respond, she closed the distance between us, her lips hovering inches from mine. The anticipation was enough to drive me mad. Was she going to make the final move, or would we be suspended in this torturous dance forever?

"What's the matter?" I breathed. "Aren't you going to follow through, or are you all talk and no action?"

Carrie's lips curled into a playful smirk at my challenge. "I can assure you I am definitely not all talk."

But still, she didn't make a move.

With a sudden boldness that surprised even myself, I closed the gap between us and captured her lips in a searing kiss, my hands tangling in Carrie's soft hair as she moaned against my lips. Our bodies pressed against each other, the heat between us intensifying with every passing moment.

I had dreamed of this moment for so long, and now it was finally happening. The taste of her on my tongue, the feel of her body against mine, it was all better than anything I could have imagined.

Carrie's hands roamed over my back and down to my hips, pulling me even closer and causing a spark to shoot through me. I couldn't get enough of her, and from the way she was responding, she felt the same way.

We broke apart for a brief moment, panting heavily as we gazed into each other's eyes. I could see the desire burning in hers, mirroring my own.

Without a word, we crashed back together in another passionate kiss. This time, there was no holding back. Our tongues danced together in a heated rhythm as our hands roamed over each other's bodies, exploring every inch.

I wanted nothing more than to rip off her clothes and ravish her right then and there.

I broke away from the kiss long enough to say, "I wish we weren't on this boat."

"What's wrong with the boat?" Carrie asked, punctuating each word with a kiss as we sank back into the soft cushions of the Turkish sofa.

"It's not a bedroom." I let out a groan as Carrie kissed her way down the side of my neck, sliding the strap of my sundress off my shoulder.

"You said it yourself before, this is the canoodling room," Carrie teased as she nibbled on my ear. She traced her fingers down my spine, causing goose bumps to rise on my skin. "We might as well make good use of it."

"Is that all you want to do here?" Maybe I was overplaying my hand thinking this would be more than a quick make-out session, but I needed to make it clear that I was looking for something more serious. Now that we'd finally crossed that line, I didn't want to stop. She was taking me to a whole new level of desire, and I wanted to explore it fully.

Carrie looked up at me, her eyes filled with lust, but also something else, something deeper. "I want to explore this, Margo," she said softly. "I don't know what it is between us, but I know it's more than just heat. These past few days, I've felt like my entire world is collapsing into you, and I can't get enough."

"What's your definition of what this would be?" I asked as Carrie's tongue slipped inside my ear. I practically melted into the pillows beneath me. "Is it a fling or something more meaningful?"

"Honestly, I can't say for sure," she whispered. "What do you want it to be?"

"I'm not... I don't..."

How could I be expected to think with the things she was doing to my neck and ear? How could I possibly be patient enough to weigh the pros and cons of this situation? Also, if I was already so turned on with all my clothing intact, what was she capable of when she had access to all of me?

Would I even survive?

"We'll figure it out," she murmured, her voice low and sultry. "For now, let's enjoy this moment and see where it leads us."

"But the staff—"

"One thing you should know about the staff on this island is that they're incredibly discreet. We're guests here, and our business is our own."

"You're saying what happens in the canoodle room stays in the canoodle room?" I joked, trying to lighten the mood.

She chuckled and kissed me again, running her fingers through my hair.

"Something like that." Carrie got to her feet. "Maybe this will give you a better idea of where I imagine things going tonight."

I watched, mesmerized, as Carrie unzipped her dress, letting it fall to the floor. The fabric pooled at her feet in a swirl of tropical floral print, revealing the lacy black bustier underneath. It barely contained her breasts, like something out of one of those lingerie catalogs I'd always assumed no one actually ordered from. I couldn't help but stare, my breath catching at the sight of her.

Sure, I'd seen her in underwear before. I'd helped her dress and undress on set. Hell, the entire world had seen her half-naked on the silver screen. But there was something different about seeing her like this. Something more intimate, more personal. Perhaps it felt like the first time because I would be able to explore her body with my fingertips, my mouth—a shiver of pure exhilaration worked its way through my insides.

"I understand if this is too much too soon," she said, her voice soft and sincere. "But I can't deny what I'm feeling for you in this moment."

I shook my head, finally finding my voice. "It's not too much," I whispered. "I want this, too."

This moment, I reminded myself. Not forever. It wasn't the way my brain was used to thinking. With Jenna, I'd gone all in, and look where it had gotten me. No, forever was overrated. This was an escape, a temporary reprieve from reality, and I needed that. We both did. It would be enough.

"Okay then," she said, brushing a strand of hair behind my ears. "Let's not think too far ahead. Let's enjoy the here and now and see where it leads us."

"Just this moment," I agreed, gently cupping her face in my hands. "No pressure."

Carrie's lips found mine again, our tongues tangling as our passion grew. I could feel the weight of the world lifting off my shoulders, replaced by a floating feeling, as if I was walking on clouds.

As our kiss deepened, I realized that for the first time in forever, I wasn't thinking about my past or my future. I was simply living in the present, lost in the heat of the moment and the embrace of a woman who made me feel alive. We were the only two people in existence. Our bodies moved in unison, exploring each other's curves and contours with a hunger that was both exhilarating and terrifying.

"Margo?" she whispered in my ear, her voice laced with uncertainty and desire.

"Yes?" I murmured, my heart racing with anticipation.

"Why do you still have all your clothes on?"

I laughed softly, my cheeks practically bursting into flames. It was a fair point. In truth, I was shy. Carrie was a movie star, the daughter of one of the most famous families in Hollywood. I was a plain girl from a small town in Minnesota. The thought of being naked in front of her made me feel exposed, vulnerable.

I knew that was ridiculous. I was about to let her discover me in ways few people ever had. Self-consciousness had no place here. Yet it did. Sure, two people, one being Carrie, had mistaken me for Alex that fateful day on set, but Alex was star material. My claim to fame was an uncanny ability to get red wine stains out of fabric. How far would that get me with the likes of Carrie?

Not taking action, though, would doom whatever was brewing between us.

"Good question," I said, my voice trembling slightly as I

rose and turned my back to her, lifting my hair. "My zipper is in the back. I'll need help."

"Gladly."

I sucked in a deep breath when her fingers took hold of the zipper. Not only did she lower it slowly, but she pressed her lips to each new inch of exposed skin as she went, all the way down my backside.

Not just kissing, but moaning like what she was doing to me was a huge fucking turn on.

How was this happening?

Caroline Fucking Jacobs was undressing me. Willingly. It was like something out of my teenage fantasies. Only this was real, and I was living it.

When her fingers finally reached the bottom, I could feel her breath on my skin, warm and eager. But what was happening? She didn't stop when the dress had fallen. Her tongue was working its way down the back of my right leg. Then up my left leg to my butt. Her fingers lowered my underwear, her teeth sinking into my ass cheek. She was literally kissing my ass.

I broke out into a nervous giggle.

"Care to share with the rest of us what's so funny?" Her voice was husky.

"I can't believe this is happening."

"Are you okay with everything? If not, we can redefine canoodling in a way that would make you more comfortable."

"I'm okay, but maybe we could settle back down on the cushions to give your knee a break?" I glanced at the troublesome joint to reassure myself it wasn't already starting to swell.

Carrie looked taken aback for a moment but nodded and stood up gingerly. The way she sucked in her breath as she flexed her knee told me she was in more pain than she'd let on.

"You're so different from all my other fiancées." She let out a soft chuckle, as if realizing how ridiculous that must sound.

I bit my tongue to stop from saying that her mom had told me almost the same thing. Talk about the worst time to bring up Vivian. No one wanted their mom mentioned during an intimate moment, but I imagine it was a million times worse for Carrie. Having a larger-than-life mother would cast an extremely long and impenetrable shadow. The woman shouldn't exist during these moments.

Carrie and I lowered to the pillows, our skin touching, causing me to let out a groan of want.

"I like the sounds you make," Carrie positioned herself on top of me, her tongue circling my nipple.

"I like... that." It wasn't the most coherent thing I'd ever said, but it was hard to focus with Carrie's warm and skillful mouth working its magic on me. My body responded more quickly than my brain, flushes of heat spreading through me.

"Such a way with words." She chuckled, her teeth delicately biting into my nipple.

My back arched. It was overwhelming, yet exhilarating, the way every touch and taste sent shivers of pleasure racing through my nerves.

"Although, I really do like a woman who isn't afraid to show her feelings." Carrie took my nipple into her mouth, sucking hard.

I gripped the back of her head, my nails scraping her scalp. As Carrie kissed her way to my other nipple, her hip slid between my legs.

This was really going to happen.

"I can feel how much you want me," Carrie whispered, her voice a low purr that made me come undone.

"So much," I breathed, our lips almost touching.

I wasn't even embarrassed to admit it. I wanted her to know how much I desired her, how her touch set fire to my skin and her mouth sent a heatwave through my veins.

I could feel her need for me, too. The tension in her body as she straddled me, her eyes locked onto mine. It was like a battle of nerves, each one trying to outdo the other.

Her hand slid down my side, her fingers leaving a trail of blazing hot caresses. Carrie was a sensitive lover. Who knew?

Her mouth was on mine again, kissing me deeply as if she wanted not simply the act of sex but a deeper connection. Or was this wishful thinking on my part?

Maybe I wanted to feel special.

As my fingers threaded through her silky hair, holding her in place, I tried not to think too much about it. I let myself be carried away by the moment, the passion igniting between us like kindling. God, the way our lips melted together was intoxicating.

I could kiss her for an eternity.

But as our lips parted, I noticed the slight uncertainty in her eyes. Had I misread the situation? Was it lust, or was there something more? I couldn't shake the feeling that we were both leaving something unsaid, some unspoken truth lurking beneath the surface of our desire.

Unless that was the effect she wanted to have on me.

After Jenna, I'd sworn I would never be with another actor. And yet here I was, falling hard and not sure what was real. Was I setting myself up for heartbreak again?

"Do you want me to stop?" Carrie asked, her eyes filled with concern as if sensing the shift in my thoughts.

"No," I replied quickly, my heart pounding with anticipation. I didn't want this to end. I wanted to lose myself completely in this moment, to feel the heat of her body against mine, to surrender to the fierce longing that raged within me.

If nothing else, that was real.

Carrie's smile widened, relief washing over her face, and she leaned in to kiss me again. Our lips met with a fierceness that sent shivers down my spine. She rocked her hip into me as I wrapped my legs around her.

"I like that," she said when she came up for air.

"What?" So much was going on at once that I wasn't sure which part had tickled her fancy.

"You holding me where you want me," she said. "The way you seem to let go and let me take control, but in reality, you're the one calling the shots. It's hot."

I couldn't help but smirk at her analysis. "I never realized I can be a bit of a control freak like that."

Carrie chuckled. "That's because you don't have a string of ex fiancés who have analyzed your every behavior. But don't worry. Being bossy totally works for you."

I groaned, feeling both embarrassed and aroused at the same time. "I didn't mean to get all dominant. I swear."

"Don't apologize for it. I think it can be quite... invigorating." Her eyes flickered down to my lips, and I felt a jolt of desire. "You should never be sorry for going after what you want."

"I don't want this to end."

"Wouldn't that be nice." As she gazed into my eyes, I could feel the intensity of our connection. It was like nothing I had ever experienced before. I wanted to stay right where I was, in this moment with her, with our bodies pressed together, our lips locked in an infinitely tantalizing dance.

More than that, I wanted to break off our fake engagement. To tell her she could keep the money she was paying me. I didn't want that. It made me feel cheap, like I was compromising myself in some way. Whatever this was between us, I wanted it to be real.

"I need you," I moaned, raising my pelvis against her hand, begging for more of her touch. I wanted her completely, everywhere and all at once.

As if to comply, Carrie inserted a finger into my wetness, knocking all words out of my head. Her sapphire eyes watched my reaction with such intensity it was like being under a microscope. For once, I wasn't terrified of what she'd see. I wanted her to know me. Flaws and all. And I wanted the same from her. If only there was a magic button I could press to see inside her soul.

"What?" Carrie kissed me as her fingers continued a steady rhythm, in and out, driving me to the edge of insanity. "What are you thinking?"

"I—" I gulped when Carrie added another finger, all remaining thoughts exiting my brain. "This... you... amazing."

"Why?" There was vulnerability in her tone.

"Because you're not afraid to be yourself around me."

"Because you see me," she said, her fingers increasing their speed. "The real me. You aren't afraid to challenge me. But you also make me feel like I'm enough, just as I am."

"I want to be that person for you." My words were laced with need but honesty as well. "And to know that you do the same for me. You make me feel alive."

"I bet I can make you feel all sorts of things." She grinned before kissing her way down my body. She didn't take a straight path but a wonderfully meandering trek. What shocked me the most was I didn't care that she was seeing me completely. Without a stitch of clothing, I couldn't hide an extra pound here and there, or disguise the parts of me that made me feel less than beautiful.

But Carrie seemed to revel in every inch of me, her fingers tracing the curves of my hips, her lips kissing the hollows of my knees. She made me feel beautiful, vulnerable, and undeniably alive.

Finally, she landed right where I needed her, in a way I'd never needed anyone before.

While my brain couldn't comprehend everything this meant, my heart was singing. I couldn't be bothered to worry. Right now, alone with Carrie, everything seemed right in the world.

Earlier, I had wished we weren't on this boat. Now, as Carrie's lips trailed down my body and her fingers expertly explored every inch of me, I never wanted to leave it. The gentle swaying of the boat and the faint sound of the waves against the hull added to the intensity of the moment.

Carrie's tongue flicked my clit, sending a jolt of pleasure through me. I let out a gasp, and my hand fisted one of the pillows beside me. "You feel so good," I moaned out, lost in the sensation. "So, so good."

She didn't speak, but she didn't have to. Her actions spoke louder than any words ever could. She was bringing me closer and closer to the edge, drawing out each moment in an excruciating yet delicious way.

Her fingers continued their dance inside me, hitting all the right spots with ease. My breaths came in ragged gasps as she brought me closer and closer to climax.

Just when I thought I couldn't take it anymore, Carrie's mouth closed around my clit and sucked gently. My body tensed as waves of intense pleasure coursed through every inch of me. It was like nothing I'd ever experienced before. Part of me wanted to dive over that edge and lose myself in pleasure, but another part wanted to stay in this moment forever.

Because what would happen when we returned to shore?

*No, Margo. Don't do that.*

As if in tune with my thoughts, Carrie slowed things down, keeping me right on the brink of a second orgasm for much longer than I thought humanly possible. Until her fingers dove in deep, forcing my eyes closed and causing flashes of light behind my eyelids.

It was the rolling type of orgasm, a new wave of bliss splashing through me. One after another.

With her free hand, Carrie threaded her fingers through mine. Once again, I couldn't believe how caring she could be. It was sexy as hell.

Carrie rested her chin on my stomach.

I glanced down at her, unable to stop myself from blurting out, "You're so fucking beautiful."

"Is this the part where you thank me for my stellar performance?" she teased with a smirk.

"If I had an Oscar with me right now, I'd give it to you," I chuckled, tracing my fingers along her jawline. "But since I don't, I'll have to show you my appreciation some other way."

Carrie chuckled, a playful glint in her eyes. "I like the sound of that."

## CHAPTER FOURTEEN

Carrie and I lay in bed, our limbs entangled with each other beneath the rumpled sheets. After returning from the cruise, neither of us had been ready for sleep. We were too desperate for the continued release of our pent-up desires, lost in each other's bodies. I had no idea how many orgasms I'd had, but I know it was more than the past few years combined.

As I stroked her back with my fingertips, Carrie let out a happy sigh, stretching like a lazy house cat.

"Morning," she mumbled, her eyes still half-closed.

"Morning," I replied, smiling at her contented expression. "I think I could stay right here all day."

No sooner had I said this than my stomach grumbled because, of course, it did. Here I was, in bed with a hot movie star that half the world was in love with, and could I play it cool for a single second? Nope.

Carrie giggled, perfectly aware of my stomach's loud-mouthed complaint. "You're adorable," she said, nuzzling into my neck. "Do you want to order room service, or should we get dressed and venture out for breakfast?"

"What time is it?" I propped up on an elbow, squinting at the clock on the nightstand. "Oh, geez. It's after noon. We missed breakfast completely."

"That's a shame." She didn't sound particularly upset about it. "You love the French toast."

I laughed. "Do you know what my second favorite meal is?"

"Tacos?"

"Close." I told her. "Lunch."

"We should get dressed then."

I sank back against her body, covering us both in the sheets. "Doesn't seem fair. I'm not sure I want this to end."

This time, Carrie's stomach rumbled. "That's life, sweet cheeks." She playfully slapped my butt, and I let out a yelp.

"Fine," I said with a groan, "but I reserve the right to come back to bed."

Carrie didn't respond, instead climbing out of bed to toss on some clothes.

Immediately, doubt overwhelmed me. Maybe I'd misread the situation. Like once we left the sex zone, it might never happen again. Did that mean Carrie had gotten a taste and that had been more than enough? That kinda seemed to be her pattern.

I rummaged through my luggage, still not having found the time or desire to put my clothing away. I was beginning to resent the fact that none of the items in my suitcase actually belonged to me. Sure, Asher had great taste and had provided me with a much better wardrobe than the one I actually owned, but I couldn't help but feel like a stranger in my own life, like I was living a lie.

As I settled on a casual pair of capris and a loose linen blouse that was still a million times nicer than I would've worn at home, I couldn't shake the feeling of unease that lingered in the back of my mind. Was I just a convenient distraction before Carrie moved on to her next conquest?

Tossing my chosen outfit onto the bed, I slipped on some underwear, or at least one of the lacy bits of nothing that passed for underwear in Asher's world. I really should have drawn the line at allowing a man to choose my underthings. I chewed my lip, fighting off the onslaught of insecurity that threatened to consume me. Who was I trying to fool with all this fancy stuff? Underneath it all, I was still plain old me.

As I reached for my bra—which matched the panties, naturally—I could almost feel Carrie's eyes burrowing into me. Slowly, I turned around, spying my reflection in the mirror at the same time I caught Carrie watching me. Her expression was completely unreadable. But based on what I saw reflected back at me from across the room, she had to be thinking she'd made a colossal mistake.

I finished dressing in record time. "Ready?" I bolted for the door, needing to break free from what I could only interpret as her disapproving gaze.

"Where's the fire?" she joked.

I almost responded, "Not in your pants," but refrained, mostly out of self-preservation. I was too afraid she would agree with me. My confidence was shattered enough already, and I doubted my ego would survive the fall from such lofty heights as I'd so recently enjoyed. It was hard to be another ordinary mortal, no longer basking in the limelight of the goddess who was Caroline Fucking Jacobs.

Heading outside, we sat at one of the tables near the pool, pouring over the menus. Neither of us attempted small talk. To me, this was more proof that Carrie had regrets. She'd never been so quiet before. It had to mean something.

When the server arrived, Carrie ordered a salad, and I got the salmon poke.

I was about to crack a joke about hoping for another kind of poke later, when Carrie's expression morphed into mortification, like she knew exactly where my mind was. She couldn't even look at me, and it bruised me to my core. Could this get any worse? I wasn't sure how many slings and arrows one person could take after the best night of their life.

"Carrie! I've been looking everywhere for you."

With a sinking feeling, I turned my head to see Sandra in a swimsuit ensemble befitting a supermodel. Because that was what happened when you dared to ask how much worse things could get. I'd practically begged the universe to give me a tutorial on the phrase "Be careful what you wish for."

"We didn't want to leave our bed but needed food," I blurted out because I was that awkward. After which I decided to add, "I'm getting the salmon poke, if you know what I mean."

The look Carrie shot me could have frozen hell over, and combined with Sandra's arched eyebrow, it told me everything I needed to know. Neither of them appreciated my feeble attempts at humor.

Apparently, neither of them had read *Lonesome Dove*, or they would've known that the cowboys in the book referred to sex as a poke. If they had, they would've found it funny.

Sandra tore her horrified expression from me, keeping her eyes on Carrie. "You know what I was thinking this morning? I want to play tennis."

There was something in her tone that immediately set off alarm bells in my brain. Playing tennis? Was that code for something else?

"Where's Kermit?" Carrie asked.

Sandra rolled her eyes at the mention of her fiancé's name. "He and Greg are taking surf lessons."

Carrie gave a knowing nod. "Groomsmen taking the groom out for a last hoorah?"

"Actually, Erik was supposed to go, but he ended up being a no-show." Sandra's shrug indicated she didn't give a damn about what any of the men were up to. She only had eyes for Carrie.

My fiancée.

Okay, my fake fiancée, but now that we'd slept together, that kind of made it more real. Or at least a gray area as far as I was concerned.

"What do you say?" Sandra asked in a coy tone. "Wanna play with me?"

I nearly choked on my water. Sandra was outright flirting with Carrie right in front of me like I wasn't a threat or even a consideration. Just who did she think she was?

"Uh, I haven't decided on my plans for the day." Carrie didn't look in my direction either.

Had I simply stopped existing?

"I'll text you." Sandra gave Carrie such a long look as she walked away, and it was one that clearly screamed, "I want you back. Please say yes."

It was enough to make me want to gag. Or punch her.

Definitely punch her.

Our lunch arrived, but honestly, I'd lost my appetite. After several failed attempts at forcing food into my body, I got to my feet. "I'm going to do some shopping."

"Should I join you?" Carrie held her overloaded fork to her mouth, and it was obvious she had no desire to leave her feast.

"No, it's fine. I need to get some trinkets for my parents, and with only a few days until the wedding…" My words trailed off as I spun around, and I started marching toward my goal, which wasn't really the hotel gift shop. It was simply to disappear so Carrie didn't have to feign finding me attractive. Once a total knock-out like Sandra was around, it seemed Carrie's acting skills could only get her so far.

It wasn't even like I could afford anything in the gift shop. But heading back to the room, with the rumpled sheets and lingering scent of sex, didn't appeal to me. Although, with the paycheck I was expecting from pretending to be in love with Carrie, I might be able to manage a T-shirt.

Which the gift shop didn't have. Did rich people not like T-shirts?

I edged my way to the back, hoping to find something with a price tag under three figures. The best I could do was a measly display of pineapple-shaped fridge magnets. Go figure.

"Oh, hey there," said a man's voice. A quick glance revealed it was that director—darned if I could recall his name at the moment—Jenna had dumped me for. How fucking fantastic. Because the universe wasn't done kicking me when I was down.

"Hey yourself." I scouted the shop, my shoulders tensing in anticipation of encountering my ex. What was it about this stupid resort and all the exes, anyway? Running into exes was like a theme to this trip.

"Where's Jenna?" I asked when I failed to locate her on my own.

He scratched his chin. "Not sure. She said she'd meet me here, but I can't find her."

"If I see her, I'll let her know you're looking for her."

He mumbled a thanks, leaving the shop.

I didn't want to bump into Jenna. This seemed like a reasonable attitude to have. Because I wasn't pining after my ex, unlike some people on this island.

My foot caught on something, and I nearly took a tumble.

"Ouch," came a voice from the floor.

The voice sounded familiar. "Asher? What are you doing down there?"

"Hiding."

This was why we were friends, because when the going got tough, we both liked to hide. In gift shops, apparently.

"What are you hiding from?" I asked, genuinely curious what had reduced a grown man to a heap on the tile floor.

"Not a what. A who." He motioned for me to take a seat on the floor, which I did. "Cagney. She's impossible."

"What does she want now? To toast her nuptials with the tears of a hundred virgins?"

"Please don't mention that idea to her." He groaned, clearly not putting it past his cousin to add to her list of demands. "She's not sure about the desserts for the rehearsal dinner. Which is two days away, in case you weren't keeping track. She wants me to go to the bakery to sample all the different options."

"You're hiding from desserts?" I placed my palm on his forehead. "You must have a tropical fever."

"I'm mentally fragile right now, okay?"

"Does this mean your wedding planning ambitions are on hold?"

"I never want to see a wedding dress or tuxedo ever again in my life." He studied me closely, suddenly keenly aware of something, though what, I wasn't sure. "You look different."

"No, I don't." It was my go-to strategy to deny things when I wasn't sure if they were good or bad.

"Yes, you do. What's up?"

"N-nothing," I stammered, not wanting to bring up my

trivial problems. Not to a guy who was traumatized by the prospect of eating sweets.

"It's not nothing. You're practically glowing—" He clamped a hand to his mouth, before releasing a squeal that his palm didn't muffle all that well. "I know what it is. You have sex glow."

"It's the sea air. It makes everyone look more luminous." I tilted my head to the side as if to give him a better view of my dew-kissed skin.

"That's not it. It's sex." He sounded awfully sure of himself on this matter, and for good reason. He was always right when it came to calling hookups. It was a talent of his that I should have anticipated would rear its ugly head. "You and Carrie had sex. I knew you two would hit it off."

"Don't get too excited," I cautioned, not bothering to deny it when he was so obviously correct. "It was a one-time thing, and I'm pretty sure she regrets it."

"Why do you say that?" His expression fell, and it was clear he wasn't just curious. He was invested in the answer. Had he been for real about thinking we would be compatible?

"Because she's chasing after Sandra," I admitted, feeling a fresh pang of jealousy at the thought.

"What are you talking about?"

"At lunch. Sandra asked Carrie to play tennis." I paused, shaking my head vigorously. "No, Sandra said, 'Wanna play with me.' I'm not a moron, ya know. I understand what she meant." A heat of blush spread up my neck and into my cheeks.

Asher scratched his head. "That she wanted to play tennis?"

"Yeah, right," I scoffed.

"You may not be a moron, but I might be," he said. "I don't know what you're implying."

"You do too. You were the one who told me Sandra always craves someone else's toys."

Asher's brow furrowed, his eyes narrowing in thought. "How did Carrie respond?"

"She said she didn't know her plans for the day," I huffed, looking at him to validate my anger.

He did not comply, offering a shrug instead. "That sounds like a blow off to me."

"Pffft." I crossed my arms. "What's your room situation?"

"Huh?" The poor guy was thoroughly confused now, and I realized my mouth was lagging my brain by several seconds.

"I can't go back to sleeping on the couch in Carrie's suite. Not after what happened between us. Do you have a spare bed?"

"I don't even have a chair. Not all of us are staying in the private bungalows."

"I'd get my own room for these last few nights, but I fear it would bankrupt me for a millennium."

"Don't you think you might be overreacting?" Asher had that infuriating calm in his tone that made me want to strangle him.

"Me? Overreacting?" I sputtered. "Sandra's a celebrity. She's gorgeous. I'm not overreacting."

"Then you're not thinking clearly. Carrie doesn't even like tennis much. I don't think she's played since she and Sandra broke up."

"Because she didn't have a partner," I pointed out, frustrated he couldn't recognize the obvious. "But now she does, which means I'm history."

Carrie and Sandra were practically tennis soulmates. Where did that leave me? Sleeping on Asher's floor, apparently. I hoped he had a spare pillow.

"Don't read into things," Asher warned me. "You always do that. Go. Find Carrie and talk to her."

"What do I say?"

"Tell her how you're feeling." He nudged my side with his elbow.

I sighed, exasperated. Asher had a point, but it was easier said than done. "I can't abandon you. You need me to taste test the desserts with you. Hell, the way my emotions are all over the place right now, I could murder an entire cake all on my own."

"Nope." He wagged a finger at me. "I'm not going to be your wingman for avoiding communication. I only ducked in here to gather my strength before I head out. This is my happy place."

"A hotel gift shop is your happy place?"

"Don't judge."

Before I could say another word, he shooed me away.

"Gosh, no one wants to be around me today." I got to my feet. "I know when I'm not wanted."

He rolled his eyes and then looked away. Tough love was... tough.

Instead of tracking down Carrie on the tennis courts like a grown-up who had a firm grasp of emotional intelligence, I hightailed it to the room to hide in peace.

Upon opening the door, I nearly crashed into Carrie.

"You're back," she exclaimed. I must have been imagining things because I could have sworn I detected relief in her tone.

"What are you doing?" I eyed her with suspicion, wondering what game she was playing. Other than tennis, that is.

"I came back to the room to change into my swimsuit."

"Not your tennis skirt?" I challenged.

"I don't have one."

I raised an eyebrow, unimpressed by her response. "The shop sells them. I know. I was just there."

"I'm good, thanks." Carrie cocked her head like she didn't know what to make of me. "Do you want to join me at the pool?"

"After what happened at lunch?" I spluttered, unable to keep cool any longer.

Carrie frowned. "Was the salmon not good? Are you not feeling well?"

"Look, you can drop the act. I don't want you to miss your tennis date."

Carrie blinked. "I feel like we're having two different conversations. What are you talking about?"

"Sandra," I nearly screamed. "And how she wants you back."

Carrie let out a howl of laughter.

I balled my fists, itching for a fight. "You know, I may not have liked you before, but I didn't peg you as this heartless. Maybe you're just relieved it's out in the open."

"What's out in the open?" Carrie seemed to be truly taken aback by my accusations. "Sandra doesn't want me back."

"She does," I insisted. "Everyone can see it."

"I don't."

I threw my hands skyward. "How can you be nine years older than I am but not understand that as soon as she learned you're off the market, it made you all the more desirable?"

Carrie shook her head. "You don't know Sandra."

"I think I do. Do you?"

"Even if you're right, it doesn't matter. I wanted to spend the day with you. At the pool. I still do." Carrie paused, looking as though a light was suddenly coming on in her head. "Wait. Was that why you rushed off in the middle of lunch?"

"Duh." I mimed my head exploding at this revelation.

"I'm sorry I didn't pick up on what upset you." To my surprise, Carrie sounded completely sincere. "I should have chased after you."

"Chased me?" I splayed my fingers across my chest, unsure she was talking to me despite me being the only other person in the room. Unless there was a ghost I hadn't noticed. "Are you just saying this so you can get lucky later today? You know, if the Sandra thing falls through?"

Carrie released a breath, and I couldn't tell if it was filled with rage or humor.

"I don't want to be around Sandra. And I'll prove it." She took out her phone and handed it to me. "After an appropriate amount of time, I texted her to tell her I couldn't play tennis."

"Because of your knee?" I asked after confirming the contents of the text on the screen. It had been sent quite some time ago, well before I'd gone on my rant to Asher.

"Jesus, Go." Carrie put her hands on my shoulders, and I had the sensation of being brought back down to earth in a whoosh. "Why can't you get it through your head that I want to spend the day with you?"

"Because..." My voice trailed off, unable to come up with a single reason that didn't revolve around my own insecurities. "You really do?"

She threaded her arms around my waist. "Yes, I do. Even if you're being weird."

A part of me still couldn't believe what I was hearing. But with Carrie's arms wrapped around me, her sincerity was palpable. For a moment, I was at a loss for words, which was a rare occurrence for me. It felt like the ground beneath me had shifted, and all my assumptions about her were proving to be wrong.

I kept expecting her to act like a superstar. Like Caroline Fucking Jacobs. But underneath it all, she was just plain Carrie.

And apparently, she kinda liked me. Even when I was weird.

## CHAPTER FIFTEEN

"Are you sure your knee's up for this hike?" I cast a worried glance at Carrie's leg, giving her hand a squeeze as we walked over the soft sand along the beach. The waves were quietly breaking on my right, the water lapping gently at the shore with a smooth rhythm that echoed back against the cliffs in the distance.

"Oh, please. It's more a stroll than hike. I may not be as spry as I used to be, but I can still outpace you any day," she teased, quickening her gait. "Besides, I want to show you Sweetheart Rock."

"You do, huh?" I waggled my eyebrows. "Sounds like a place to make out. Did teenagers name it?"

She chuckled. "Not exactly. The official name is Pu'u Pehe. But that's kind of a mouthful for the tourists."

We reached the end of the Hulopo'e Beach portion of the hike, hitting a dirt trail with tire tracks and footprints intermixed. Much to my relief, the terrain wasn't that rocky. Carrie's face didn't show any strain, and her steps seemed pain free.

"Did you do this hike as a kid?" I asked, curious to hear more about Carrie's past.

She nodded, her eyes distant as if reminiscing. "Yeah, the whole family used to do it every summer when I was little. Well, minus Cagney. She wasn't born yet. I try to visit at least once each time I'm on the island."

"How many sweethearts have you brought here?" I immediately regretted my joke. Honestly, I didn't want to know the answer. Not if it meant hearing about more exes. I didn't need a history of every fling she had ever taken to this spot.

Carrie shot me a sly grin. "You know me. I have a little black book filled with secret rendezvous spots all over the world," she quipped, making me laugh despite my best efforts to keep a straight face.

"Forget I said anything," I begged. "I don't want to know about your extensive list of romantic hideaways. It might make me jealous."

Carrie let out a melodramatic gasp, placing a hand over her heart. "Jealous? You? Why, I can't even picture it. You're so not the jealous type."

"Laying it on a little thick, don't you think? And before you answer, I'm pretty sure anyone would have reacted the way I did if a viper like Sandra started to encroach on their territory," I retorted, trying to keep things light despite the underlying truth that her past relationships were undeniably a sore subject for me.

Carrie's expression softened, and she reached out, her hand gently brushing mine. "The answer is only one. You."

My heart skipped a beat at her words, a warm glow spreading through my chest. "What makes this place so special for you?"

Unless I had misread the situation and there were some other reasons she'd never brought anyone else here. But no, this was exactly the kind of negative thinking I had promised Carrie I would try to steer clear of. Trust was the name of the game, and I needed to learn to take her affection for me at face value.

"Let's just say I can relate to the story behind it." She looked forward, slowing her gait so we walked side by side. "I probably should tell you now that the legend doesn't have a happy ending."

My heart seized in my throat, all my earlier doubts rushing to the surface once more. "You're bringing me here why?"

"To watch the sunset," she said softly, giving my hand a squeeze. "It might be our last peaceful night on the island, and despite the tragic story surrounding it, this is my favorite place at this time of day." She cast a side glance at me, a small smile playing on her lips. "I know you're looking for a hidden meaning, but don't. Not everything I do is to fulfill an agenda."

"It's like you get me." I couldn't help but laugh a little at how accurately she'd pegged my suspicious nature.

"I'm starting to."

"And you don't want to run away?" Again, I regretted my statement. It made me sound like I was always expecting the worst. Which I probably was, but she didn't need to know that. At least not more than she already did.

"Run away? Are you kidding me? Not with this knee." She gently whacked her bad leg and rolled her eyes. "But seriously, Margo, I brought you here because I wanted to share something special with you. No hidden agendas or ulterior motives. Just us, enjoying a beautiful sunset together. Think you can handle that?"

I couldn't help but chuckle at Carrie's lighthearted jab, the tension in my chest easing at her words. "I'll do my best.

But no promises on resisting the urge to overanalyze everything all the time."

Carrie laughed. "I'll take what I can get."

"I imagine you can get quite a bit, if you play your cards right." I winked, wondering when I had become so comfortable openly flirting with her.

It felt like we had known each other for years instead of just a few days. Although, technically, it had been much longer. We'd worked together on the set, after all. But we'd never had the chance to really connect until now. To be honest, even if we had, I would have avoided it. I had been too stuck on the notion that all actors were untrustworthy.

Now I could see that maybe, just maybe, my preconceived notions were wrong. Carrie's presence was slowly chipping away at the walls I had meticulously built around myself. She had proven me wrong in so many ways, and I was grateful for that.

As I smiled at her, I couldn't help but take in the sights around us. "Could you see yourself living here?" I asked, genuinely curious how she felt.

"I've considered it, but..." Her voice trailed off as she looked to the horizon, where the light was starting to turn a deep shade of orange. "We're almost there and just in the nick of time."

We must have reached the end of the road because Carrie motioned for me to take a seat on some rocks overlooking the water.

"Right there is Sweetheart Rock." She pointed to a rock jutting out of the water, towering as high as an eight-story apartment building.

It was impressive to see, so tall and sheer that it seemed impossible for anyone to climb. The fading sunlight bathed it in a warm, golden glow, making the rock look like a beacon in the ocean. I couldn't tear my eyes away, but as I glanced at Carrie, I realized she was watching me instead.

"Beautiful, isn't it?" she said softly.

I knew she meant the rock, but some small part of me hoped she was referring to me as well. I couldn't help the blush that rose to my cheeks at this realization. I was so far gone over this woman I would probably never recover. And I didn't seem to care.

"It's absolutely stunning," I replied, trying to play it cool despite the fluttering in my chest. The way she looked at me made me feel like I was the only one in her world at that moment, and I found myself getting lost in those mesmerizing eyes of hers, so much more vibrant in person than they ever looked on screen.

As the silence between us grew, a sense of anticipation hung in the air. I could hear the soft lapping of the waves against the rocks below and distant seabirds calling out as if they were reminding us of the passing time.

"Now that we're here," I said quietly, almost afraid to break the spell that seemed to surround us, "can you tell me why they call it Sweetheart Rock?"

Carrie's gaze softened as she turned her attention back to the rock, a wistful smile playing on her lips. "Legend has it that a warrior fell in love with a young woman from one of the other islands. He was so enthralled by her he brought her home with him and hid her in one of the caves below."

My eyes traveled downward as Carrie gestured to the shoreline. "A cave doesn't sound like the most romantic accommodation, but I suppose it was different back then."

"Not exactly a five-star resort, but it was secluded and private. So, I guess it had its perks," Carrie agreed. "One day, the warrior had gone off. He'd left his lover alone in the cave so he could gather supplies. Too late, he noticed a terrible storm approaching, turning the sea into a raging monster. The warrior rushed to the cave, but he couldn't make it back in time. The woman cried for him, her voice lost in the howling wind as the waves crashed against the rocks, threatening to swallow her whole."

Carrie's voice had taken on a haunting quality, and I was reminded of the immensity of her talent for bringing stories to life. I watched her, captivated by the emotion in her eyes as she continued the tale.

"Finally, a wave as big as a mountain came crashing toward the cave. The woman was swept out to sea and drowned."

I gasped. "That's terrible."

Carrie nodded gravely. "The warrior was so distraught. He knew he couldn't ask the gods to bring her back to life, so instead, he pleaded with them to give him the strength to climb Sweetheart Rock so that he could bury her body at the top where no one could ever reach it."

"Did the gods hear him?" I asked, my heart heavy with the tragic tale Carrie was spinning.

"They did. The warrior climbed Sweetheart Rock with the woman's lifeless body, his heart aching with grief. When he reached the top, he buried her. And afterward, he was so overcome with his loss, he threw himself over the edge and plummeted to his death."

"That's tragic." I shivered, feeling the weight of the story settle over us like a heavy cloak. "But here's what I don't get. Why'd he keep her in the cave if it was so dangerous?" I peeked over the side of the cliff at the expanse that separated us from the rock, my vision blurring a little at the drop. I could picture the crashing waves in my mind, and the small cave filling with salty water from the sea. It was enough to give me heart palpitations.

"That's a good question. My guess is he didn't want other people to see her because she was so beautiful, and he wanted to keep her all to himself." Her shoulders folded inward, and I could tell this was the part of the story that hit home for her.

"It sounds like you can relate."

"I've dated some people who wanted me all to themselves. I usually have a heart-to-heart with them before we get serious."

"Is this our heart-to-heart?" I asked, suddenly grasping the weight of Carrie's words and the vulnerability she was showing me.

"Maybe it is. You see, everyone says they're cool with the way my life is. The adoring fans. The movie roles—especially the sexy ones. But when push comes to shove and fans nearly knock them over to get to me for a selfie? Or they see one of those sex scenes on the big screen? That's when they start to show their true colors. Every single time."

"But you've always dated other actors," I said. "Surely they know what they're signing up for."

Carrie let out a bitter laugh. "That's what I thought, too. But it turns out, even actors can be insecure and jealous."

"You mean, that's not the exclusive property of wardrobe supervisors?" I joked.

"Touché." Carrie blew out a breath, and I could almost feel the years of frustration she'd experienced. "I thought other actors would get it, but I was wrong."

"That's not fair. It's your job."

She bobbed her head sadly. "And if I'm doing my job well, the sex scenes look real. Too real. And then it's off to the cave with me."

"I was thinking. What if the warrior had a different reason for hiding the woman?"

"Such as?"

"Maybe he didn't think he was good enough for her, so he hid her away to keep her from falling for someone else. His own insecurities were the cause of his doom."

"Hmm." Carrie's gaze practically burned. "Who does that remind me of?"

"Er..." I swallowed, belatedly realizing how well that particular shoe fit me. "I'm really sorry. I know yesterday with the whole Sandra thing—it wasn't my best moment. It's just... I have no idea what you see in me."

"Someone who's honest, for starters. Who isn't afraid to speak her mind, even if it can be annoying." She bumped her shoulder into mine, perhaps as a way to soften the blow from her words. "You're beautiful and amazing, Go-Go. I only wish you could see what I see."

"You know what I see right now?" I pointed to the sky, bathed in deep pink and purple hues as the sun slipped below the horizon. "I see the most stunning sunset I've ever experienced. I'll remember this for the rest of my life."

Carrie wrapped her arms around me, pulling me closer as we watched the sun disappear beyond the horizon. The silence between us was comfortable, the tension from before dissipating into the evening air. As darkness settled in, I could feel her heartbeat against mine, a rhythm that synced with my own.

"What is that island over there?" I pointed to the land mass in the distance that was barely visible in the dimming light.

"That's Maui."

"Wow. Maui, really? I still can't believe I'm here. Never in my life did I think I'd vacation in Hawaii with—"

"Caroline Jacobs?"

"No. Caroline Jacobs is a movie star. You're just Carrie." I began to laugh. "I probably shouldn't say this—"

"But you're going to anyway," Carrie guessed, proving how well she knew me. I loved that about her, just as I loved that she would no doubt find what I was going to tell her amusing.

"In my head—mind you, mostly after I thought you had me fired—I always referred to you as Caroline Fucking Jacobs. With a capital F, like it was your middle name."

She laughed but without as much humor as I might have liked. "You aren't the only one, I'm sure." She sucked in a deep breath. "Sometimes I think I'm crazy for staying in this business."

"Why do you do it?" I asked. "You could quit right now and live comfortably the rest of your life. Maybe buy a little place on the island and, I don't know, grow pineapples or something."

"As nice as that sounds, I was born to act. Not just because of my mom. I know deep inside." She clutched the front of her shirt. "This is why I'm here. No matter how much pain and frustration it causes me."

"The warrior should have trusted her," I said, my voice low and filled with quiet sympathy.

"Why's that?"

"If you love someone, you have to trust them. No matter what. Don't you think?"

"I do." Carrie whispered, her eyes searching mine. "Does that mean you'll start trusting me? Even when you feel insecure?"

"I'll do my best, but I reserve the right to be irrational sometimes. I mean, I gotta be me, right?" I offered her a shrug paired with my best attempt at a grin.

"I suppose I can let you be you. As long as you let me be me." She put her pinky out as if to seal our pact.

"A pinky promise." I locked mine with hers. "The most solemn of promises."

"Can I confess something?" Carrie leaned in closer. "I liked you before this trip."

"No, you didn't." A nervous giggle escaped me.

"I did," she insisted. "I know I was with Alex then, so I wasn't going to act on anything. But each day, I prayed it'd be you, not Gilly, who'd dress me."

I blinked, unable to hide my surprise. "Wait, really? You never said a single word to me."

"You don't believe me?" She arched one eyebrow.

"It's not that. I'm just trying to decide if that's a compliment or not. Gilly wasn't anyone's favorite."

Carrie let out a hoot of laughter. "She's infuriating, but that wasn't my reason. I felt... safe when you were around. In good hands. And you're pretty cute, too, not that that factors into it or anything."

"You think I'm cute?" I smirked, raising an eyebrow playfully.

"You have the sincerest eyes I've ever seen and the most adorable nose." She kissed the aforementioned body part and then pressed her forehead to mine. "I'm glad we came here."

"To Hawaii? Or here to watch the sunset at your special rock?"

"Both." Carrie kissed me. The type of kiss that was sweet but full of meaning. "I'm happy my cousin thought to hire you as my fake fiancée. I may never have pursued you on my own."

"Asher fancies himself as a matchmaker."

"He's had some luck on that front."

I tilted my head. "Did he get Cagney and Erik together?"

She shook her head. "Definitely not."

We sat in silence, our shoulders pressed together, and waited as the sun finished its descent below the horizon.

"I wish we could stay." Carrie's eyes swept the water with a longing that matched my own.

"Me too." I looped my arm through hers. "Although, we didn't bring food, and I'm getting a little peckish."

"Poor planning on our part. Should we get back?" Carrie got to her feet without waiting for a reply.

"You really are amazing, you know that?" I leaned in for a kiss.

"So you don't plan on hiding me in a cave?" she asked when we parted.

"Of course not. I wouldn't want to have to carry you to the top of that rock when my inevitable jealousy led to your untimely demise. Looks hard to climb."

"Next time we're here, I'll take you below to show you the caves."

What did she mean by next time? Tomorrow was the rehearsal dinner, and the next day was Cagney's wedding. After that, we would be heading back to Los Angeles. Back to real life. There would be no time to make it to the caves before then.

Unless she meant she wanted to make another trip in the future. We hadn't discussed it yet, but did she want to continue seeing me when we got back home?

I wanted to ask her about this, but I couldn't gather the courage to bring it up yet. Instead, we walked in silence in the twilight, holding hands, until we once again found ourselves in the tropical oasis of the resort. The sky was a dark purplish black, and the pool lights glimmered. In the potted palms were twinkly lights. It was practically a magical night.

Aside from one thing.

A young woman sat in a lounge chair with her knees

pulled to her chest, her arms wrapped around them as she rocked back and forth, a sobbing mess.

Carrie stopped abruptly, narrowing her eyes. "Is that Cagney?"

I sucked in a breath as recognition set in. "I think it is. What on earth could have happened?"

But Carrie had already taken off at a trot, favoring her knee but not letting it slow her down. I followed behind her as quickly as I could.

"What's wrong?" Carrie folded her sister into her arms.

"It's over," Cagney wailed. "The wedding is off."

## CHAPTER SIXTEEN

"What happened?" Carrie sat on the lounge and patted Cagney's back, letting her sister cry it out as I stood awkwardly a few feet from them, not wanting to intrude on this family moment.

Poor Cagney's body shook with sobs, her face buried in her hands. Her signature blond hair was tangled, and I was almost certain that her makeup was running down her face—even the best waterproof mascara in the world couldn't stand up to this kind of abuse. Cagney didn't seem to care. And I couldn't blame her. Life had taught me that sometimes a good, ugly cry was the only thing that got you through the most difficult moments.

"I went back to the room to get the menu cards for tomorrow night's rehearsal dinner," Cagney explained through her sniffles. "And that's when I found him in bed with another woman."

"Who?" The way Carrie sounded, I almost pitied the other woman, and Cagney's now-ex-fiancé, too, for the wrath they were clearly about to have unleashed upon them.

"Some social climbing, D-list actress nobody," Cagney

wailed. "She's been floating around here all week with that director who keeps pestering me, saying he's got the perfect project for my next role."

Well, shit. I knew exactly one person who fit that description. Jenna.

Carrie's eyes met mine, and for a flicker of a moment, I feared she would somehow lay the blame on me. But Carrie's gaze didn't hold an accusation. That was all projection on my part. And no wonder. Even though I had played no role in bringing Jenna here, I was racked with guilt by association.

"He tried to say it was all h-her fault," Cagney said through her sobs. "Like he played no role in cheating on me at all."

"He clearly doesn't know how to take responsibility for his own actions," Carrie remarked, her voice laced with disdain.

But I knew Erik's excuse, as flimsy as it was, held a kernel of truth. It was all starting to make sense now. Jenna was an ambitious and conniving woman who had her eyes set on advancing her career by any means necessary. She'd done it to me when a better option came along. I had no doubt she would have jumped at the opportunity once again to seduce her way to the next level of the Hollywood food chain. Jenna was the type to step over anyone in her way, morality and loyalty be damned.

What had I ever seen in that pathetic excuse for a human being?

"This is completely Erik's fault," I assured Cagney, feeling a surge of protective instinct toward Carrie's little sister. I thought of her as so much younger than me, even though we were about the same age. "I don't care how tempted he was. He should have had the backbone to resist, to see her pathetic social climbing for what it was."

Cagney looked up at me, her face shiny from what appeared to be equal amounts of tears and snot. "I feel so stupid. All this time, I've been trying to put on the perfect wedding just to hold onto him."

"What do you mean by that?" Carrie demanded. Her tone was fierce, protective. "He was lucky you so much as glanced his way, let alone agreed to marry him. That man doesn't know what he's losing out on."

"You're only saying that because you're my sister." Cagney slumped forward, looking utterly defeated.

Carrie scoffed. "No, I'm saying it because it's the truth. You're a catch, Cags. Smart, beautiful, talented—you've got it all. And you're a Jacobs. Well, a Blythe, but you know what I mean."

"I know exactly what you mean because that's the only reason anyone pays any attention to me in Hollywood." Cagney wiped her tears with the back of her hand, but I could tell Carrie's pep talk had not hit its mark. "Hell, the only reason I got my debut role was because of you."

"Honey, that's not true," her sister said.

"It is. I know what the director said to you. That he needed you but ten years younger." There was another gut-wrenching sob. "I don't even know how I managed to play that role. I felt like I was in this fugue state this whole time. Whatever it was, I can't ever repeat it. I'm a one-and-done star. I'll never be that good again." Cagney's voice was heavy with resignation as she stared blankly at the ground.

Carrie knelt in front of her sister, her expression softening as she met her sister's eyes. "Hey, none of that self-pity talk, okay? You were incredible in that role, and you're capable of so much more. That fugue state you mentioned? That's the mark of a true actor. Mom taught me that, so you know it's true. If you could tap into it once, you can repeat it."

Cagney shook her head. "Maybe you can, sure. You've been in the business for decades. You've worked hard for everything you have. I'm just a nepo baby who's riding the coattails of my family members because I couldn't figure out anything else to do with my life."

"Nonsense," Carrie grasped Cagney's hands firmly, her eyes locking onto her sister's. "You're not a nepo baby, and you're certainly not riding anyone's coattails. And if anyone dares to say that about you, well you should know they all say the same about me."

"I don't know what to do," Cagney admitted. The weight of her insecurities seemed to press in all around us, adding to the humidity of the tropical air.

Was this what I sounded like when I went on a rant about my own doubts and fears? Poor Carrie, forced to play therapist to the both of us. And her parents, too, with their never-ending feud. I wondered how many other people in her life leaned on her for support without realizing how much she herself needed someone to lean on sometimes. She hid it well. Too well, like she hid her need for a cane when her injured knee threatened to give out.

"The first thing you need to do," Carrie said gently, "is break the news about calling off the wedding to Mom."

"I can't." Cagney buried her head in her arms again, muffling her voice. "She's been so excited about it, planning everything down to the tiniest detail. She'll be devastated."

"She'll understand," Carrie assured her, but Cagney shook her head.

"The only reason Mom is giving me all this attention the past several months is because of this wedding. I'm the first one of the three of us to finally get married. She wants it to be the wedding that people talk about for the rest of their lives.

It's why I shoved down all my fears about Erik and went full steam ahead with everything."

"What do you mean?" Carrie asked in a sweet but firm tone. It was clear she was not going to let her sister say something like that without going into detail.

Cagney's expression became pained, her fingers twisting the hem of her shirt in her trembling hands. "I'm not a fool. I know Erik can be a charmer when he wants to be, but that's all it is—an act. I convinced myself I was in love with him, that our relationship was solid. After all the times you got engaged and then balked, I guess I wanted to be the first to actually get married."

"Oh, Cags." Carrie reached out and squeezed her sister's hand. "You deserve so much more than settling for someone who isn't right for you. If there's one thing my pathetic romantic history can teach you, it's that."

"Did you have any signs this was coming?" I asked, feeling tentative to break into a conversation where I was little more than a bystander.

Cagney bit her lip, her eyes filling once more with tears. She hesitated before finally speaking. "There were little things, you know? Like how he would snap at me for the smallest things. He's been so distant, too. Like, he's been MIA so much since we got here. He even missed surf lessons with his bros, and that's so unlike him."

Fuck. I remembered how Luke Abbot had been looking for Jenna the other day. I had a feeling I knew exactly where both of them had been. The clues were there, but I hadn't put them together. Not that any of that would bring comfort to Cagney.

"I'm so sorry I haven't been there for you during all of this," Carrie said softly. "And I have to confess something. I've let jealousy cloud my actions, all because of that stupid movie role and you winning an Oscar when I haven't. I should have seen how hard it's been for you. You're my baby sister. It's my job to protect you, especially from jerks like Erik."

"I agree with your sister," I said. "He's not good enough for you. I've always got jerky vibes from him. I hope the tabloids rip him apart when they find out."

"The tab-tabloids?" Cagney stuttered. It was clear my attempt at a pep talk had had the opposite effect. "They're going to have a field day with this."

"No. It's going to be fine." Carrie assured her. "We'll think of something."

"What?" Cagney stared at Carrie with imploring eyes. "I can see the headlines now. With all your broken engagements, and now this? They'll call it the Jacobs family curse. I will never live this down."

"I'm sure it will all blow over," I said cheerily, hoping my optimism would rub off. "People's attention spans these days are shorter than a TikTok video. They'll find something else to gossip about in no time."

"Are you kidding? I could live to a hundred, and this would probably be in my obituary. These stories never go away. Even in death I won't be able to escape this scandal." A fresh wave of sobs took over.

I looked to Carrie, but instead of her backing me up and assuring Cagney she was being melodramatic, her mouth had hardened in a grim line.

"They're vultures," Carrie said through clenched teeth. "But we won't let them define us. We'll write our own story, and it will be epic. Trust me, Cagney. You're more than just a headline in a tabloid. You're part of the Jacobs dynasty, and we always rise above the drama."

"Hello, darlings!" Arriving at the pool in a one-piece suit, flowing wrap, and a massive sun hat—despite it being pitch black by now—Vivian, far from rising above it, was drama personified.

"Oh God." Cagney buried her face into her knees.

"What's going on?" Vivian looked from one daughter to the other, finally settling her gaze on me with a *someone needs to explain this right now* expression that gave me chills.

Carrie swallowed hard before saying, "The wedding's off, Mom."

"Again? Oh, Carrie, I can't understand how you keep—"

"Not mine," Carrie corrected. "Cagney's."

"What?" Vivian gasped before rushing to Cagney's side and enveloping her in a fierce, mama bear hug. "Darling, what happened?"

"He cheated," Cagney sobbed.

"Erik's been caught sleeping with... someone." Carrie's eyes briefly slid to mine, letting me know she, too, had figured out Jenna's identity but wouldn't share my connection. It was a small mercy given the range of colors in Vivian's cheeks.

"That little tramp!" Vivian seethed, her protective instincts in full force. She whipped her sun hat off as if she planned on strangling the nearest person with it. "I'm not sure if you can call a man a tramp, but I don't care. That's what he is. And he's never going to work in Hollywood again. Not even as a waiter. Why, I'm going to tell everyone I know—"

"No, Mom." Cagney looked stricken. "Please. No one can find out about this."

It was then that I glanced around, belatedly realizing this entire conversation had taken place in public and expecting to find a sizable audience. But there was no one at the pool. In fact, a red rope blocked the entrance to the area with a *Closed for Cleaning* sign dangling from it.

Vivian met my confused expression and shrugged. "They do this for me every night so I can go for a swim."

Of course, they did because she was Vivian Jacobs. I imagined everyone she encountered bent over backward for her every whim.

"Mom," Cagney repeated, "promise me. Promise me you won't tell anyone what's happened. I can't bear for this to leak to the tabloids."

"They'll call it the Jacobs curse," Carrie repeated the earlier line, as serious as a heart attack.

Vivian took a step back, the fire in her eyes dimming. She was still fuming, but I could tell her protective instincts for her daughter overshadowed her desire to expose Erik's infidelity to the world.

It hit me that none of them had it nearly as easy as people probably assumed. Their glamorous lifestyle was all a snow-job. They had a lot of money, sure, but even more scrutiny. They were prisoners of their own making. Okay, not of their own making entirely. Society played a major role. But whoever was at fault, it was a fucked-up way to live.

"We need to spin this." Vivian's expression was terrifying, and I pictured the inner workings of her mind, conjuring up all the ways she'd make Erik pay. Not simply denying him work, but possibly feeding certain body parts to hungry crocodiles.

Perhaps this vision should have terrified me, given that I was currently posing as Carrie's fake fiancée, with an inevitable calling off of the engagement in my future. Instead, I found it oddly comforting that Vivian Jacobs was trying to put her daughter first.

"How are we going to spin this?" Carrie asked. And I'll admit I was also dying to know.

Vivian Jacobs straightened up, her eyes alight with a plan

forming rapidly in her mind. "We say this is what we had planned all along. A ruse to get our friends and family to the island for a family reunion without paparazzi swarming the place."

"Not going to work," Carrie said. "It's too extreme, even for us. No one would believe that."

"How about a vow renewal? Your father and I—"

"Haven't spoken directly to one another in two years," Carrie reminded her. "Or were you planning to renew your vows via an intermediary? That would definitely be a headline-grabber."

The corners of Vivian's lips turned upward in an almost wicked grin. "I know. We claim the Cagney and Erik engagement was all a fabrication, like I said before. We were using it as a cover for the real bridal couple, to throw off the media's scent. Like it was planned exactly like this all along."

"Erik's family and friends would be livid," Carrie said, making a valid point. No way would any of them take kindly to finding out they'd traveled all this way as a ruse.

"I'll make sure Erik sees the value in explaining the situation to his guests privately so they won't make a fuss. If he knows what's good for him and his future prospects." The chilling way Vivian said this made me suddenly remember I'd once assumed she was a mafia crime boss. The role would have suited her perfectly. I had no doubt Erik and his kin would do exactly as they were told to avoid facing consequences beyond my wildest imagination.

"Who are you going to get to play the part of this unknowing, yet essential, cover couple?" I interjected, unable to contain my curiosity as I leaned forward, drawn into the theatrical plot unfolding before me.

Vivian slowly turned around to face me and then looked pointedly in Carrie's direction. "If only I could think of a different daughter who was engaged and who might have reason to hate the tabloids to the point of developing such an elaborate charade."

As her meaning belatedly became clear to me, my mouth dropped open in disbelief. Could she be suggesting what I thought she was suggesting?

Carrie's eyes widened in shock as she glanced between her mother and me, a flicker of realization dawning in her expression.

"You can't be serious, Mother," Carrie spluttered, breaking the stunned silence, but there wasn't defiance in her eyes like I thought there would be. More curiosity.

Cagney seemed to pick up on Vivian's plan, a smile creeping across her face. "I think it's brilliant! This could actually work."

Was I the only one who thought this was a cockamamie plan? Because it was. I couldn't marry Carrie. I'd only started liking her less than forty-eight hours ago.

And no way would Carrie go for it. Would she? As much as she loved to get engaged, she was the epitome of a runaway bride. She'd never let herself actually get hitched. Never.

I hated to break it to Vivian and Cagney, but they were going to have to come up with another plan.

## CHAPTER SEVENTEEN

"I can't believe you said yes." I paced the main room of our suite, rubbing my temples as I glared at Carrie and tried to keep my voice steady. "Are you out of your mind?"

"It's funny. When it comes to marriage, most people would be happy with a yes." Carrie sat on the arm of one of the chairs, giving me that damn smile of hers, the one that undid me in the most delicious ways. This was absolutely not the time for it.

"Don't do that!" I shook a finger at her, determined not to let her charm distract me from my point. "We barely know each other, and now you've told your mom we're cool with getting married in two days. Like, legally married."

Carrie tilted her head, her blond locks falling over one shoulder. "It's not about how long you know someone. It's about the connection. Don't you agree?"

"You're doing it again," I snapped, unable to tear my eyes away from her lust-filled grin.

"What?" Carrie placed a hand over her heart as if ready to

swear she was innocent, even though the twinkle in her eyes told a different story.

"Stop smiling at me like that. Like you want me." I flipped around and paced in the other direction, my breathing coming in short, rapid bursts. "It confuses me."

Carrie stepped into my path, taking both of my hands into hers. "Breathe."

"I am breathing," I growled. "Too much. I'm likely to hyperventilate and pass out."

"Slow and steady, honey," she cooed, her voice soft and soothing. The warmth of her hands sent a shiver down my spine, a sensation I tried to ignore. "I know this is unexpected and maybe a bit crazy, but everything's going to be okay."

"Everyone thinks we're really engaged. We're getting legally married in less than forty-eight hours," I tried to wiggle my hands free, but Carrie held on. "How is it possibly going to be okay?"

"Because it has to be. We need to do this to protect my little sister's reputation," Carrie said, her explanation making as little sense now as it had the first fifty times I'd heard it. "We can quietly get an annulment in six months, if that's what you want."

"Of course, that's what I want. Isn't it what you want? I mean, do you actually want to be married?" My heart ping-ponged in my rib cage, unable to decide what answer it actually wanted to hear.

"Yeah, of course not. At least, I don't think so." Carrie hesitated, her brows drawing together as she searched my face. "I mean, it's nuts. I know that. For all the reasons you've said. On the other hand, I've never actually been married—and not for lack of trying—so I don't have anything to compare it to in order to make an informed decision on what my preference would be."

"Carrie, we're about to walk down the aisle in front of your family, friends, and the entire world. This isn't some quirky rom-com plot line that will neatly wrap up in two hours," I blurted out, the weight of the situation crashing down on me like a ton of bricks. "There's no script writer to get us out of this jam."

"It's kinda perfect, though. Isn't it?" Carrie flashed a mischievous grin that made my heart skip a beat despite the impending doom.

Damn it, why did she have to be so infuriatingly charming and sexy all the time? It made this a hundred times harder.

"How can you possibly think anything about this is perfect? Nothing about this is even slightly okay. It's a disaster waiting to happen," I snapped, my patience wearing thin as the reality of the situation sunk in even deeper. "We are about to commit fraud in front of hundreds of people just to save face for your sister, all because of the damn tabloids and something about a Jacobs family curse. How is that remotely perfect?"

"Because, for once, I'm in control of the narrative. For years, my life has been this chaotic, over-analyzed mess. People dissect every word I say, every relationship I have, as if they're entitled to be a part of it. Like they own me. But they'll never guess the first time I actually make it down the aisle it's with someone I paid to be my fiancée. They don't get to have that."

I understood what she was saying, at least as much as anyone could who had never lived it. But my expression fell as the reality of our relationship hit me in stark contrast to whatever fantasy was playing out in my mind. I was being paid to be here. This wasn't right. It felt deceptive and wrong in ways I couldn't fully articulate.

But the biggest problem was that deep down, some small part of me—the part that had watched the sunset at Sweetheart Rock with Carrie a few hours ago and imagined a future together that extended beyond this trip, one that was independent of a paycheck—wanted it to be real. But how could it be if we were starting off on such dishonest terms?

"I know this is so far above and beyond what you signed up for," Carrie said quietly, a hint of pleading underlying her tone, "but I have to admit I'm not completely unhappy with the way things are working out. I can't think of another person I'd want to marry in two days' time, aside from you, Margo. But I don't want you to feel like you're stuck with me."

I swallowed hard, trying to rein in the tumult of emotions swirling inside me. Carrie's words hit me like a freight train, catching me off guard with their sincerity.

"It's not that. I would be lucky to be stuck with—no, that doesn't sound right. But you know what I mean. It's happening at warp speed." I sucked in a breath, this time holding it and counting to five before letting it out so I wouldn't get lightheaded. Arguing about it wasn't going to get us anywhere, and as my blood pressure lowered a bit, I knew what I had to do. "Okay, let's talk details. What kind of prenup will I have to sign? I don't have a lawyer I can call, so I'm going to have to take it on faith."

"None." Carrie shook her head. "No prenup."

I shot her an incredulous look. "I'm being serious."

"So am I. I don't believe in prenups. I always felt like that was a sign of mistrust, planning for things to end before they even begin."

"We're literally planning for this to end." I gaped at her. "Without an agreement, I could screw you over."

"I don't think you would do that."

"You have no way of knowing that," I argued. Not that I planned to, but it was a valid point that needed to be driven home. What if she had some other fake fiancée who wasn't as scrupulous as I was? She needed to learn caution. "I could take you for everything you're worth and leave you high and dry."

Carrie sighed, reaching out to gently cup my cheek with her hand. "You are not one of those people. You're nothing like anyone I've known." She kissed my forehead, and I melted a little, leaning into her warmth. "I don't trust people easily, but I trust you." She kissed my right cheek, brushing her soft lips against my skin. I felt a flutter in my chest, a mix of disbelief and something dangerously close to hope. "You are one of a kind."

Her lips brushed my left cheek, and I let out a gentle sigh.

"Are you always this reckless, or am I a special case?" I asked.

As if to answer my question, she tilted my head up and captured my lips in a tender yet passionate kiss. The world around us seemed to fade away as I dissolved into the moment, savoring the taste of her in my mouth.

"Does that answer your question?" she asked once we had parted.

"Not without raising at least a thousand more," I admitted. My heart raced, and I longed to feel her lips on mine again, but it would be beyond reckless to give in under the circumstances. Wouldn't it?

"What kind of questions?" she asked, her eyes sparkling with amusement. I couldn't help but admire how effortlessly she shifted the mood, turning a serious conversation into an exchange of playful banter. It was one of the many things that intrigued me about her.

I took a moment to compose myself, clearing my throat

before replying, "Questions like, how can I possibly be considering going along with this charade when any fool knows it's a terrible idea? Questions like, why does your touch make me forget all the reasons I should say no? Or what could possibly go wrong if I let myself enjoy this moment with you?" The words spilled out before I could stop them, and I mentally cursed myself for being so candid.

Carrie's gaze softened as she studied my face, her thumb gently brushing my cheekbone. "Because maybe deep down, you don't really want to say no," she whispered, her voice barely above a breath.

The vulnerability in her eyes mirrored the tumult of emotions swirling inside me. She was right, of course. Each moment spent with Carrie felt like a glimpse into a world I never knew existed, a world filled with possibilities and risks that simultaneously thrilled and terrified me. But was I ready to take that leap of faith with her, to trust in the unknown and embrace the chaos that seemed to follow wherever she went?

"Maybe you're right," I whispered, unable to tear my gaze away from hers.

The air between us crackled with unspoken promises, and I found myself leaning closer to her, drawn by an invisible force that seemed to pull us together. In that fleeting moment, all doubts and reservations vanished, leaving only the raw desire that flickered in Carrie's eyes.

Her hand slid down to intertwine her fingers with mine, a silent gesture that spoke volumes. Her touch was warm and reassuring, grounding me in a way I hadn't thought possible.

Before I could contemplate the consequences of my actions, our mouths crashed together. Honestly, it was the best thing that could've happened. The only way to still my mind was to block out all thoughts, and Carrie had a way of doing that to me. It might not have been the most mature way to handle stress, but she was Caroline Fucking Jacobs, after all.

And she was all mine.

"I need you," I said when I broke for air, and then I went back for another kiss.

"You have me." Carrie lifted her shirt over her head.

The feel of Carrie's skin against mine was electric, sending shivers down my spine and igniting a fire within me. Our bodies moved together in perfect synchronization, each touch and kiss fueling our passion even further.

My mouth still devouring hers, I reached around her to undo her bra, desperate to feel all of her against me. Carrie's breathing hitched as I slowly slid the straps off her shoulders and tossed the garment aside. She arched her back, pressing herself closer to me as I trailed kisses along her collarbone and down to where her bra had been.

Meanwhile, she worked on her shorts, pushing them down until they fell to the floor with a soft thud. By the time we made it to the bed, both of us were naked, leaving a trail of clothes in our wake.

On the bed, I was on top of Carrie. The thought still blew my mind—that I got to make love to this incredible woman who happened to be famous. But in that moment, she was just my Carrie. Absolutely gorgeous and irrefutably mine.

My hand roamed down her side, her skin soft and inviting. My mouth made its way to her nipple. When I took the nub into my mouth, it quickly hardened. Making me let out a gasp.

"You're so beautiful, Carrie," I whispered, my hip rubbing into her center.

"We're beautiful together." She cupped my face with both of her palms. "We're amazing."

I believed her. Was I fucking crazy? Right now, I didn't give a fuck. How could I when I felt this incredible?

Our bodies moved together with an intense rhythm as if we had been doing this for years. But really, it was only our second time being intimate like this. Yet it felt so natural and right.

Carrie's hands roamed over my back and shoulders while mine explored every inch of her body, committing every curve and dip to memory. Each touch between us seemed to ignite a deeper level of desire until it was almost too much for me to handle.

And through it all, a single word echoed in my head: forever.

Was I crazy to believe in that word? Maybe. But in this moment, as we were entwined in each other's arms, I couldn't help but feel that anything was possible. It was just us, two people from very different worlds, finding solace and passion in one another's arms.

As if sensing my thoughts were wandering, she pulled my head to hers. Our lips met in a blur of desire, quickly escalating from longing to intense heat.

We kissed as if sealing our bond for an eternity.

Our bodies rocked together, her wetness increasing with each thrust of our hips. The room was filled with the sounds of our passion—the kisses that turned into moans of pleasure, the sweat that dripped from our brows, and the sheets that rustled beneath us.

"I can't believe I'm here with you," I whispered into her ear before sinking my teeth into her lobe.

"I feel the same, although I'm still shocked how the

Wardrobe Warden left a trail of clothes on the way to bed." Carrie ran her hand through my hair. "All the actors were terrified of your strict rules when we were working together. And to think, you were just one of us slobs all along."

"Are you going to bust me on the next set?" I joked.

"Your secret is safe with me." She slid her hand between my thighs, and I shuddered at the pleasure her touch sent coursing through me.

"Is my heart?"

"One hundred percent."

"You promise?"

"We pinky swore. I don't do that with just anyone." She kissed me. Hard. Passionate.

My hand slipped between her legs, her need for me palpable, but in case the wetness wasn't a big enough clue, Carrie groaned in a way that made my heart skip a beat. This wasn't merely physical desire; it was deeper, something that reached the very core of both of us.

"Fuck me," she begged. "Now."

She didn't need to tell me twice.

My lips made their way down from Carrie's earlobe, along her collarbone, my tongue dipping into the hollow of her neck as I feasted on the delicate skin, teasing the spot that made her shiver.

Carrie's breath hitched as I trailed kisses down her chest. My fingers tangled in the silky strands of her hair, guiding her head back so she could look into my eyes. "You know there's no going back from this, right?"

Carrie's eyes locked with mine, her own gaze filled with equal parts lust and vulnerability. "I wouldn't have it any other way."

I took her nipple in my mouth, sucking gently, and then

ran my tongue around the hard peak, my teeth nibbling enough to make her moan. She arched her back, her hips bucking wildly beneath me.

"I want this so much," I whispered, my voice barely above a breath. "Not just this, but everything."

I wasn't sure if she could hear me, and I was too afraid to repeat myself, scared I would tempt fate if I said it too loudly. But in that moment, I understood that the words didn't matter. It was the feeling that mattered, the connection that radiated between us.

I wanted to explore every inch of her creamy skin. The tiny freckle right above her belly button. The birthmark on her thigh. The scar on her knee. Every part of her, even her imperfections, lured me in and made me want her more.

This was the difference between Carrie and Jenna. With the latter, I always thought I was on borrowed time. I was afraid to be anything but the best version of myself I could be. And even that was never enough.

But with Carrie, I wanted her to know I was as flawed and imperfect as she was. We were both human beings, vulnerable and damaged, but somehow stronger because of it.

With Carrie, time spread out before us as an invitation. No rush. No expiration date.

Well, there was one immediate situation that needed to be dealt with. Carrie needed a release, and I was more than happy to oblige.

Pressing my head between her thighs, I dove in, savoring the taste of her. My tongue landed on her clit, slowly circling it, causing Carrie to arch her back. I never knew I would have this power over her, but now that I did, I didn't want to lose it. Ever.

I eased a finger inside her, feeling her muscles tightening around me as if welcoming me, holding me tightly. It was an unbelievable feeling, one that I knew I couldn't get enough of if I lived a thousand years.

Carrie let out a moan as I moved deeper, her voice filled with an intensity that sent chills down my spine. I wanted to keep going, to explore every inch of her, but instead I kept my tongue concentrated right where Carrie needed me most.

She reached for my free hand, threading our fingers.

Since that first night, she had been finding ways to touch me, I realized. Yes, part of it was she literally needed my support for her bad knee, but I now understood that wasn't the only reason. She loved being near me.

I felt the same. Right now, I couldn't get enough of her musky scent, her pungent taste, and how wet I made her.

I added another finger inside her and began to pump them slowly, while continuing to suck and lick her clit.

Carrie's moans grew louder, and her fingers tightened around mine.

She was getting closer and closer.

"Go-Go," Carrie gasped, her voice shaking. "I can't... I'm going to..."

I smiled against her sensitive flesh, knowing exactly what was coming. Carrie's body was so responsive, so in tune with mine. It was an intoxicating feeling, this power she allowed me to have over her.

My tongue circled her clit.

Our interlocked fingers tightened.

Carrie's ragged breaths increased in intensity until finally, she cried out, her body trembling violently as the first waves of pleasure crashed over her.

Her hips bucked, arching into my face as her body writhed under my touch. Her scent filled my nostrils, and I could feel the waves of her orgasm pouring through her.

I reveled in it.

"Oh!" Carrie's legs started to shake, and she writhed under me. "Right there... don't stop."

Nothing in the world could get me to stop.

My tongue never broke contact, continuing to tease and pleasure her. I wanted nothing more than to rock her world.

At last, she went over the edge, taking me with her.

# CHAPTER EIGHTEEN

"Hold still." An intimidating woman with a mouthful of straight pins clenched in her teeth snapped at me while pinching one shoulder strap of white lace fabric and scowling.

"Sorry," I said, willing my limbs to freeze in place. "I'm not used to being on this side of things."

I stood on a box of printer paper in the middle of the hotel suite, unable to blame the designer for being tense. Given my line of work, I knew exactly what it had taken for her to show up in Hawaii with two custom wedding dresses in hand a mere twelve hours after Vivian had placed a frantic middle-of-the-night phone call.

Seeing myself in a wedding dress was a shock, but what I was really trying to wrap my head around was that a well-known designer had flown on a private jet to deliver these dresses personally because Vivian Jacobs had asked her to. What would it be like to hold that kind of power?

If I were in Vivian's position, I wasn't sure I would be able to control myself. I might start barking orders simply to see what would happen. I'd like to think I'd wield my power for good, and not for something silly like scoring extra fudge sauce on a sundae. But realistically, I had my doubts.

When the designer stepped away, I turned to inspect my reflection in the full-length mirror. I was blown away. The gown hugged each and every one of my curves like it had been made for me. Delicate lace cascaded down to form an intricate train. It was a dress fit for a princess, or in this case, for someone marrying into Hollywood royalty.

The designer stroked her chin, admiring her work. "Sublime."

I had a feeling she was talking about her dress and not me, but I still basked in the compliment. "Thank you," I said, mustering a smile. "It's beautiful."

She gave me one last critical look before nodding in approval. "You'll do. Just don't spill anything on it before the ceremony."

With that parting shot, she left me alone in the suite. But I was only there a moment before Asher came in, a long white veil draped over one arm. He stopped in his tracks when he caught sight of me.

"You look beautiful, Margo." Asher spoke with a level of reverence in his tone I wouldn't have thought him capable of.

"I expected it to be held together with a thousand pins, but your aunt's designer worked a miracle."

"My aunt can be a force to reckon with, as I'm sure you now fully understand." He handed me the veil, and I lifted it to my head, hands shaking as I felt the weight of it settle gently on my hair.

I stared at my image in the mirror, almost unable to recognize myself. Never would I have imagined that a wedding dress and veil could make me feel this way, like a stranger in my own skin. Was I really about to go through with marrying a woman I barely knew?

Yet, somehow, it didn't seem like that was what was happening. Part of me felt I'd known Carrie forever. And standing there in that wedding dress didn't strike me as nearly as absurd as it should have.

"Do you think I've lost my mind?" I asked, genuinely curious how he would answer.

"Oh, absolutely. I still stand by my belief that you and my cousin are a good match, but..." It was as if he lacked the words to complete his thought, or possibly he reckoned whatever he was thinking was better left unsaid.

"But maybe we should've tried dating first?" I supplied. "I'll admit I never imagined our first date would be our wedding day."

"You did go zip lining with the family," Asher pointed out as if being strapped into a harness and flying over a Hawaiian volcano was akin to a casual cup of coffee at a corner café.

"Second date, then." I went to run a hand through my hair but didn't want to wreck it. Not after having Vivian's hair and makeup person work on me for hours on end. "Oh, God, Asher. I'm afraid to move in this getup."

Asher chuckled, a genuine warmth in his eyes. "If you need a hand to hold while you walk down the aisle, I'm your guy."

"Would you?" Tears pricked at the corners of my eyes, surprising me with their sudden appearance. I blinked carefully, desperate to keep my expertly applied makeup intact. "My dad isn't here, of course, but I always thought he would walk me down the aisle. I didn't think it would hit me like this. I mean I know it isn't a real wedding, but it feels real, doesn't it? The dress, and the hair, and..." I swept my hand down my side to indicate the whole ensemble. "It all feels so... permanent."

"Are you okay with this? Really, truly?" He'd finally asked the question I'd been mulling over in my head but was afraid to answer.

Taking a breath, I thought it over before replying. "I'm more okay with it than I would have thought I'd be if you had floated this idea a couple weeks ago."

A lot more, in fact, though I wasn't certain if I should tell Asher that. Part of me was downright excited by the prospect of being married to Carrie, for however long it lasted.

"I'm not sure that means much," he pointed out. "A couple weeks ago, you thought Carrie was the spawn of Satan who'd gotten you fired."

"I may have exaggerated slightly," I admitted sheepishly. "She's more like a minor demon at best."

Asher chuckled, shaking his head in amusement. "From minor demon to future spouse, it's still quite the turnaround."

"Life is funny like that," I said with a smile. "You know what they say. One moment you're wishing curses upon someone's lineage, and the next you're walking down the aisle."

"Pretty sure no one says that." He gave me a *get real* stare.

"At least I can say without hesitation that Carrie is nothing like I believed before I got to know her."

"Don't judge a book by its cover might be the phrase you were searching for that time. You know, something people actually do say."

"Never heard of it." I gave him a playful eye-roll. "Not to gross you out talking about your cousin like this, but her cover's not half bad, if you know what I mean."

Asher raised an eyebrow. "Careful there. It almost sounds like you're about to confess your undying love for the bride-to-be."

"She's a book I thought I'd never want to read, but now that I've flipped through the pages, I can't seem to put it down," I confessed with a chuckle.

"So we're clear, when you say flipped through the pages, is that a euphemism for—"

"Asher," I scolded, playfully smacking his arm. "I'm confessing my evolving feelings here, not giving you a play-by-play of the past week's bedroom activities."

"Fine. Fine." He raised his hands in surrender. "We'll keep it PG-rated. But seriously, are you sure you haven't been pressured into going through with this?"

Asher's tone was more serious now. I almost thought I detected a hint of guilt, as well. Maybe that made sense. If it hadn't been for him suggesting the fake engagement to begin with, I wouldn't be standing here now, in a designer wedding gown, ready to get hitched.

"I'm a grown woman," I assured him, not wanting him to carry the weight of my decision on his shoulders. "Carrie made it clear if I wasn't comfortable with the idea, we didn't have to do it."

Although, there was the Vivian factor. That woman scared the fuck out of me.

But that wasn't why I'd agreed to go through with it. There was something about Carrie that put me at ease and drew me in. No matter what, I felt in my heart she'd make things right between us when the day was done. Look what she was doing for her sister. What she'd been doing for her loved ones all along. She would take care of me, too.

At least, I hoped so.

I wished Carrie were here right now instead of getting ready in Vivian's suite. I never would have pegged her mother as the superstitious kind, but Vivian had insisted on following every wedding superstition in the book. The 'something old, something new, something borrowed, something blue' was stretched to its limits with heirlooms from their family vault that made me nervous just touching them.

I was pretty sure it was impossible to jinx a fake wedding by catching a glimpse of the pretend bride, but I couldn't exactly say that to Vivian, so I'd been forced to play along.

Only this isn't fake, I reminded myself, my stomach doing a flip. It was very real, at least on paper. We'd applied for a marriage license the day before, and Vivian—who was certain she was the only one with enough dramatic skill to convince the guests that our wedding had been planned all along—had received her officiant's permit. This was going to be one hundred percent legally binding.

Caroline Fucking Jacobs was going to be my lawfully wedded wife.

After Asher excused himself to go check on Carrie, I waited nervously in the suite, willing myself not to fidget with the expensive lace of my gown. Every second felt like an eternity as I waited for these final moments before the ceremony to pass.

I glanced nervously at my reflection in the mirror, adjusting the veil that cascaded down my back. My heart raced in anticipation, unsure of what the future held. Would this faux engagement turn into something real? Was I making a mistake by putting my trust in Carrie?

A knock on the door interrupted my thoughts. Asher's voice echoed into the room. "Margo, it's time."

Taking a deep breath to steady myself, I met him at the door.

"You ready?" Asher held out a hand.

I stared at his hand, trying to figure out the meaning of his words. Ready to put one foot in front of the other and walk out the door? Yes. I could manage that. But my brain spluttered when contemplating the next steps while my heart was spinning like a figure skater.

"I... I hope so." I'd never heard my voice shake so much.

Once we were outside, Asher led me down the walkway to the resort's private beach. The sun was starting to dip below the horizon, casting a warm glow over the sand. Tiki torches burned brightly, illuminating the makeshift aisle leading to a beautifully decorated arch adorned with tropical flowers. I had to hand it to Cagney. She'd planned a picture-perfect wedding.

As we approached the crowd, I couldn't help but steal glances at the guests, all seated and waiting for the ceremony to start. The crowd wasn't as large as originally planned, given that all of Erik's side of the aisle had had the good sense to make themselves scarce after Vivian had forced him to confess his misdeeds in private. They'd each had to sign a nondisclosure agreement first, of course.

Still, there were plenty of people attending—Hollywood producers, actors, and other elites—and I didn't really know a single person aside from Asher. None of them were here for me. I wondered what they would think when they found out about the switcheroo being pulled on them. At least I could rest assured that a well-heeled group of people like this one wouldn't cause a scene. They probably wouldn't care. They were here to network and hobnob, nothing more.

As soon as my eyes spied Carrie waiting for me at the back of the assembly, hidden by some carefully placed potted palms, my heart stopped. In a simple white sheath dress, she was the epitome of elegance and poise as the last rays of sunlight caught in her blond hair like a halo. Despite all the doubts swirling in my mind, seeing her there, waiting for me, made something inside me melt.

I was certain that she had never looked more beautiful

than she did at that moment, whether in person or on screen. And when her eyes spied me, the widest grin spread across her face. She seemed honestly thrilled to see me. As I walked closer to her, feeling the soft sand under my feet, it was like being in a dream.

She held out her hands to me, and I swallowed as I took them, not believing I was marrying this goddess.

The tension that had been coiled in my chest slowly unraveled as our fingers intertwined. I could feel the softness of her skin against mine, the warmth of her touch like a soothing balm to my unsettled nerves.

"You made it," she whispered, her voice barely audible over the distant lull of the ocean waves. "I was scared you wouldn't show."

"Fortunately for you, I'm not one to back down from a challenge. Plus, I didn't want to miss the chance to finally see you in a wedding dress," I teased and was rewarded by a heartfelt laugh.

"If all of my exes knew what was really happening, they'd be taking bets on whether or not I would show," she joked back.

The music started playing, signaling the beginning of the ceremony. We turned our gazes toward the arch, where Vivian stood in her impeccable suit, looking every bit the part of an officiant. That woman really could play any role.

Carrie's father stood at the edge of the aisle, waiting to take her arm. Before going to him, Carrie leaned close to me, whispering in my ear. "I haven't said this yet, but I need you to know, I love you."

My heart swelled at her words, and I could feel the sincerity in her voice. Carrie in love with me? It was a moment I had never allowed myself to imagine, and I was frozen in place for lack of a proper response.

But it was too late for me to say anything anyway. She was already gliding down the aisle, and I was left standing there, trying to process the weight of her words. Love. She said she loved me. A rush of emotions flooded through me as I became fully aware of the most improbable reality: I loved her, too.

I was nearly blinded by unshed tears as I took Asher's arm, and we began the wedding march.

The people in the crowd murmured, likely surprised by the sight of two brides, along with the dawning realization that neither of us was the one they had expected.

My steps were slow and deliberate, timed to the music, so I wouldn't freak out. A glimpse of a reddish flower on a hat caught my attention, and my heart started beating erratically. Ever since the incident on set with the mysterious person in red, the color had sparked unease within me, like a bad omen. A wave of anxiety washed over me, and I nearly stumbled, causing Asher to tighten his grip on my arm to get me the rest of the way to the altar.

"Our beloved guests," Vivian began, her commanding presence causing a sudden hush to fall over the crowd. "You might notice this isn't my daughter Cagney getting married today. Please excuse our little subterfuge, but after Carrie's previous missteps in the matrimony department, she didn't want to risk anything ruining her special day."

A murmur echoed among the guests, and a pang of sympathy shot through me. Carrie must be feeling like a spectacle, with all eyes on her right now as her mother made public mention of her many failed engagements.

"Yes, it's true," Vivian continued. "Cagney and Erik's engagement was simply a ruse to get you all here. The plan had always been for my darling Carrie and her beloved fiancée, Margo, to get married tonight."

"Hold on a minute." A woman in the crowd stood up, too far back in the sea of chairs for me to see her face clearly. "When the fuck did you come up with this plan, Carrie?"

My blood ran cold as I spied the red flower on the woman's hat, even as I belatedly recognized the speaker's voice. It was Alex Franklin, Carrie's most recent ex-fiancée.

"Excuse me," Vivian began, but Alex wasn't about to be silenced.

"Oh, hell no. I got the invitation to this wedding months ago. Back when you were engaged to me."

The crowd erupted into whispers and gasps at this revelation. Vivian's usually composed expression flickered with a mix of surprise and dismay, but she quickly regained her composure.

"I'm sorry, young lady, but you really need—"

Alex butted in again. "This is rich. You accused me of being a hussy, and you were with... her?" It was the most devastating pronunciation of the word *her* I'd ever heard in my life. Like I was completely unworthy to be standing where I was.

"Please sit down," Vivian commanded, but Alex didn't comply.

"Were you cheating on me the whole time?" Alex demanded, becoming more and more irate. "Did you use me for this?"

The man beside Alex, whom I assumed was Richard Thompson but I couldn't see him clearly through the tears in my eyes, pulled on her arm to get her to stop making a scene. But you know the phrase: 'Hell hath no fury like a woman scorned'. Nothing would stop Alex from having her say.

"Either this is all a crock of shit," Alex raged, "or you're the worst person to ever walk this earth."

Carrie raised her hands in a placating gesture, her voice

barely loud enough over the rising tension. "Alex, please, this isn't the time—"

"No, I think it's the perfect time," Alex interjected, her tone laced with hurt and anger. "This whole thing is an elaborate fraud. The Caroline Jacobs I know is too in love with grand romantic gestures to agree to some sneaky scheme like this. I want answers!"

It was clear from the sounds of the guests that they did, too.

Vivian did her best to cow everyone into submission, but it wasn't working. It seemed her power to control the universe did, indeed, have limits. At the worst possible moment. Chaos was descending. Rapidly.

"Everyone, sit the fuck down!" Vivian screamed.

It was the proverbial straw that broke the camel's back. All hell broke loose from every direction at once. To be frank, I'd seen better behaved crowds at Monster Truck rallies.

Vivian crouched beneath the floral arch, curling into a fetal position before my eyes.

A moment later, Asher was back at my side, his tone urgent. "We need to get you out of here."

Cagney motioned for her father, saying to him as he stood, "Dad, you have to help Mom. Get over this ridiculous grudge, and be there for her."

He started to protest but, after a deep breath, did as he was told.

Carrie took my hands in hers. "Go with Asher."

"What about you?" I asked, my bottom lip quivering.

"I need to fix this."

"I don't want to leave you alone."

"Which is why I love you," Carrie said. "But trust me. It'll be better if you aren't here. Don't worry. I'll come for you. I'll find you, Margo. Please trust me."

With that, Asher whisked me away.

It was like the Daniel Day Lewis scene in *The Last of the Mohican's*, but instead of the threat of being shot by a militia, Carrie was going to be torn to shreds by the tabloids.

Before I could fully comprehend what was happening, I was on a private jet, taxiing down the island's small runway, fleeing paradise.

And I had the gut feeling I was flying straight to hell.

## CHAPTER NINETEEN

Rain poured from the sky as I stood outside the West Hollywood bar. They say it never rains in California, but they—whoever they are—have no fucking clue what they're talking about. Not only was it raining, but my umbrella had decided to turn inside out during a sudden gust of wind, leaving me completely drenched. I cursed under my breath as I tried to wrestle the umbrella back into its proper shape, the rain plastering my hair to my face.

Somehow, I was certain this was all one big metaphor for my fucked-up life.

The bar was the same one Asher and I had met in when he had come up with his cockamamie fake relationship scheme. Part of me wanted to turn around and ride off into the soggy sunset on my own terms, leave this whole sorry chapter of my life in the past.

The other part was desperate for information. It had been two weeks since the wedding fiasco in Hawaii, and in all that time, Carrie had been radio silent. Not a single peep.

Play it cool, Margo, I told myself as I reached to open the

door. Do not waltz in there and beg Asher for intel about Carrie.

Inside, Asher sat at a high-top table in the corner near the bar, giving us a semblance of privacy.

"Hey, stranger." He got to his feet and pulled me into a hug. It wasn't an unusual gesture—we were friends, after all—but this time the close human contact was enough to break down all my defenses and leave me shaking like a wet puppy.

"Fuck," I sobbed into his shoulder.

"What's wrong?" He held me tighter. "Jesus, you're soaking wet."

"My umbrella betrayed me," I cried, though I was smart enough to know my tears had nothing to do with the broken object in my hand and everything to do with a different broken object residing in my chest. "It's over, isn't it?"

So much for playing it cool.

"What is?" Releasing me from his embrace, Asher's face was the picture of confusion. "The rain? I'm afraid it's forecast to continue for the rest of the day."

I shoved his shoulder. "Don't be cruel."

"Not something people usually accuse me of." He retook his seat, waving for me to join him.

I dragged my palm across my damp face and pretended that only the rain was to blame for its sorry state. I reached for the martini he had waiting for me without bothering to sit down first. "Who sent you?"

He tilted his head in confusion, but then his eyes softened as understanding set in. "You still haven't heard from her?"

"Not a word in two weeks." I collapsed onto the barstool, my feet dangling. The stupid chair didn't even have a bar to rest them on. It made me feel childish and hopeless. "I'm starting to wonder if I'm frigging losing my grip on reality. We did go to Hawaii together, right?"

"We did," he confirmed.

"And I almost got married to your cousin, who's a famous actor, right?" Some wild part of me almost hoped he would tell me this was a total fabrication. Maybe I'd been bitten by a rare tropical mosquito and was suffering from delusions caused by brain swelling.

"Also true."

Damn it. No matter how many times I wished for an escape hatch, the reality remained the same. My life was straight out of a bad soap opera.

"And now I'm back here, crying my heart out over a woman who can't even be bothered to give me the courtesy of a breakup text. Unless—" I paused to take a sip of my drink. "Did she join a cult at the airport and forgot to send me an invite?"

Asher chuckled, and I half expected him to play along with my ridiculous theory if only to make me feel better. "Not to my knowledge," he replied, dashing that hope and possibly my last shred of dignity.

"She said she'd come for me," I choked out as tears threatened to fall. She'd said she loved me, too, but I found myself unable to tell Asher that part. It sounded too pathetic coming from my own lips. Instead, I gripped the martini glass tighter as I attempted to muster some semblance of dignity. "But here I am, abandoned like a soggy napkin at a fancy dinner party."

"Have you texted her?"

"Twice and not a peep. I don't want to text again. That'll make me look desperate."

His laughter was gentle, but I could tell I hadn't fooled him. Everything about me reeked of desperation, but that didn't stop me from trying to save face.

"I've got a smidgen of pride left," I insisted, despite all

evidence to the contrary.

"Of course, you do," he said soothingly, reaching across the table to squeeze my hand. "But sometimes a little desperation can be a good thing. It shows you care."

I gave him a weak smile, knowing he was trying to lift my spirits but feeling like I was beyond repair at this point. "Have you heard anything about what happened after I left the island? I've been checking the tabloids in the grocery store every day, but there hasn't been a peep about Cagney's wedding." I stifled a sob before adding, "Or mine."

"The power of Aunt Viv." He wiggled voodoo magic fingers in the air.

My eyes narrowed at the mention of my almost-mother-in-law's name. "No offense, but does she have that much power? She was losing it at the wedding."

"Vivian Jacobs could probably make the sun rise from the west if she put her mind to it." Asher leaned back in his chair, swirling the remnants of his drink.

I gave a snort. "What a useful super power. Tell me the truth. Did she send you to talk to me? Are you here to let me down easy?"

Asher shook his head. "I'm here to have drinks with you. That's my only mission. I haven't heard from Carrie or Aunt Viv since we left Hawaii."

I studied his eyes, looking for a trace of deceit but not finding any.

As if sensing the truth behind my glare, he said, "There's a reason I went into theater management. I don't have an ounce of acting skills."

"Not even by osmosis?"

"Pretty sure that's not a thing." He patted my hand.

My phone, which I'd placed on the table so I wouldn't miss a message, buzzed. Instantly, I jumped and grabbed it.

"Is it her?" Asher seemed as anxious as me.

I read the perplexing message twice before speaking. "This can't be right."

"What is it?"

I stared at the automated message from my bank, alerting me to an unusually large deposit in my checking account. Unable to form words, I handed Asher my phone so he could read the message himself.

He let out a low whistle. "Holy shit, that's a lot of Benjamins."

"Who deposited that money into my account? I don't recognize the name. Is it a scam?"

"It's not a scam. That's Vivian's production company."

"Vivian paid me off." My heart plummeted to my stomach as I realized what this meant. "She's trying to buy my silence, isn't she?"

Asher raised an eyebrow and handed back my phone. "Or she's trying to make amends."

"You can't just throw money around like it's a fruit basket," I scoffed, bitterness creeping into my tone. "I guess that's the message I've been waiting for. It's over, and Carrie didn't have the heart to tell me herself. I didn't mean anything to her, and once I was out of sight, she forgot all about me. She does that. Carrie told me herself."

"I'm sure that's not true." But Asher avoided my eyes when he said it, and I had to admit, he hadn't been lying earlier about the acting gene skipping over him.

I swallowed half of my martini in one gulp. "Carrie's not going to talk to me or even send a Dear Jane text. She's leaving it to her mommy to kick me to the curb."

"Look at the bright side." Asher painted on a buck-up smile. "You have more than enough money to stay in LA now."

"Why should I? The director's strike is still ongoing with no end in sight. I don't have a job. All I do is sit around, waiting for a message from Carrie. Which has been received, loud and clear. I have nothing keeping me here."

"What about me?"

My expression softened as I took in his heartbroken demeanor. "You know what I mean."

He looked down, fiddling with the coaster beneath his drink. "I hate seeing you like this. And I hate that you're giving up on your Hollywood dreams because of something my cousin did."

"I hate Hollywood," I reminded him.

"Okay, but you're a costumer. This is where the jobs are. Where else would you go?"

"Such a typical Californian. We have theaters in the Midwest, too, Asher." I was about to launch into a lecture about his west-coast-centric myopia when a flicker on the TV screen above Asher's head grabbed my attention. I pointed, my mouth gaping.

Asher turned around, slow motion style, right when the tabloid TV show started to display grainy footage of Carrie and Sandra holding hands, ducking into a party. The chyron read: *Are the lovebirds of the century back together for good this time?*

"She really is a heartless bitch." I flagged down the server, requesting the drinks to keep coming. "At least I can afford to pay for another few rounds. I just can't believe I fell for it."

"Fell for what?"

"Carrie's act. I know better. I never should have trusted an actor. I'm telling you right now, I will never trust her, or any woman, ever again. This—" I tapped my shirt in the spot over where my heart was—"is closed for good."

"You can't mean that," Asher said, his brow furrowed.

I shook my head, a bitter smile playing on my lips. "But I do. Fool me once, shame on you. Fool me twice—well, I shouldn't have let it happen. Not after Jenna."

"You know you're really bad at quoting common sayings." After his attempt at a joke fell flat, Asher's expression grew serious once more. "You can't let one bad experience close you off from the possibility of finding happiness again."

"Maybe I am." I shrugged. "I don't care. It's time to go home and concentrate on my career. Kiss LA and Caroline Fucking Jacobs goodbye. The universe is telling me to run, and that's exactly what I'm going to do."

---

"Are you sure you want to do this?" Asher placed a box into the back of the U-Haul. "You've made a career for yourself here."

"All I've done is fuck up my life," I corrected. "I never should have moved here. It was always Jenna's dream to move to California. Not mine."

"You're here now, though. The directors' strike can't last forever." He followed me back inside my place to load up the dolly again.

"I got fired from my last job, remember?" I wished I could blame Carrie for that. I really did. Unfortunately, even if she'd lied about loving me, I was pretty sure she'd told the truth about that.

"I'm sure Carrie—"

"No." I held up my hand to stop his words. "I've always loved live theater more than movies, anyway."

"Dinner theater, darling." Asher's nose wrinkled. "There's a difference."

"You're right. Do you know what it's like working for the dinner theater? It's heaven. They treat me well. Everyone knows my name. Half of the staff is going to help me unload the truck when I get there. The other half is helping Sally, whose granddaughter just had twins." I licked my lips, placing a box onto the dolly. "I need to be around people who care about me."

"I care about you." He casually slid his phone out of his pocket to check it.

"Uh-huh." I stared pointedly at the device in his hands.

He shoved the phone back into his pocket. "I'm easily distracted. It doesn't mean I don't care. It's just… if you leave because of Carrie, aren't you letting another woman dictate your life? You've always resented Jenna for dragging you out here. Now you're letting Carrie chase you away."

He wore a cocky grin as if he'd come up with an argument I couldn't rebut. And he sort of had. I just didn't want to listen to him. I was done with people of any gender dictating how I should live my life. The thought of being dependent on anyone else for my happiness grated on my nerves.

"Shut up and carry this box to the truck," I told him. "I don't need your input."

"It's only been three weeks, Margo. Don't you think you should stop a minute and think everything through? It's not wise to make a major life decision when you're angry."

"I'm not angry." I practically shouted it, which probably didn't bolster my case. "Maybe I'm a little angry. I'm also hurt and sad."

"I get that. I do." He placed a hand on my shoulder, but then his face went completely white. "Right. I'm out of here."

"You're not going to help me with the rest?" I couldn't believe he was leaving me when I needed him the most.

He stared pointedly behind me, forcing me to turn around.

Caroline Fucking Jacobs was standing in my doorway.

I blinked, assuming it was a mirage.

She was still there.

"What are you doing here?" My throat closed around the words. The last person on Earth I expected to see in my cheap apartment was standing right in front of me, looking as out of place as a swan in a duck pond. Although, in her simple white shirt and jeans, her hair a bit windblown and frizzed, she looked like an ordinary person—like Carrie—and not a glamorous movie star at all.

"I bet you two have a lot to catch up on." Asher gave a *call me* motion before hightailing it down my walkway and almost diving behind the wheel of his car.

"You're really leaving." Carrie said it as a statement, but like one she could hardly comprehend, as she peered around me, looking into the truck at the piles of furniture and boxes.

"I am."

"I don't understand. I told you I'd come back and find you."

"When? I haven't heard from you in twenty-three days, and every night there's some new photo of you and Sandra hitting up a nightclub. You're out there living your best life while I'm eating Ben and Jerry's three meals a day." I wrapped my arms around my belly to hide the evidence.

"I haven't been to any nightclubs." Carrie's lips formed a thin line, and the hurt look in her eyes was so believable I almost bought it before remembering she was an actor. "I don't know who's leaking those photos, and I don't remember them ever being taken. I think they're fake."

I blew the loudest raspberry I could muster, and let me tell you, it was a doozy. Which regrettably left some drool on my chin. I swiped it with the back of my hand. "Tell me another one. Clearly, I'm a sucker."

"I know you're upset, Go-Go, but will you give me a minute to explain? I've been hunkering down with my family, letting this blow over."

"Are you kidding me? As far as I can tell, the only news about your family is you swanning around town with Sandra."

"I haven't seen Sandra since Hawaii!" Carrie clenched her fists, trying to regain her composure. "I admit I may not have handled things as well as I could have in the immediate aftermath."

"You make it sound like a natural disaster," I remarked. "You know, you could have answered one of my messages."

"No, I couldn't. I don't trust my phone, or yours. I have no idea who is watching. I never know what's private and what isn't. I was afraid if I texted you from the number you had for me, someone might learn of your identity. I didn't want that—"

"Yes, that message was received loud and clear." But something she'd said, the number I had for her, stuck in my brain like a splinter. I'd forgotten all about her second phone, the real number she'd alluded to at Sweetheart Rock. Had Asher messaged her on the phone number I didn't have access to? I felt my heart start to melt and forced myself to think cold, icy thoughts.

"Margo, please believe me. It's not like that. I don't want to throw you into the deep end of my life. That's all."

"Didn't you think marrying me was going to do that?"

She started to speak but quickly zipped her mouth shut

and closed her eyes. Was she counting to ten to control her frustration?

"I know being with me is difficult, and I don't know how to change that, but I want to be with you, Margo. More than anything."

I think she honest to God meant it, and my heart practically burst from my chest.

My brain, though, took over.

"I want to be with you," I said, my eyes downcast.

"There's a but coming, isn't there?"

"Even if I did buy that the photos of you and Sandra are fake, I don't know how I fit into your life." Was that why I was running? Because I couldn't figure it out and it was easier to scram than deal with reality?

"By my side." She took me into her arms.

I nuzzled into her, the tears flowing now. "My heart can't take all of this. It's too much. This isn't a normal life."

She pulled back to gaze into my eyes. "To me, it's normal life."

"That's the problem. For me, it isn't." I let out a shaky breath. "I want you, Carrie, but I don't want everything that comes with you. I don't want to have a burner phone just to send you a text. I don't want to worry about someone snapping a photo or creating ones to make me or you look bad. I never wanted to be famous. Truthfully, it sounds more like a prison than anything."

Carrie sucked her bottom lip into her mouth.

"We'll always have Hawaii. It was a magical time, and I'll think of it often. But I can't change who you are, and I don't want to hide you away in a cave until the sea comes to claim you."

Her eyes filled with tears, and she let out one lone sob

before a mask descended over her face. "I understand. More than you know." She took a step closer, kissing me on the cheek and whispering, "I love you, Go-Go."

And then she was gone, and I wanted to collapse into a puddle.

# CHAPTER TWENTY

I'd been back in Minnesota less than a week before it was time to report to the costume shop for my first day of work. The sun was barely up as I plopped into a chair at the breakfast table across from where my mom sat with her massive mug of coffee. At least that hadn't changed.

"Good morning," she chirped, looking up from her newspaper. It was possible my mother was the last person in America to get her news in print. I wondered if it had apartment listings. I was going to need to find a place for myself as soon as I settled in.

"Hrmf," I responded, not bothering to hide my envy as I eyed her steaming mug. Something about coffee made facing the day slightly more bearable.

"Still not a morning person after all those early call times in Hollywood?"

I grunted in response.

She poured me a cup of coffee from the carafe, and I accepted it gratefully, feeling the warmth seep into my palms. That was another thing that hadn't changed about Minnesota. It wasn't even fall yet, but it was fucking freezing this morning, at least by LA standards. Another few weeks, and I would be wearing a winter coat. After five years in California, I didn't own a winter coat anymore.

"Did you hear Tilly Swanson is having a baby?" Mom asked as if I was intimately acquainted with the soap opera star.

I thought about it for a moment, finally having to ask, "Isn't she like sixty?"

"Yep. It's a miracle baby." Mom tapped the news article, and my eyes narrowed.

Upon closer scrutiny, I realized it wasn't a proper newspaper she was reading but a tabloid from the grocery store checkout. And it had pictures of Carrie's and Sandra's heads on the cover, each in its own half of a heart with a jagged split down the middle, accompanied by the headline "Trouble in Paradise?" My stomach did a somersault, and I rushed to look away.

"You're still reading that crap?" I asked accusingly.

"It's not crap," my mom responded indignantly, flipping the page. "Look at this photo of Bigfoot. If that's not proof he's real, I don't know what is."

I shook my head, chuckling at her misplaced trust in tabloid journalism. "I hate to break it to you, but I don't think Bigfoot is posing for pictures in the wilderness for a quick buck."

"I wouldn't blame him if he did. Times are hard."

I blinked, unable to ascertain if she was yanking my chain. "Please tell me you don't believe Bigfoot exists and that he's besties with Nessy."

"Wouldn't that be something?" Her eyes gleamed with mischief, and I was relieved to see she was messing with me. "Are you going to tell me what's wrong? Because you're in a foul mood all of a sudden, and I don't think it's because of Bigfoot."

"These stories"—I tapped Carrie's photo, the blood draining from my finger as I pressed down on it—"are all bullshit. These are real people. It may seem like harmless entertainment, but it impacts them, and the people who care about them."

My mother raised an eyebrow as my voice cracked. "Sounds like you have personal experience. Is this about Jenna? Because I never much liked her."

"No, it's not about Jenna." I almost laughed at the thought of Jenna ever being a big enough star to merit tabloid coverage. I had a feeling after Vivian got through with her for wrecking Cagney's wedding, Jenna would be lucky to get hired to clean the bathrooms on a low-budget web series. "It's about someone else," I admitted, tears stinging my eyes.

My mother set the tabloid aside, her gaze softening as she studied me. "Is it about that actress you used to work with? The one that got you fired?"

"She didn't get me fired," I said through the lump in my throat. "And it was never going to work out, in part because of these stupid tabloid stories."

"Did you have feelings for her?"

"Yes." There was no point lying about it.

"Did she reciprocate?"

I squeezed my eyes shut. "I believe she did."

"Then what the heck are you doing here in Minnesota instead of trying to work things out back in LA? I mean no offense, honey. It's nice having you home. But have you lost your darn mind?"

"I made a rational adult decision," I argued, wondering as I said it whether that was really true. Had it been rational or just safe? "I don't want you to see my photos in the tabloids while drinking your morning coffee and wonder what kind of sleazy stuff I'm getting up to in Hollywood."

"Now, Margo, I know most of this stuff isn't real. It's just entertainment."

"At a cost, Mom. At a cost."

My mom's face fell, and she reached across the table to take my hand. "You really loved her, didn't you?"

I nodded, feeling the weight of unshed tears threatening to spill over. "I did. I still do."

"Then tell me the real reason you're here."

"I did," I insisted. "Because I couldn't live that kind of celebrity life."

"You don't sound all that convincing," my mom informed me. "And don't get me started on your furtive eye movements."

I rested my head on bent elbows. "Fine. I admit I may have made a big mistake in rejecting her, but it's too late to change things. So please, let it go."

"Okay. But before I drop the subject for good, did you at least learn a lesson for next time?"

"There's not going to be a next time. I'm never falling for another person in my life."

"You know what that tells me when you can't think about a next time?" She didn't wait for me to reply. "It tells me this time probably isn't as over as you think it is. You need to figure out a way to make things better."

"Yeah, sure. Let me get right on that."

She looked expectantly at me like she thought I was going to do that.

"That was sarcasm."

"Is that what it was?" The sarcasm in her own tone reminded me where I'd learned that particular trait.

"The relationship can't be fixed. I broke it beyond repair

the day I left to come home." I gulped my coffee. "And now I need to get to the theater to see about some big shake-up coming down the pike. I've had a hundred texts this morning already. It's my first day, and I'm stressed out beyond belief."

"It's only a job, Margo. Don't let work define you."

"It's all I've got now. Sorry you won't get any grandkids out of me. And don't rot your brain with that trash." I snatched the tabloid from the table, kissed the top of her head, and ran out the door before she could tell me to try to fix things with Carrie.

Like how was that even possible? Carrie had put her pride aside and chased after me, and what did I do in return? I told her she wasn't enough. It was a shitty thing to do, and as soon as I drove out of LA, I knew I'd made the biggest mistake of my life. But there was no turning back the clock. I would have to live with my mistake.

---

"THIS PLACE IS A TOTAL DISASTER!" Martha, the costume shop manager, ranted immediately upon my arrival.

I cast my eyes over the cluttered space with a certain fondness. True, it was disheveled but not more than usual. It felt like home.

"It's not that bad; trust me." I shuddered, remembering what it was like in some of the costume trailers I'd worked in. "I've seen much worse."

"You don't understand." She placed a hand on her hip. "The theater's been sold. The new owners are coming in today. Some kind of surprise inspection, I think."

"Back up a minute. Sold? I didn't even know we were on the market," I replied, a sense of dread creeping up my spine at the thought of even more change than I'd already endured.

"Who are the new owners? Do you know anything about them?"

"It's all super hush-hush," Martha said. "All I know is they're a rich husband and wife team who are kind of a big deal, at least from the way people in the know like to hint around. Whoever they are, they can't see the place like this."

"What are they gonna do, fire us for leaving the scissors out?" I laughed over such a ridiculous idea.

Martha didn't join in, her face losing all its color. My smile faded as I realized this was more serious than I thought.

"I was kidding," I insisted. "That's not possible, is it?"

Martha cast a shifty glance at the door, lowering her voice. "There was a theater about our size in Illinois that was bought out last year. The new owners wanted to cut costs and axed the entire costume department. They started buying outfits made in China and paid for one seamstress to do all the fittings when they came in."

I couldn't believe the horror story Martha was recounting. My stomach churned. What was going to happen to me? I'd moved here for a steady paycheck, and now that was in jeopardy.

"That can't happen here, right?"

Martha pursed her lips. "I don't know, Margo. All I know is that we need to impress these new owners."

Asher had been right. There were jobs aplenty in LA, but this was the only theater with a full costume shop for hundreds of miles. If I lost this job, I'd be working at the family dry cleaners the rest of my miserable life.

The old phone on the wall trilled, and Martha and I stared at each other for a long second before she answered it.

I gnawed on a hangnail, dreading the news that might come from the other end of that call.

"I understand." Martha's expression was grim. "Right away." She hung up the phone.

"Everything okay?" My heart raced.

"You're wanted in the main office."

"Me?" I squeaked, a hand on my chest.

She simply nodded, and my heart sank.

This was it. I was getting canned. For the second time in less than a year.

My legs felt like lead as I forced myself to make my way to the main office. With each step, all I could think was I was cursed. How else could you explain such a shitty year?

The hallway seemed longer than I remembered, every step echoing my fears. With a deep breath, I knocked on the door and heard a muffled "Come in."

The door swung open, and I nearly fainted when I saw Vivian and Tom standing in the middle of the room as if they'd been beamed from a spaceship to a new planet.

Because my life hadn't been cursed enough. Now Carrie's parents were here to destroy me. What other reason could there be for them coming here?

"Are you okay, darling? You've gone pale." Vivian whacked Tom in the side to get him to help me to a seat.

I sank into it, my knees giving out halfway down. "You're firing me, aren't you?"

Vivian and Tom exchanged a glance that I could only assume meant they hadn't thought I would figure it out on my own so quickly.

"Now why would I do that?" Vivian asked, her face seeming sincere. But on the other hand, she hadn't denied it.

"Because of how I treated Carrie," I answered, resigned to my fate.

"Do you think we bought this theater so we could fire you out of revenge?" It was Tom who spoke.

I nodded, my eyes unable to meet his.

"My goodness. That would be extreme." Vivian waved a hand.

Again, not exactly a denial.

"The truth is," Vivian continued, "Tom wants me to retire, but I don't know if I can fully commit to that. After Asher told us about you taking a job here, I looked into it. I had no idea how exciting the world of dinner theater could be."

I gave her an incredulous look. "You want me to believe you bought this place because you want to run a dinner theater?"

"Of course. This is our retirement plan." She made air quotes as she said the word retirement, as if to make it clear she had no intention of slowing down. "The Jacobs family name is synonymous with the stage, you know. This way, I can get back to my roots with live theater whenever I want. What do you think?"

"I have absolutely no idea what to think."

"Hmm. I see what Carrie meant about you." Vivian perched on the lip of the desk right in front of me, her eyes staring down into mine. I had no idea what Carrie had said about me, but it couldn't have been good. "Speaking of Carrie..."

Here it comes.

I absolutely knew what it must have felt like to be led to a guillotine for execution.

"She's miserable," Tom supplied, catching me by surprise. "I've never seen her like this."

"She's been living in the same pajamas and robe for weeks," Vivian continued, wrinkling her nose. "If something doesn't change soon, we're going to have to call in the health department to shut her place down."

"It's starting to smell," Tom added.

I sank deeper into the chair, feeling like the worst person on the planet.

"Don't take this the wrong way, but on our way here, I had my heart set on discovering you're as miserable as she is." Vivian's eyes were kind, but her words came out with a hopefulness that seemed odd, considering. "So, tell me. How are you?"

"I've been better," I confessed, seeing no point in not being honest.

"Are you sad?" Tom questioned.

"Heartbroken." My shoulders slumped.

As Vivian grinned, Tom patted my shoulder tenderly. "Does that mean you're still in love with our daughter?" he asked gently.

I buried my head in my hands. "Of course, I am."

"I have to fix this," Vivian declared.

"By firing me?" I moaned.

"And people accuse me of being dramatic," Vivian said with a laugh. "For the last time, I don't plan on firing anyone, least of all my future daughter-in-law."

My jaw fell open. "Surely Carrie told you it was all a lie."

"Oh, yes. That." Vivian waved it off like she was swatting a fly. "I'm sure we can fix that."

My head spun as I tried to piece together what was happening. "I'm sorry if I seem dense, Vivian, but what are you trying to fix? Why are you here?"

"Other than to check on our new investment?" Vivian smiled indulgently. "Because I wanted to talk to you."

"Did you ever consider making a phone call?" Rich people were so weird. Like did it never cross her mind to simply stop by for a chat instead of shelling out millions to buy my place of employment?

"I have a plan for you to win Carrie back. Are you in?" Vivian waited for my reply.

My eyes slid to Tom who gave me an encouraging grin.

I didn't like the look in Vivian's eye, and considering her last plan ended up with me jetting out of a total shitstorm dressed as a runaway bride, I had some serious doubts.

I also didn't have any other solution, and I was desperate for a second chance to make Carrie mine. This time, I wouldn't let anything screw it up.

"Yes, I'm in," I finally answered, steeling myself for whatever Vivian had up her sleeve.

After all, what's the worst that could happen? Famous last words. Vivian's grin widened, and I couldn't shake the feeling that I had made a deal with the devil herself.

# CHAPTER TWENTY-ONE

Four weeks of preparation passed in the blink of an eye, and suddenly, it was the night of the gala to celebrate the grand opening of the newly renamed Jacobs-Blythe Theatre.

I could hear the orchestra warming up in the pit above my head as I waited downstairs in the theater's green room. I'd spent countless opening nights in spaces like this, running from dressing room to dressing room for last-minute adjustments to straps and hems before the curtain went up. But this was the first time I would be going on stage myself.

In a hula skirt and a coconut bra, no less.

I tugged at the plastic grass at my waist, feeling ridiculously exposed. My hands were clammy, and my heart pounded in my chest. Why had I ever agreed to Vivian's plan to publicly humiliate myself?

Because I wanted Carrie back.

The orchestra finished warming up, and in the relative silence, I could hear the chatter of the audience as they filled their seats. Nerves clutched at my stomach like a vise, but I couldn't give in to the temptation to flee before places were called. Desperation had driven me to agree to the kind of grand romantic gesture I had always abhorred. But if wearing this absurd outfit and humiliating myself in front of half of Minnesota meant a chance to win Carrie back, I was willing to endure anything.

"Are you ready for your close-up?" Asher came up behind me and gave my shoulders a squeeze.

"Puke." It was the only word I could force out. "Going to puke."

"Nonsense. You got this." He tossed an arm across my shoulder. "We've been rehearsing for a week, and you're starting to sound..." He visibly struggled to choose his next word before landing on "decent."

"Wow, that's high praise, indeed. Thanks for the vote of confidence." I tried to muster a smile, doing my best to summon some bravado, but it faltered on my lips. My self-doubt was threatening to drown me.

"The point isn't to be good," he reminded me. "The point is to get her attention. And trust me, this performance is definitely going to achieve that."

"I still can't believe you relocated to Minnesota," I said, changing the subject before he could make any more attempts at inspiring me. I'd been shocked when Asher accepted the position of manager for his aunt's theater, certain he was an LA guy through and through.

"I can't believe it either." He let out a surprisingly contented sigh. "Why didn't you tell me about the fried cheese curds before? I feel like that should have been the first thing out of your mouth when you said you were from Minnesota. Don't even get me started on the Kolaches. They're fruit-filled doughy delights. I'm in love, Margo. In love."

"I'm glad it's working out for you. Me on the other

hand..." The weight of the coconut bra felt heavier now, and I longed to shed this ridiculous costume and run far, far away from the theater. "I'm about to make an ass out of myself in front of thousands of people."

"Don't be ridiculous. The theater seats three hundred, tops." A distracted look came over Asher's face, and he placed a hand over his earpiece. "What? Absolutely not!"

"Trouble?" I asked.

He nodded at me, his eyes widening over whatever he was hearing from the headset. "Tell her it's way too late to incorporate live doves into the finale. I don't care if she has them on standby. This isn't a magic show." With that, he stormed off in the direction of the stage.

I didn't mind being left alone as he put out another fire, more than likely caused by Vivian's exuberance. The woman had grand visions and didn't like the word no.

I'd certainly learned that the hard way over the past month. If there was any other way to accomplish the goal of convincing Carrie to take me back, I would've done it. But sadly, Vivian knew her daughter, and her plan was foolproof. Emphasis on the fool part. Thinking of what was to come, a wave of nausea washed over me. Fortunately, I was distracted by the sight of my mother wandering around backstage.

"Mom!" I waved her down.

Her face broke into a wide smile as she caught sight of me. "There's my girl." Mom rushed toward me, giving me a hug.

"Where's Dad?"

"Camped out in the buffet line, getting his fill. He's not much for live entertainment, but he loves an all-you-can-eat spread." Mom wrapped one of my hands with her own. "Are you ready for your big number?"

"You mean flop?"

"Now, now. None of that negativity," Mom chided

gently, giving my hand a reassuring squeeze. "You were really sounding so much better this morning in the shower."

Great.

Unfortunately, neither my mom nor Asher was the best at pep talks, probably because they weren't the type to outright lie. And right now, a massive lie was what I needed.

"There's the star of the show!" Vivian approached, pulling me in for one of her crushing hugs. I was still getting used to being smothered by the sheer force of her personality on a daily basis. Tom was several paces behind her, doing his best to blend into the shadows.

"Vivian, I'd like you to meet my mother, Jeanette."

"Jeannette." Vivian pulled my mom into an embrace. "I feel like I know you already from all the wonderful stories Margo has shared about her family."

"Me too," said my starstruck mom, "but probably for different reasons. I'm sure my daughter has told you about my tabloid addiction."

I most certainly had not said a word about it and was completely mortified, but Vivian took it in stride.

"You come along with me," she said, grasping my mother by the elbow. "I'll tell you all the really juicy celebrity gossip."

With that, Vivian and my mom walked away, leaving me to battle my stage fright all on my own. Taking a deep breath, I tried to shake off the nerves and focus on the task ahead.

"You look like you're about to face a firing squad," Tom said as he sidled up next to me, apparently having gained the courage to approach only after his wife had made her exit. "Chin up."

"Have you ever wanted the power to teleport?" I asked, letting out a nervous chuckle. "Because right about now, I'd give anything to be anywhere but here."

"I feel the same at pretty much every red-carpet event," he confessed.

"How do you keep doing it?"

"Love." He gazed across the way, where Vivian stood holding court. "She's not perfect, believe me—despite what the world likes to think. She can be downright infuriating, but she loves me with her whole heart, and I feel the same."

"That's the secret?" I'd been hoping for something more life-changing, to be honest. Not the type of cliché that could be embroidered on a pillow. But it seemed Tom was sincere in his conviction.

"Here comes Cagney. Hopefully with a Carrie update." He waved his youngest daughter over as my stomach did a series of somersaults at the mention of Carrie's name. "Is she here?"

"First row, just like requested," Cagney confirmed. "You should probably go sit with her, Dad."

Tom nodded and offered me a reassuring smile before making his way to the stairs that led to the main floor.

"Carrie's really here?" I asked Cagney. It felt like my lungs were collapsing.

"And she's not wearing her bathrobe. That was a battle; let me tell you." Cagney waved a hand in front of her face to illustrate the odiferous situation she'd been tasked with. "I want hazard pay from Mom after that one. I wasn't half this pathetic after I dumped Erik."

Cagney laughed, but I felt suddenly overcome by guilt at the inadvertent part I'd played in that fiasco.

"I'm really sorry about how things turned out in Hawaii," I said. "If I'd realized what Jenna was capable of..."

"Don't be sorry. I've never felt better in my life. It's important to find the person you're supposed to be with, and Erik wasn't it." Cagney's expression softened. "Carrie loves you. Like, she really does. You'll win her back. Break a leg tonight!"

The lights backstage flickered, meaning the show was about to begin. With a quick wave, Cagney dashed off to get to her seat.

My number was last on the program. It was for dramatic effect, or possibly because Vivian wanted the customers to get their money's worth and be fairly drunk on the complimentary champagne before I went on stage and made an ass out of myself.

Out of all the romantic gestures to choose from, it occurred to me that Vivian believed utter personal humiliation was the best way for me to win her daughter's heart. Maybe I should have gone for the classic boombox-over-the-head move.

The show—a musical revue including some of Vivian and Tom's favorite show tunes from Broadway musicals—was going smoothly. As the cast sang their hearts out and the audience clapped along, I could feel my nerves building up to a breaking point. It was almost time. Time for me to step onto that stage and prove to Carrie, and maybe to myself, that I loved her enough to risk doing something that scared me more than anything I could think of. Even zip lining.

As I waited for my cue, I paced backstage, resisting the urge to peek into the audience to see if I could spy Carrie. What was she wearing? Not her bathrobe, I knew that much. But I couldn't think about that right now. It didn't even matter. I would've been fine with her wearing the damn robe, smell and all.

I ran the lyrics of "I'm in Love with a Wonderful Guy" from South Pacific through my head for the millionth time. Naturally, we had changed the word guy to gal. Vivian thought the number was perfect as a callback to our time in Hawaii. Did she not remember how that had worked out?

The spotlight flickered, signaling my entrance. The entire cast was assembled on stage for what promised to be a heart-stopping finale, even if the only heart that actually stopped was my own when I keeled over from a heart attack.

"You're up, Margo." Asher was at my side, doing his best to shove me on stage.

I shook my head, blinded by fear. "I can't do it. You do it."

"I don't think it'll have the same effect if I serenade Carrie on your behalf. She's my cousin." He not so gently shoved me through the curtain, and I practically stumbled.

The crowd laughed as if this had been planned. I couldn't blame them. With my grass skirt and coconut-enshrouded tits, I must have looked like a tropical circus clown.

I tried looking for Carrie, but the lights were too blinding. Why did they have to be so bright? And hot?

The orchestra started up, but when I was supposed to sing the first line, I didn't. I was too terrified to make a peep. So they started again.

I got maybe four words out before my voice cracked, and I wanted to die. I held up my hand to signal for the music to stop.

"I'm sorry, everyone," I said, addressing the audience that was somewhere behind the blinding lights. "I'm not an actor. I'm a costumer. And, no, I was not responsible for this one." I fanned out the hula skirt and then patted the flower in my hair.

There was an uncomfortable chuckle from the crowd, like they wanted to find me entertaining but had no clue where my rambling monologue was going to take them. I would have liked to know that, too.

"A little while back—about thirty-six days and ten hours ago, but who's counting, right?—I made the worst mistake of my life. A woman told me she loved me, but I said that wasn't enough. She's really famous, and I'm just plain Margo, not used to the limelight. If you hadn't guessed that."

There was sympathetic murmuring from the crowd.

"Vivian Jacobs happens to be the mother of this woman, so in case you were hoping management was going to send someone to escort me off stage, I have bad news for you. Vivian kind of put me up to this. Well, not this rambling speech, precisely. There was supposed to be a song and choreography. And maybe doves? I don't know. I heard a rumor."

This got a laugh, which bolstered my confidence a little.

"Anyway, Vivian is a really persuasive person, so I agreed to come on stage tonight because, honestly, she scares me a little. Not as much as the thought of never seeing Carrie again or holding her does, though. It's just too much. So I agreed. Let me tell you Vivian had much grander ambitions. You should have seen the fight Tom put up to prevent her from installing a swimming pool in the orchestra pit so there could be synchronized swimmers. All so I could stand here and make a fool of myself. At least I got that part right."

There was actual laughter this time, loads of it.

"If you don't know who I'm talking about, allow me to let you in on a little—er, big secret. I'm madly in love with Caroline Jacobs, and I hope she still loves me. I know for a fact she loves grand gestures. Me, I'd rather die. It's possible I have, and this is my spirit speaking right now. From hell."

More laughter.

"I don't know what else to say, and I'll spare you from trying to sing again. I'll simply say what's in my heart. Carrie, I love you. I was a fool to leave LA. If you'll give me a second chance, I won't blow it this time. Unless you want me to sing in a musical. In which case, no can do."

There was a rustling in the crowd, and all of a sudden, Carrie was jumping onto the stage, pulling me into a hug. I nearly knocked the microphone stand over in my surprise. The crowd erupted into cheers and applause as Carrie held me tightly, her eyes shining with tears.

"You idiot," she whispered in my ear. "I can't believe you did this."

"No one is more surprised than I am," I whispered back. "Does this mean it's a yes?"

"You're such a fool. It was a yes as soon as you came on stage and missed your first cue."

"Why did you let me do this whole song and dance? Well, so to speak."

"I had an evil desire to see how far you'd get with it," she confessed, her hand squeezing mine. "I couldn't resist watching you squirm."

A surge of joy and relief washed over me.

"I seriously could kill you right now." I sank into her arms, pulling her as close as I could like I feared ever letting her go again. "But I think I'd rather kiss you instead."

The room around us seemed to fade away until it was only me and Carrie wrapped up in each other's arms. We shared a passionate kiss, and I felt the weight of uncertainty lift off my shoulders as if the world had finally righted itself. The crowd erupted into cheers and claps, but I barely heard them. I was too busy savoring the moment.

It was as if everything I had been through, all the heartache and doubts, led me to this moment of pure clarity, that Carrie was the one I had been searching for all along.

# CHAPTER TWENTY-TWO

"Open that bag and die!" I gave the hanger in my hand a menacing shake as a startled Carrie, wrapped in a robe of thick, white terry cloth, twirled around to face the door of her wardrobe trailer. Her expression was like a toddler caught reaching into the cookie jar as her hands gripped the top of a fresh bag of forbidden nacho-cheese-coated chips.

Not on my watch.

"What are you going to do, Wardrobe Warden, hang me?" Carrie ripped the bag open with a defiant smirk, as if daring me to follow through on my threat.

Ignoring her bravado, I tossed the hanger aside and sauntered closer, my lips curling into a sly smile. "You're impossible. You know that?"

Carrie's chuckle filled the small space as she popped a chip into her mouth, orange dust settling onto her chest like snow, before setting the bag down on the makeup vanity. "I've been told that a time or two. But you love it."

I raised an eyebrow, fighting a smile. "Who said anything about love? I'm just here to make sure you don't ruin the costume for today's scene. It's a masterpiece."

Fortunately, the chic 1940s-era evening dress hung safely on a hook on the far side of Carrie's trailer, nowhere near the open bag of contraband.

"Does it have a scarf?" Carrie batted her lashes with an innocence that belied the mischief in her eyes. "It will make it much easier to strangle me with it if it does."

"Shoot." I gave an exaggerated stomp of my foot. "I knew I was missing something."

"Yes, you are. This." Wrapping her arms around me, she pulled me in for a kiss, her mouth tasting lightly of nacho flavoring.

"I really hope you don't have any kissing in today's scene," I told her, wrinkling my nose, though I made no attempt to extricate myself from her embrace.

"Why? Jealous?"

"No, just feeling sorry for anyone else who has to put up with that much nacho breath," I teased, leaning back slightly to look into her gorgeous eyes. How had I gotten so lucky?

"Oh, please. You love how I make your life spicier." She grabbed the bag once more and held it out like an offering. "Let's see if you can handle the heat."

Something told me she wasn't really referring to the chips. For a moment, I regretted the strong work ethic that kept me from stripping off her robe right here and now so I could feel her bare skin against mine. As much as I tried to maintain a professional demeanor now that we were back to work, Carrie had a way of breaking down my barriers with her infectious smile and playful banter.

"Handling you is a full-time job," I quipped, grabbing the bag from her hand, rolling it shut, and tossing it far out of reach.

Carrie stuck out her tongue as she realized I had out

maneuvered her. "And yet, here you are, back in Hollywood with me and not applying for other positions."

Now that the directors' strike had ended, we were racing to finish up Carrie's movie, though there had been several changes. For one thing, Dennis had been sacked. And instead of filming an artsy black and white snoozefest, the film had been transformed into an action-packed spy thriller. I knew Carrie didn't want to jinx it, but I was privately convinced this would win her an award, and I was thrilled to be a part of it.

Not that I would admit such a thing to her, of course.

"After all the groveling you must have done to get me my job back after so callously having me fired, it would just seem rude to quit."

"Me? Grovel?" Carrie let out a hearty laugh at this. "A Jacobs does not grovel, darling."

"You sounded exactly like your mother just then." My observation earned me a playful sock to the bicep. "What? It's true. Although, I could've sworn when she stopped by the house the other night, I caught the start of a Minnesota accent creeping in."

"I think you're right, doncha know," Carrie agreed, unable to hold back a snicker at her own sorry attempt at the accent in question. "She's counting the days until she heads back to the land of ten thousand lakes. Can you believe it? I would never have thought the great Vivian Jacobs would find her life's calling working in a Midwestern dinner theater."

"I keep telling all of you Hollywood snobs not to underestimate the power of a good hot dish and Jell-O salad."

Carrie playfully rolled her eyes at the mention of these potluck staples, which were a major point of disagreement between us when it came to doing our menu planning. Fortunately, in the two months since I'd moved into her Hollywood Hills home, groceries were about the only thing that caused an argument, and even then it felt more like a well-rehearsed comedy routine than a real fight.

A reminder beeped on my phone, and I reluctantly stepped out of Carrie's embrace to attend to my costume duties while Carrie settled into a chair to go over her lines.

"Can I say again how much better this film is now that Luke Abbott has taken over?" I held out the hem of the gorgeous period gown, lightly puffing steam at a stubborn wrinkle. "The new costumes are to die for. I mean, not literally, luckily. Not like last time."

"No, Luke's much more concerned about not killing off his stars," Carrie said with a laugh, looking up from her script. "And the changes to the script are amazing. It's like *Ocean's 8* meets *Casablanca* but with some serious sapphic undertones."

"I still can't believe the transformation this project has undergone," I agreed. "Who knew ol' Abbie would actually have some good ideas?

"I'll admit I was skeptical," Carrie said. "But I felt a little bit bad for him after getting caught in the middle with the whole Erik and Jenna thing. I know you weren't as keen to hear him out."

I shrugged, no longer bothered. Once I'd figured out the director had known nothing about my existence when he'd started seeing my ex, it had been easy enough to muster some sympathy for the guy. At least enough not to freak out when Carrie came to me with his idea for taking over Dennis's doomed film.

"Are you sorry Richard was given the boot?" I asked. "I mean I know he had an affair with Alex and all that, but he's a popular leading man, and I know it was a strategic career move for you to star with him."

"Are you joking?" Carrie scoffed. "Remember that he used to eat garlic bread before every intimate scene. He loved to blow garlic breaths in my face. Such an asshole."

"He really was." I, for one, was glad both he and Alex were no longer associated with the film. "I would like to point out, however, that you're not much better if you continue with your nacho-flavored chips obsession."

"At least I brush my teeth afterward," Carrie retorted playfully.

There was a knock on the trailer door, and a voice called out, "Fifteen minutes, Miss Jacobs."

"Showtime," I said, carefully removing the dress from the hanger.

Carrie rose and stripped off her robe as she crossed the space, the sight of her vintage undergarments setting off a flutter in my belly that I would be forced to ignore, at least for now. I quickly eased the dress over her head, in part to remove as much temptation as possible.

"Before I forget," she said from somewhere inside the dress, "my parents want to do dinner before they head back to Minnesota."

"Sure," I said, already having guessed a final catch-up with her parents would be on the agenda. "They're leaving next weekend, right? I hope so, because my mom is jonesing for the latest gossip. She's been texting me saying, 'I need juice beets.'"

"Juice beets?" Carrie made a disgusted face. "Is that another example of Minnesotan cuisine?"

"As much as it sounds like something that would be served with lutefisk, I think she meant to type juicy deets, but she never checks her spelling before she hits send."

Carrie's laughter was soft and reassuring. "Asher tells me Cagney's rehearsals for the fall performance of *Annie* are fantastic. She's enjoying acting again and is killing it in the role of Miss Hannigan."

"I'm excited to see that." I let out a tiny groan as I contemplated the coming months, which seemed to be rushing by now that we were back at work. "What I'm not excited for is Christmas in Minnesota."

"It won't be that bad. Both our families will be there."

I raised an eyebrow. "Is that supposed to be a selling point?"

"There might be snow," Carrie offered with a shrug. "I love it when the mountains here get a dusting. It's so pretty."

I motioned for her to turn so I could do up the side zipper of the gown, closing it with a gentle tug. "Clearly you have never experienced a winter in Minnesota."

A bit of the color seemed to drain from Carrie's face as worry clouded her expression. "Exactly how cold is it?"

"Even when taking a scolding hot shower, you'll never feel warm." It was true, but I may have been taking a bit more pleasure than necessary from the horror in Carrie's eyes. She quickly rallied, offering a brave smile.

"Is it weird I'm almost looking forward to that? It'll be like a normal holiday. Away from here. Far from the limelight. Just us with our loved ones. I doubt the paparazzi are crazy enough to brave the freezing cold."

"One can only hope. It's still weird seeing my face on the covers when I'm at the grocery store."

Carrie's expression clouded, a crease forming in her brow. "I'm sorry about that."

"No need to apologize. It comes with the territory," I replied, brushing off her concern. But deep down, I appreciated her empathy. And I was determined not to let the trappings of fame come between us. "And, you're right. It'll be a nice change of pace to have some quiet family time."

As I finished adjusting the gown on Carrie, she stood up and took a step back to admire the results in the mirror.

"What do you think?" she asked, twirling slightly to see the full effect of the gown. The emerald fabric clung to her curves in all the right places, accentuating her figure.

I couldn't help but smile at how effortlessly stunning she looked. "You look breathtaking, as always."

"I love that this film allows me to look great and kick ass at the same time," she said. "Do you think Luke will let me do that skydiving scene next week, instead of giving it to a stunt double?"

"Sure, because doing your own stunt went so well last time." I cast a meaningful look at her injured knee, though I was happy to know it hardly ever gave her trouble these days.

"That was Dennis's fault. The car wasn't safe." Carrie reached down and massaged the top of her knee as she spoke, an action that made me wonder how often the accident still haunted her.

"Jumping from a plane isn't safe, either. I don't even know why you keep suggesting it." I had an inkling, though. The closer Carrie got to turning forty, the more she seemed determined to prove she was as fearless as ever, regardless of the past mishaps. I also suspected that chasing adrenaline-fueled roles was a way to prove she wasn't just the same old romantic comedy darling everyone expected her to be.

"I guess that means we'll finally have to do that tandem skydive we told everyone we did." Carrie batted her lashes, seeming to play innocent, even though she was fully aware how I felt about heights.

"You're the one who came up with that whopper," I said, shaking my head as I retrieved her robe from the floor. It had landed beside the bag of Doritos, which I scooped up as well. "I'm not beholden to you to make your lies come true."

"Come on. It'll be fun. You liked zip lining with me." Carrie flashed the kind of winning grin that went straight to my heart, even as I rolled my eyes at her antics.

"Jumping from a plane is a whole other level of insanity. I don't want to tempt fate. I'm finally happy in life. I'm already waiting for the other shoe to drop. I don't need to spur my death along."

"You're happy in life?" Carrie threaded her arms around my neck and treated me to a close-up look into her stunning blue eyes.

My heart skipped a beat. "Very much so."

"Is there a reason behind this happiness?"

"Yes." My mouth had gone dry, and it was all I could do to say that single word.

She tilted her head to one side. "And what reason is that?"

"Doritos, naturally." I held up the bag, which was still clutched in one hand. "As soon as you're on set, I plan to finish these off so you can't be tempted by them again."

"You're incorrigible. Now kiss me so I can go to work." She leaned in, pressing her lips gently against mine in a kiss that was brief but brimming with promise. "I should be home tonight in time for dinner."

As she pulled away, her smile lingered, imprinting itself on my mind.

"Try not to be late," I urged, wearing what I was certain was the goofiest grin on the planet. "I'm making my famous Tater Tots hot dish."

---

"I COULD GET USED to this life." From my seat on the deck, I stretched my legs, lacing my hands behind my head. Below us were the twinkly lights of Hollywood. "The view is spectacular."

"You're not used to it yet? You moved in with me months ago." Carrie set two full wineglasses on the table between our chairs.

"I don't think I'll ever take it for granted," I said with a dreamy sigh.

She settled into her chair, grinning like a fool.

"What?" I asked, a little unnerved by her response.

"Nothing. It's just that I like the sound of that. When people start to take things for granted, the shine has worn off."

I gave her a sideways look. "We're not talking about the view anymore, are we?"

"Nope."

I reached for her hand. "I'll never get tired of you. Never."

"Ditto."

"Such a romantic." I picked up the glass of wine, taking a long, slow sip of the deep red liquid, letting it dance on my tongue before swallowing. "I won't tire of this either. You buy the good shit."

"Now who's the romantic?" She winked at me before standing and walking to the railing, holding on with both hands. A soft breeze made her blond hair swirl around her.

I joined her. "It's so peaceful here. I never associated Hollywood with peace."

"Neither did I. Not until you." She turned her gaze to me, lighting my insides up like a pinball machine. "You have that look."

"What look is that?"

"Like you want to eat me."

I couldn't help but chuckle at her comment, my eyes

roaming over her body, taking in every detail. She was right, I did want to devour her. She was my everything.

I wrapped an arm around her waist, pulling her closer to me. "You caught me," I whispered into her ear, planting a soft kiss on her temple. "I do. All the time. I think it might be an unhealthy obsession."

"Like Doritos?" She boosted one eyebrow, giving me a look that brought a giggle from deep within me. She always had a way of lightening the mood, even in the most intimate moments. I loved that about her.

"Don't sell yourself short. You're better than Doritos." I added, "You don't stain my fingers orange."

"Is that the only difference?" She pinned me with those gorgeous blues, and I grinned, feeling the familiar warmth of her teasing seeping into my bones.

"You're definitely more addictive than Doritos. Once I start, I can't stop." I let my fingers trail lightly down her arm, reveling in the way her skin raised in tiny bumps beneath my touch. "But I may need another taste to answer this more definitively."

She let out a laugh that filled the air around us, a coy expression on her face. "I don't know. I have to be up so early tomorrow."

"Me too," I argued.

"We should behave and go to bed." I must have looked too excited by this suggestion because she quickly added, "To sleep."

I pulled her into my arms. "Who can sleep with you next to me?"

Her lips met mine in a passionate kiss, sending sparks of electricity through my body. The heat of her touch and the intensity of her gaze promised that sleep was the last thing on her mind.

"What if someone has a telephoto lens?" I whispered as I peppered her neck with kisses.

"The cat's out of the bag with our relationship. If people want to see how in love I am with you, let them."

She kissed me again with such hunger I went weak in the knees. Every nerve in my body tingled with desire as I surrendered to her. My hands glided beneath her shirt, tracing the contours of her smooth skin. Each touch sparked with that special Carrie magic. She was truly irresistible.

Carrie fisted the hair on the back of my neck. "I can't get over this..."

"Do you plan on filling in the blank?" I ran a finger down her cheek, gazing into her eyes. Loving how much emotion I saw in them.

"How perfect this feels? I've never had this before." She patted her heart. "I never knew this was how love was supposed to feel. I don't think I've truly been in love before you."

I ran my fingers through her hair. "You can tell me that every day."

"Do you need me to?"

"*Want* might be the better word choice."

Our mouths found each other again, the passion in her kiss making it clearer than the breath going into my lungs that this woman loved me with her entire soul.

Again, I went limp in the knees.

"Care to move this to the bedroom?"

"What took us so long?"

# EPILOGUE

$\mathcal{I}$ shifted on my feet as I watched the boat dock, the reflection of tiki torches dancing on the water as the Hawaiian sunset painted the sky in hues of pink and orange.

"I think I'm going to pee my pants," I whispered to Carrie as the passengers began to disembark. "Why am I so nervous? It's just our family, for goodness sake."

Carrie put an arm around my shoulders and gave me a reassuring squeeze. "I'm right here. Everything's going to be okay."

Vivian came down the gangway, wearing her big sun hat and glasses, despite it being nearly dark out. But she looked like a star, which was the point, of course. I'd come to love this little quirk about the woman who was soon to be my mother-in-law. Even if she didn't know it yet.

"Darlings!" she cried out in that gregarious voice of hers, sweeping me into a hug that smelled of expensive perfume. "It's so good to see you! You both look amazing."

Joining her at the end of the dock, Tom gave a fatherly wave. Before I could speak to him, several of Carrie's other relatives emerged from the boat, and Asher jumped into action to coordinate the family reunion.

"Alright family!" He called out, projecting his voice without need of a microphone. "You have one hour to get presentable for tonight's luau. I'm looking at you George. Looks like you haven't been sleeping."

There were a few chuckles from the assembled crowd as George gave Cagney a sheepish look.

"I don't want details man," Asher assured him. "I want action."

"That's what I tell him," Cagney deadpanned.

"Do you find it as weird as I do that one of your ex fiancés is dating your sister?" I whispered to Carrie.

Carrie simply shrugged. "Given how many of them I have and how incestuous Hollywood is, it was only a matter of time."

"At least he's nice," I offered. "I always liked George. Not once when we were here three years ago for Cagney's wedding did he make me feel unwelcome."

"I'm just happy my sister has finally found happiness," Carrie said.

"There's my girl!" My father ran down the gangway as if he'd just woken from a deep slumber.

"Dad! Mom! You made it." I pulled both of them in for a hug, my heart pounding. The last I'd heard, my dad didn't want to fly and then take a boat to the island. He treated it like it was an either-or situation, because that was how he was. I'd been terrified he'd back out of the trip altogether.

"I had to bribe him," Mom confessed, and I'd never been so grateful.

"So this is the fancy place you're always talking about." My father tried to act unimpressed, but I saw the excitement in the crinkles around his eyes. "I heard there's zip lining. I kinda want to try that."

Mom jabbed her elbow into his side. "You know she's terrified of heights!"

Asher stuck two fingers into his mouth and let out an insanely loud and ear-piercing whistle. "I'm not kidding, people. All of you now have fifty-seven minutes to meet us on the beach. Those who are late won't get free cocktails."

With that threat, the crowd dispersed in a hurry, leaving Carrie and me alone except for Asher.

"Ladies," Asher said, addressing us both with the seriousness of a general before battle. "You know what you need to do. I've done all that I can."

"You're a prince," Carrie kissed his cheek before taking my hand and leading us back to our room. Once the door was shut, she fell against it. "I can't believe the moment is finally here!"

I couldn't help but laugh as she let out a high-pitched squeal. "I don't think I've ever heard you make that sound before."

"Yes, you have." She waggled her brows as if to suggest something naughty.

"Correction. I've never heard you make that sound with all of your clothes still on." I could feel my cheeks growing warm.

Carrie gave me a mischievous grin. "Do you think anyone suspects what we have in store tonight?"

"They probably think you're going to pop the question, not that we'll actually host a surprise wedding."

"Having a public engagement never worked to my benefit."

"True." I had to stifle a chuckle as I recalled the many times Carrie's love for grand romantic gestures had fizzled. "I would like to point out our first surprise wedding didn't work out either."

"Are you sure about that?" She closed the distance between us. "We're here now. With only the people we want at our wedding. No Jenna. Or Alex. Or Sandra. Or Kermit."

"We'll make an exception for George," I added. "I'm just glad my parents are here."

"And we're about to have the wedding we want," Carrie pointed out. "Nothing against my mom's designer, but I don't want to get married on the beach in a wedding gown. I want us to be real. It's something I've always admired about you. How you can look so beautiful and elegant without wearing flashy fashion."

"If my memory serves, you once said I looked like I had wandered away from a homeless encampment, wearing a grungy T-shirt."

Carrie's eyes widened, and she pressed a hand to her chest. "I would never say something so rude!"

"You said that with such sincerity I almost believed you. Almost." I couldn't help but smile at our matching dresses made of festive Hawaiian prints. "Not having to have wedding gowns designed did help us keep this whole thing a secret. Is your mom going to be disappointed that she's not officiating this time?"

"She'll have to get over it if she is," Carrie said emphatically. "I've been living in her shadow long enough. My wedding day doesn't have to be about her."

"It's not just today that you stepped out of her shadow," I said. "Your latest movie has so much award buzz. Just like I told you it would."

Carrie sank her teeth into her bottom lip, clearly pleased. "It's nice to read an article that simply says my name, instead of calling me the daughter of Vivian Jacobs. I love my mom, but—"

"But you've earned your own spotlight."

Carrie grinned, her expression saying that I understood where she was coming from and that she appreciated it. "Today is about us. I can't wait for you to make an honest woman out of me."

Before I had a chance to argue, she kissed me with the type of passion that made me forget my own name, let alone why I wanted to get snippy. It took my breath away, and for a moment, I forgot everything else. It was the kind of kiss that made me weak in the knees and left me feeling like I was floating on air. When she pulled back, her eyes were sparkling with love and excitement.

"I love you," she said in a low, sultry voice that made my heart skip a beat. "Let's go get married."

"I love you, too," I whispered, my heart fluttering in my chest. "Let's do it."

As Carrie smiled and took my hand, I realized this was the moment I had been waiting for my entire life—to marry the woman I loved more than anything in this world. There was a time I wouldn't have believed that woman would turn out to be Caroline Fucking Jacobs. But now, I couldn't imagine it being anyone else.

# A HUGE THANK YOU!

Thanks so much for reading *Posing in Paradise*!

We couldn't have done this without the support of our generous Gold-level Patreon supporters, including: Diva007, Jackie L Disch, Zaïna Adam, Patricia Barcena, Debbie Fahlman, Georgia Becker Scheve, Anne Lawler, and Marie Clifford.

This book owes its beginning to a string of very cold days last winter when TB, who does not do well in extreme weather, started sending Miranda links to travel sites for tropical islands. Miranda finally had to point out the exorbitant prices on these getaways, which TB struggled with for a little longer because she's not great at math. Finally, a compromise was reached and we decided to set a book in the type of resort we would spend the winter at if money were no object. Throw in some quirky characters and a few snippets from Miranda's costuming days, and Posing in Paradise was born!

We've cowritten so many books now and we're often asked how we manage to work so well together. What many don't realize is that we go way back. How far back? We were actually born in the same hospital, just nine weeks apart,

## A HUGE THANK YOU!

although TB keeps insisting it was seven weeks because math... While we may quibble about plot points, we're often laughing as we do.

If you want to stay in touch with TB, sign up for her newsletter. She'll send you a free copy of *A Woman Lost*, book 1 in the A Woman Lost series, plus the bonus chapters and Tropical Heat (a short story), all of which are exclusive to subscribers.

You'll also be one of the first to hear about her many misadventures, like the time she accidentally ordered thirty pounds of oranges, instead of five. To be honest, that stuff happens to TB a lot, which explains why she owns three of the exact same Nice Tits T-shirt. Yes, we're talking about birds here. TB loves birds.

Here's where to join: https://tbmarkinson.com/newsletter

And, if you want to follow Miranda and find out the full scoop of what TB is really up to, sign up for her newsletter. Subscribers will receive her first book, *Telling Lies Online*, for free. Seriously, you don't want to miss out on Miranda's heartfelt and funny newsletters.

Here's where to join: https://mirandamacleod.com/list

Thanks again for reading *Posing in Paradise*. It's because of you that we are able to follow our dreams of being writers. It's a wonderful gift, and we appreciate each and every reader.

TB & Miranda

# ABOUT THE AUTHORS

TB Markinson is an American who's recently returned to the US after a seven-year stint in the UK and Ireland. When she isn't writing, she's traveling the world, watching sports on the telly, visiting pubs in New England, or reading. Not necessarily in that order.

Originally from southern California, Miranda MacLeod now lives in New England and writes heartfelt romances and romantic comedies featuring witty and charmingly flawed women. Before becoming a writer, she spent way too many years in graduate school, worked in professional theater and film, and held temp jobs in just about every office building in downtown Boston.

TB and Miranda also co-own *I Heart SapphFic*, a website for authors and readers of sapphic fiction to stay up-to-date on all the latest sapphic fiction news. The duo won a Golden Crown Literary Award for *The AM Show* in 2022.

Get to know this dynamic duo better by following their Patreon account, where you can get weekly free content as well as opt-in for premium behind the scenes material you won't find anywhere else.

Printed in Great Britain
by Amazon